Running Everest

*For Lodge Group A*

Foreword by DEAN KARNAZES,
*bestselling author of Ultramarathon Man*

# RUNNING
# EVEREST

## Adventures at the
## Top of the World

## Holly Zimmermann

MEYER & MEYER SPORT

British Library Cataloguing in Publication Data
A catalogue record for this book is available from the British Library

**Running Everest**
Maidenhead: Meyer & Meyer Sport (UK) Ltd., 2020
ISBN: 978-1-78255-197-3

© 2020 by Meyer & Meyer Sport (UK) Ltd.
Aachen, Auckland, Beirut, Cairo, Cape Town, Dubai, Hägendorf, Hong Kong, Indianapolis, Manila, New Delhi, Singapore, Sydney, Tehran, Vienna

Member of the World Sports Publishers' Association (WSPA), www.w-s-p-a.org
Printed by C-M Books, Ann Arbor, MI
ISBN: 978-1-78255-197-3
Email: info@m-m-sports.com
www.thesportspublisher.com

# CONTENTS

# FOREWORD

As a longstanding member of The North Face Global Athlete Team, I've been immersed in the world of adventure and mountaineering for many years. Epic tales of the Himalayas and Everest have been shared fireside at our annual athlete meetings, and I've always been captivated and awed be these stories; tales of hellacious winds, unimaginable cold, and thin, ever so thin air that makes breathing labored and arduous. On Everest, the dangers are very real, and the consequences of a mistake can prove terminal. Everest commands your respect, and it deserves it. Many have never returned.

So when I heard about a group attempting to run a marathon on Everest, you can imagine my surprise. How was this possible? Having raced and competed on all seven continents, twice over, I've been exposed to some of the most extreme environments on earth, from running across Death Valley in the middle of summer to running a marathon to the South Pole. But the thought of running a marathon on Mt. Everest seemed out of the question.

Yet that's exactly what Holly Zimmermann and a group of intrepid runners set out to do, to run a long-distance footrace at the highest place on earth. Though she quickly learned that much of the challenge would be just getting there. In this book, she describes—with sometimes hilarious and sometimes nail-biting detail—the lead-up to the race and the many gaffes and misadventures along the way, from food-borne illnesses to being run off the trail by an obstinate yak.

Getting to the starting line became a battle with the elements and with the sometimes less than opulent living conditions. Sleeping in cold, cramped quarters with limited fresh water and no toilets made for a mental and physical fight, and morale among the group ebbed and flowed as the days dragged on. Holly describes the psychological warfare taking place insider her head as she struggled to stay focused and composed, sometimes with only a few hours of sleep a night. Her attitude remained positive, despite numerous setbacks and unanticipated hindrances, like dealing with a pompous, narcissistic doctor, taking cuts in line and acting like God's gift to humanity.

When the race finally commenced, after weeks of travel, the challenges were multiplied. Spending two nights in tents at 17,000 feet on a glacial moraine field, the racers were hardly fresh when the gun went off. But away they ran, contending with impossibly sparse air and rocky, technical terrain that had to be navigated cautiously, each footfall placed with added care. Despite it all, Holly's performance was admirable, finishing as the first international female. Nailed it! as one of the other runners was fond of saying.

But that wasn't the end. Controversy arose when it was announced that the first five international male finishers would receive cash and prizes, but nothing would be awarded to the top international female finishers. Apparently the #MeToo movement hadn't made it all the way to Nepal. How could this injustice be allowed? Holly broached the subject with the race organizers—rightly so—and they claimed to be "looking into it," though the ultimate resolution was less than settling, if not a bit more disturbing.

Despite it all, the Everest Marathon was a memorable experience, with all the high drama and emotional twists of a true epic. Holly tells the tale with candor and honesty—who she came to admire and who she came to despise—as any odyssey with strangers during trying times can reveal inner character strengths and flaws. A fascinating read, I'm sure you'll enjoy it as much as I did. Whether you run at high altitude, at sea level, or not at all, there's something here for everyone as the allure and mystique of Everest alone is captivating, and placing a bunch of marathon runners in the midst of this hallowed place elevates the intrigue to spectacular heights.

–Dean Karnazes
Author of *Ultramarathon Man*
Winner of the Badwater Ultramarathon, 2004
Eleven-time 100-Mile/1 Day Silver Buckleholder at the Western States Endurance Run, 1995-2006
*Competitor* magazine Endurance Athlete of the Year Award winner, 2008, 2006, 2005
ESPN ESPY Award winner, "Best Outdoor Athlete," 2007

# PROLOGUE

*"Invited (to join) ... Everest expedition. Could not refuse. Please forgive erring son."*

–Telegram from Edmund Hillary to his family in 1951 after having been asked to join the British Everest reconnaissance expedition

What motivates people to undertake extraordinary adventures? To travel far from home and place themselves in completely foreign environments, taking on endeavors that no one has ever accomplished, endeavors that are challenging both physically and mentally? Are these people rare exceptions or can that thirst for adventure be found in all of us?

My youngest daughter was named after Amelia Earhart, the first woman to fly solo across the Atlantic and who disappeared over the Pacific Ocean in 1937 during her attempt to circumnavigate the globe. Although I adore the name *Amelia* in its own right, it was the fascination with this pioneering, adventurous woman that inspired me to give her name to my own child.

But what exactly is adventure? Breaking it down into three facets, an adventure can involve danger and the unknown, an exciting or remarkable experience, or even a financial risk. For the sake of argument here, we'll let all things be financially equal and focus instead on the first two definitions. Drawn by some of the tallest mountains on earth where they encountered yawing glacier crevasses, crushing avalanches, and extreme cold, the initial explorers entering the Khumbu valley in Nepal were certainly facing danger and the unknown—and so was Amelia Earhart, trusting her life to the mechanics of her aircraft and her own navigational skills.

Today, adventure has become more attainable, with less danger and fewer risks for those who seek it. Certainly life-risking danger is still lurking out there for those who are willing—all you need to do is pick up Jon Krakauer's *Into Thin Air* to confirm this—but for most of us the excitement of the *Everest* movie is satisfying enough, so why would we put our lives in jeopardy to experience that in real life?

Now let's focus on the second definition of adventure: an exciting or remarkable experience. This can have a million diverse interpretations and mean something completely different to everyone on the planet. Watching your child take his or her first steps, embarking on a new career, jumping from an airplane. Depending on the person, these examples could be boring or ridiculously out of the question, but each instance could unquestionably be remarkable and exciting.

Adventure tours are booming today. People are taking multi-week vacations to exotic destinations that would previously have required months of travel. Not only are we travelling more but we are challenging our bodies with new physical fitness regimes and diets. We are testing our boundaries whenever we get the chance and as the envelope gets pushed, the norm goes right along with it.

Does this mean that we are more adventurous than our forefathers? According to our general definition, probably not.

But let's find out.

This book describes the journey of a group of people (let's not call them adventurers yet) who spent three weeks in Nepal, trekking in the Himalayan mountains for hours a day, sleeping in lodges with no heat in temperatures below freezing; having no access to fresh fruits or vegetables; no coffee; no alcohol; while enduring deplorable sanitary conditions and facing high-altitude sickness and the risk of injury, all with very limited access to medical help. And once they reached their destination and spent two nights camping in tents on a glacial moraine field at over 5,000 meters (17,000 feet) above sea level, they turned around and ran a marathon (yes, 42.2 km or 26.2 miles) back the way they came, back to that warm hotel, Internet access, that morning coffee and fruit bowl, that hot shower, that glass of Chardonnay, and those Portobello mushrooms.

Are they adventurers? Or a random selection of today's average human being?

And, last question…Could that be you?

# CHARACTERS

**Holly**  Me; born in the United States; living in Germany; adventure chaser

**Beatrice**  Italian-born Zurich-based fashionista; down-to-earth diva; believer in karma

**Shaun**  London-based bodybuilder; humorist; cover model; everybody's best friend

**Ricky***  Nepalese mountain guide; leader of Lodge Group A; naturalist; rock star

**Harry***  Even-keeled Dutchman; experienced mountain trekker

**Jesper***  Danish world-traveler and philanthropist; expert on most everything

**Raemonde***  Canadian realist; gorilla activist; only Everest ultrarunner in our group

**Niki & Carolyn***  Canadian girlfriends; running addicts; foul-mouthed

**Mark & Jill***  Couple from the American South; road runners; movie fanatics

**Hendrick & Cindy\*** South African; reserved; lovers of extreme sports and dogs

**Ray\*** Self-diagnosed obsessive-compulsive native New Yorker; forcing himself to see the world; Harry's roommate

**Dave** New Yorker; stranger to Ray though they live around the corner from each other; Shaun's roommate

**The Mexicans** Clara, Gris, Veronica, Pedro; three women and one man from Mexico; spoke mostly Spanish amongst themselves…when not laughing

**Kiki** Chinese-born American; energy-laden drama queen

**Pemba** Raccoon-tail-capped Sherpa

**Prajwal** Humble, young Nepalese doctor assigned to Lodge Group A

**Kyaron** Nepali environmentalist; emergency helper post-earthquake; trail runner

**Ash** Activist, sportsman, businessman; world-changer via *Run7.global*; Shaun's buddy from England

**Maggy & Anja**   German travel addicts; nature lovers; best friends; Insta giants

**Aayush & Anuj*** Nepalese cameramen; non-athletes; talented *yak-shitters*

**Thuan Na, Thi Thu Ha, Bluesky, Michael, Pierre, Jianqi**
Remainder of Lodge Group A

*See Appendix II for audio transcripts of personal interviews

# CHAPTER 1

*"To travel, to experience and learn: that is to live."*

–Tenzing Norgay

## Days 1 and 2: Arrival in Kathmandu

After the overnight Etihad Airways flight from Munich, in which I didn't get any sleep, I was not thrilled at having a three-hour layover in the Abu Dhabi International Airport. It was 8:00 am local time as I found a seat at the gate for the connecting flight to Kathmandu. The coffee didn't help much to lift my spirits, but Beatrice would be meeting me shortly and I was full of anticipation about seeing her again after more than a year.

If you are not familiar with Beatrice, this may be a good time to go buy my first book, *Ultramarathon Mom,* and get acquainted with us; otherwise, here's what you need to know. Beatrice and I met in 2016 at the Marathon des Sables, a 257-kilometer (160 mile) 7-day stage race across the Moroccan Sahara Desert, where we were tent-mates. She was born and raised in Tuscany but now lives in Zurich after a stint as a bond broker in London. She is spontaneous, outgoing, and daring, while I am the complete opposite, an introverted pragmatic planner. In the Sahara we were nicknamed Salt & Pepper by some of the other runners. The comparison suits us perfectly, a blond and a brunette, basic and spicy. The only thing we seem to have in common is our thirst for adventure, which was what was bringing us together again.

Our current quest: The Mount Everest Marathon.

The Everest Marathon is known for its extremes. Extremely high, extremely technical, extremely remote and, above all, extremely, breathtakingly beautiful.

The trip entailed a couple of days in Kathmandu, a ten-day trek up to Mount Everest's South Base Camp, two night of sleeping there on the glacier, a marathon trail race from Base Camp down to Namche Bazaar, and then a few days of recovery in Kathmandu before flying back to reality. All told, we'd be away from our families for three weeks. And our families are not small, with seven kids in total between us.

So there I am in Abu Dhabi, completely wrecked after missing an entire night's sleep, and here comes Beatrice bouncing along like a schoolgirl, looking fresh as a daisy since she had flown in the night before and slept a wonderful eight hours in the airport hotel.

So much for me being the pragmatic planner.

Although, to my credit, I had managed to get us seats together on our flight from Abu Dhabi to Kathmandu. Beatrice was surprised when I handed her a new boarding pass, and she happily tossed away her old ticket that had us separated by half a plane.

I was seated by the window, with Bea in the middle and a stranger on the aisle. He was probably about 30 years old, looked as though he was from somewhere in the Middle East, as were most on that flight, and he sat cool and relaxed. After about an hour, the man fell asleep with his arms crossed on his hips and his legs spread out somewhat provocatively.

After a while, Bea and I had to go to the bathroom. I'd had to go for some time, but had been waiting for the guy to wake up so he could let us out into the aisle. Bea said she couldn't wait anymore and that she would climb over him. I laughed and told her I'd give her 10 euros if she could do it without waking him up. With excitement in her eyes, she immediately hopped up onto the armrest in the middle, then, facing him, she carefully side-stepped across to the outside armrest and jumped down into the aisle. Then she looked at me smugly, rewarded at the sight of my dropped jaw. I was impressed. Now what? How should I get out? *Whatever.* I followed suit as quickly as possible, climbing just like she did onto the arm rests, but a flash of fear shot through my mind as I briefly paused mid-straddle while looking down at a stranger's head between my legs. What if he were to wake up *right now*? I hastily jumped down into the aisle and Bea and I skipped back towards the rear of the plane, startled by the astonished looks from the dozens of passengers seated behind us who'd just gotten some free entertainment. From their intense stares, I thought we were going to get a round of applause.

Returning to our aisle we found that Mr. Cool had woken up, and though he looked confused when we asked him to let us back into our seats, he never said a word.

Finally, after what seemed an eternity—but was only four and a half hours—we reached our final destination: Kathmandu, the city of organized chaos.

The scene in the airport was farcical, too many people not knowing how to get a visa and too few people there to show us how. I thought that I was smart by getting my visa in Munich before the trip, but since Beatrice hadn't had a chance to get one back in Zurich, I'd have to wait anyway. Somehow, in what can only be described as an unjust twist of fate, after we got all her forms filled out for her visa, then stood in separate lines for those with and without the entry visa, she was actually processed faster than me and, to top it all off, after she passed through customs, she stood behind the counters laughing and snapping photos of me trying to keep a straight face while frustratingly answering the redundant questions of the customs agent.

Then down to baggage claim and the same deal. Beatrice squealed with delight as her suitcase was one of the first to appear. I waited. And waited. The place was a zoo. Massive amounts of trekking equipment, bundles of who-knows-what tied up in rope, plastic wrap, and miles of tape, and monkeys swinging from the rafters. I needed to use the ladies' room but was afraid to miss my bag, so with crossed legs I waited for an eternal ten minutes until it arrived. Then after a quick stop in the loo, we were outside and being propositioned by taxi drivers, hotel reps, and luggage schleppers. We found our trekking company representative and he ushered us across a chaotic park-whereever-you-want-since-there-are-no-lines-anyway parking lot to a minivan that had a few from our group already waiting inside. We were given a flower-wreath lei necklace and asked to take a seat since we were waiting for others who had also been on our flight.

We chatted with the guys in the transfer van. There were two men from New York City, Ray and Dave. Complete strangers to each other up until that point. They had traveled separately, but on the same flight, and were surprised to learn that they live in the same neighborhood, just around the corner from one another. Who knows, maybe they pass each other every day on the street on their way to work or the gym, but it took a flight to the other side of the planet for them to have a conversation with each other.

After 15 minutes of waiting, it was beginning to get hot in the van.

Next came a Welsh dude, whose English was next to impossible for the rest of us to understand. Really. He asked if any of us had a pen, which resulted in dead silence and blank stares until he mimed a writing motion and then it clicked. Forty-five minutes later, the last two, Polish men, finally got there. They had been buying phone cards. Super. We had just traveled for a full day and wanted nothing more than a shower and a change of clothes, but we had to wait in the sweltering heat while our comrades were doing personal errands. Then, when they finally got there, not only did they not thank us for waiting but they did not even say hello! I commented lightheartedly that they owe us a beer, but there was no reaction. I suppose there was a language barrier in addition to the politeness gap.

At 6:00 PM we finally arrived at the Hotel Shanker! Drinks were handed out while checking in and then the confused nonsense started up again.

And why were the Polish guys being attended to first? Ugh.

We were approached by a very young and fragile-looking Nepalese woman, who told us that there was to be a short info meeting for our group at 6:00 PM. I looked up at the clock on the wall that now read 6:15. She followed my look and said, "Whenever you can get there." Beatrice and I hurried to our room to drop off our bags, so it was another 10 minutes before we arrived in the conference room for the info session which was already well in progress. The speaker looked at us skeptically. "Did you just arrive?" he asked. Yep, we responded. Clearly they'd scheduled the meeting at a time when all group members should have already arrived and had time to check into the hotel, and he'd apparently not been informed that some were delayed. But by now we were a little frustrated since we would have gladly skipped the hour wait in the bus at the airport to have made a timely appearance at the meeting, but hijacking the vehicle was not a viable option—even in the post-era Kingdom of Nepal.

Apparently there were different groups with the trekking company and the meetings were subdivided amongst these smaller units, so our meeting was an assembly of everyone in Lodge Group A. We were 25 people. I alternated between listening to the speaker and scouting out the other members of our trekking group. Shaun was sitting in the back row. We'd had some email contact prior to the trip and I recognized him from Instagram, so I was looking forward to finally talking to him face-to-face after the meeting. Two women who sat close together in the front also caught my eye, and my initial impression was that they were a couple. Another woman in the back row kept asking questions about information that had already been provided to us and that even Beatrice, who only reads for pleasure, had studied. The organization had been thorough, and on the Internet they supplied a very detailed itinerary along with a two-page pack list of essential items, so the woman's questions were redundant at best. She must have been nervous. Who wasn't? Sometimes we just need that personal interaction to ease our minds in stressful, foreign situations, even if we are fully prepared in all other aspects.

Then we were given our start numbers, trekking bags, and polo shirts. The trekking bags—giant red and black bags made of heavy-duty canvas with our start number on it and printed with the Mount Everest Marathon logo—rocked! I was so excited! That bag was going to follow me on every trip when I got home. I could already foresee my kids fighting over it.

We then spent a couple of minutes chatting with Shaun. Shaun is a rare breed, with more charisma than everyone I know, and built like the Incredible Hulk—though not green—with shoulder-length blond hair and, in somewhat of a contrast to his tough-guy body, a very boyish face that is nearly always wearing a smile.

After the meet and greet, Beatrice and I brought our trekking bags to our room and took well-needed showers. And although by then we were really getting tired after the long trip, we needed to eat before we crashed, so we went down to the hotel restaurant. We ordered way too much food, and it was all delicious.

With one exception.

Beatrice had some veggie tempura as an appetizer and, given that the vegetables weren't discernable under the thick crust, she unknowingly bit into a spicy pepper which had her in agony and temporarily speechless. (Note to self: this is one way to shut Beatrice up.) We quickly got some yogurt over to our table which she smothered all over her palate. The wait staff were practically doing backbends to help her.

We weren't able to finish everything, but we had given it our best shot and then shuffled up to our room where Beatrice got to work. She disappeared into the bathroom where she hand-washed her tiny black string thong in the sink and hung it out in the shower to dry overnight (I would get used to seeing Beatrice's tiny sexy garments hanging everywhere).

Though it was only 9:00 PM and despite the excitement of our upcoming adventure, we were barely able to keep our eyes open while texting family and friends. A few minutes later, just after turning the lights out, we were both sent swiftly into dreamland.

# CHAPTER 2

*"I needed to go . . . The pull of Everest was stronger for me than any force on earth."*

–Tenzing Norgay

## Day 3: Kathmandu City

At breakfast on the morning of our first full day in Kathmandu was when we first really got a chance to meet some of the other members of our group. I sat next to Cindy and Hendrik (Henni), who were a couple from South Africa but currently living in Japan. They had both done the trek before—the same route we were about to do—but they had done it without tagging the marathon on at the end. They loved the region and wanted to come back, and this time instead of *trekking* down from Base Camp, they would *run* back. Cindy warned us about one major downside of the trek: the sanitary conditions were apparently deplorable. She recommended that a neck warmer could be used not only for warmth and filtering dust in the air but also, when pulled up over your nose, to keep smells at bay. *How bad can it be?* I wondered. That bad and even worse was what I'd soon find out.

Right after breakfast there was another short info meeting. Beatrice and I were sitting next to Shaun, well, Beatrice was sitting next to him (she'd developed a little bit of a crush), while Mark and Jill, a couple from the US, were directly in front of us. Mark had a full, graying beard and mustache and Jill had ultra-long jet-black hair woven into two tight braids. Both kind of had a hippie look and when they spoke I detected southern accents, but then again, coming originally from Rhode Island, most everyone sounds southern to me. Some of the others in the room looked familiar from the night before including the female couple and the uniformed question-asker. There appeared to be a healthy cultural mix from around the globe, but discerning conclusively who comes from which country is impossible at first sight in the 21st century.

Before the meeting started, Shaun began telling us about getting separated from his buddy, Ash, with whom he had planned to be on the trip, share a room, and so on, but each had unwittingly registered via different tour groups; Ash was flying up into the mountains that day whereas our group would be a day behind. Shaun was hoping that he could switch into the other group, but he was told that the logistics would be difficult. In order to do that, roommates, lodging, and food would have to be adjusted for the entire three weeks. Not as easy as it sounds especially since in the higher villages lodging is limited and some of our food would be transported via yak alongside our trekking group.

Once all assembled, we were introduced to the man who would be our group leader for the entire trek. A Nepalese man in his mid-30s who'd worked in the tourist industry for several years, his name was Ricky, though I assume that is a westernization of his given name. He was very calm and succinct when he spoke in fluent English, and I immediately felt that we were in good hands.

After a recap of the pertinent information from the night before, the floor was open to questions. The uninformed question-asker was naturally the first to start, and she brought up the hypothetical event of one of us getting sick or injured and not being able to go on. What would happen then? But before Ricky had the chance to answer, Mark made a Rambo-type comment about how *No one gets left behind!*

Shaun laughed out loud. I think he was beginning to realize he might be happy in our group after all, with or without his friend Ash.

When there were no more questions, Ricky gave us the itinerary for that day. We would have a guided sightseeing tour of Kathmandu and then a press conference back at the hotel. Our bus would be leaving shortly, so Beatrice and I dashed off to our room to change into comfortable clothes and grab our cameras.

I was really looking forward to our first stop scheduled on the tour, the Pashupatinath Temple, because it was one thing that I had not seen on my visit to Kathmandu a few years earlier. In 2015, my husband and I had taken our four kids, who at the time were between the ages of 7 and 13, on an amazing trip to Nepal. We visited the capital city of Kathmandu and the ancient temples of Bhaktapur, hiked in the Himalayan foothills of Dhulikhel, took a wild ride cross country to Pokhara, and ended up in Chitwan National Forest where we rode on elephants, saw rhinos, and were even lucky enough to get up close to a Bengal tiger in the wild. We left that beautiful country just ten days before a massive earthquake struck which devastated the country's historical sites and infrastructure. I'd done some fundraising at home to help with their restoration efforts and had regular contact with a friend in

Nepal (Kyaron, introduced in *Ultramarathon Mom*), but I was eager to get back myself and see first-hand how the country was recovering.

So on that first day back in the capital city, we were planning on visiting a few sites that I'd been to before and one that I'd not yet seen: the Pashupatinath Temple. A Hindu temple dedicated to Lord Shiva, it lies on both banks of the Bagmati River and is the holiest Hindu temple in Nepal. Only Hindus are allowed in the main pagoda-style temple, which has four sides covered in silver and a gilded roof and is surrounded by many other temples to various Hindu and Buddhist deities.

Among tourists, the temple is best known for its public cremations. Along the river at least ten ghats (cremation pedestals) can be seen where the last rites of Hindus are performed before cremation. After a procession from the temple to the steps of the river bank, the body (which is wrapped in white except if it is a woman whose husband is still alive, then it is wrapped in red) is washed with the holy water of the Bagmati River and some is poured into the deceased's mouth to make sure they are dead. *You have to wonder if that is ever a show-stopper.* Next, a Tilaka (traditional marking) is placed on the forehead, the big toes are tied together with a string, and family and friends then carry the body to a ghat near the river. Finally, the deceased is placed on top of the ceremonial pyre with feet facing south.

Our temple tour guide told us that the bodies must be cremated within hours of death, and several ceremonies took place in the time we were there. Our group stood across the riverbank for at least an hour, mesmerized by what was going on at the other side. The body is left to smolder and then the ashes are swept into the river. After the ashes of one of the deceased had cooled, a man took a handful of the ash and placed it in a plastic bag. He then waded knee-deep into the river, bent down into the water, and buried the bag underneath the sediment of the riverbed; apparently that is done with every ceremony.

The ghat is then washed clean and ready for the next ritual. There were extravagant ghats for the wealthy and plain ones for the poor, but the mourning of the relatives was the same, with the male relatives surrounding the body and the women in the sheltered porticos behind.

Despite the many distractions of the palm readers, fortune tellers, and card readers, as well as women selling bracelets, artwork, and suspicious looking bottles of drinking water, the ten-minute walk back to the bus was a somber one. I don't think I've attended as many funerals in my entire life as I'd just witnessed that morning.

Our next stop was the Boudhanath Stupa. The term *stupa* refers to a mound-like or hemispherical structure containing relics that is used as a place of meditation. The Boudhanath Stupa is one of the largest in the world and the original dwelling is thought to be about 1,500 years old. Atop its whitewashed dome, a gilded tower with the eyes of the Buddha watches all who come to visit. The stupa dominates the plaza and allows worshipers just enough space to walk its outskirts, before the surrounding walls close in with shops, cafes, and homes, giving it the feeling of a ship in a bottle. As one of Kathmandu's busiest tourist destinations, it is now well maintained in a fresh coat of paint and bright prayer flags flying from its highest points.

Bea, Shaun, and I strolled around the base of the stupa, spinning prayer wheels as we went, then up a set of whitewashed steps to walk directly around the perimeter of the dome itself, prayers flags by the dozens flapping in the breeze just above our heads and towering up to the top of the golden spire. It's a magical place, and the energy you feel swirling around you is completely humbling.

The contrast of the brilliant colors of the flags against the white and gold of the stupa makes it clear why such images are so often photographed. We took plenty of photos, some striking a pose, but other times we captured each other simply entranced by our surroundings and, after Shaun took a series of Bea and me together, a female tourist asked him to take photos of her as well. I think it was just an excuse for her to talk to him. Of course, he couldn't say no.

Back down at the stupa base we met with Anuj, who had been hired by the marathon organizers to do the photography as well as make videos of the trek and marathon. While chatting with him, a huge flock of pigeons settled down next to us and suddenly Anuj had a cinematic vision of Beatrice and me running through the flock of pigeons and how they would majestically take flight. Unfortunately, the pigeons were not well-trained actors and were apparently very used to being around people, because as we took off on a jog through the flock, they didn't budge. I nearly tripped while tip-toeing through the cluster, trying to avoid stepping on them. A few of them took flight but swooped around and immediately rejoined their group. Anuj said we should try it again, but this time run faster and make noise. At a full sprint and screeching like canaries, we still didn't ruffle any feathers of those winged rats and, not wanting to break any beaks or risk a fall into pigeon poop, we ceased our moviemaking bid after just two takes.

Once the group had rejoined, I talked to Dave while waiting for the bus. He was in his late 20s, from NYC, and though he spoke English with no foreign accent, due to his straight dark hair and Asian features, my guess was he had some Chinese ancestry (later confirmed as first-generation American, often speaking Mandarin with the two Chinese-born women in the group). He was travelling alone on his first overseas trip. "Whoa! First trip overseas, and you come here to run a marathon at the foot of Everest?!?" I asked with astonishment. He nodded, slightly embarrassed. Then he said that he liked my sense of humor. Seeing my confused expression, he clarified. He had been in the minivan the day before on our ride from the airport to the hotel, and it was my comment to the Polish men that they owe us a beer for making us wait.

Apparently, he didn't get a beer either.

Back at the hotel, though we were all starving, we were ushered straight into the banquet hall for a press conference. Bea, Shaun, and I sat right in the front row. Local cultural dignitaries were seated at a long table up on the stage along with the race organizers and each was given a few minutes in the spotlight, describing the history of the race, the importance of tourism to Nepal, and the efforts that are being made to keep the region eco-friendly. Then several runners with impressive stories from the various trekking groups were subsequently called forward to make some comments. Shaun was first to be called up to speak about his fundraiser. He described how he was raising donations for The Himalayan Children's Charities (HCC). I thought that he knew about the press conference and planned a speech since he did not appear to be at all surprised when he was called up front to speak and he seemed to know exactly what to say. Once he sat back down the race organizer started talking about two friends who met at the Marathon des Sables. Oh! That was us! Caught a bit off guard, Beatrice and I were called up front to say a few words. Although Beatrice can strike a pose with the world's best, she is not an impromptu speaker, at least not in English, though she may have fewer hang-ups in Italian. Anyway, I took one look at her face and knew I needed to be the one with the microphone. So I talked for a minute about the MdS itself, which is not known to everyone, and then about our friendship and what brought us to Nepal. Then Beatrice made a few upbeat comments and we dashed back to our seats. After us there were a couple of others brought forward, mostly people raising funds for charities, using the race to raise awareness for their cause.

Then, finally, we were free to enjoy a late lunch, and Bea, Shaun, and I made a beeline to the hotel restaurant. Jesper sat down alone at the table next to us so naturally we invited him to join us. In his early 50s, clean cut and well dressed in good quality sporting clothes, he told us that he was originally from Denmark, but had been living in Poland for years with his Polish wife and family.

"Ever done anything like this race before?" I asked him.

"Well, I ran the Antarctic Ice Marathon."

That answered that.

Then Shaun got a phone call from his wife and their two-year-old son, the cutest little kid imaginable. Shaun turned the camera around and introduced his son to the rest of us. I heard his wife say in a sweet voice, "Have you made yourself some friends?" Since she was talking to quite possibly the most gregarious person on the entire planet, she must have been joking with him.

After lunch we had some work to do, namely, packing our trekking bags and day packs to weigh cumulatively 15 kilograms (33 pounds) or less. Mind you, this is for two weeks, with clothing items for four seasons. Most of us had apparel ranging from shorts and tank tops to hats, gloves, and thick winter jackets. We'd have to be prepared for anything. Our trekking bags contained not only our clothes, shoes, and personal items, but also our thermal mattresses, sleeping bags, and any other gear we thought we'd need in the great unknown. Protein bars were also a major contributor to the gear list for the majority of us since no one was quite sure what we'd be served to eat along the way. These trekking bags would be carried by the porters or by the yaks.

So, while the porters suffered for our vanity, we each burdened ourselves with only a small day pack containing rain gear, a jacket, water, cameras, and snacks.

A bunch of the others in our group were planning on going into Thamel for dinner, but I didn't want to risk anything before setting out for the trek and marathon, figuring that the food in the hotel may be safer on my stomach. Beatrice agreed. Then I texted Shaun to see what he was up to. He also wanted to stay put, so we settled on 7:15 in the hotel restaurant, which gave me time enough beforehand to get in a quick 5K run!

I was happy to find that the driveway of the hotel was actually a loop around the pool and gardens. It was almost 400 meters long. My own track! After a short warm-up, I did some accelerations before jogging it out, then finished it off with some yoga and stretching in the garden. It felt great to move after the traveling and languorous sight-seeing.

And after a super-soapy hot shower and hair washing—the last for a few days—we were down in the restaurant drinking Everest beers, filming boomerangs, and enjoying the excitement and anticipation of the upcoming adventure.

# CHAPTER 3

.....................................................................................

*"I have discovered that even the mediocre can have
adventures and even the fearful can achieve."*

–Edmund Hillary

.....................................................................................

## Day 4: Flight From KTM to Lukla (2860 m); Trek Downhill to Phakding (2610 m)

The 3:50 AM wake-up call threw me for a loop.
*Good Lord, where am I?*
Once I realized that the woman lying next to me was my
friend Beatrice and we were about to embark on the adventure of
our lives, I hopped out of bed and took a quick shower, and then
we hurried down to the lobby to catch the shuttle bus leaving at
4:30 AM.

Beatrice grabbed a spot next to Shaun, and I took an empty
seat next to a guy with dark skin and hair. I greeted him with a
smile, which he gave in return before resuming his staring out
the window at the rain. I wasn't even sure if he spoke English at
first, since I had only heard him speaking Spanish with a group

of women, but I began to make small talk and was surprised to find out that not only did he speak English, he spoke it very eloquently, and that although he grew up in Mexico, he now lived in New York City where he worked as a journalist—apparently of some notoriety. *Who knew?* His introduced himself as Pedro. We soon discovered that we'd both run the Boston Marathon—though not in the same year—which gave us some common ground. We also talked about our specific training for the Everest Marathon. He said he was satisfied with his fitness level after having trained at altitude on a volcano in Mexico. I was imagining him as a Taramuhara, with red cape and sandals, running tirelessly for hours on end through the hot Copper Canyons. (I was wrong on the sandals, but he did in fact wear a red, white, and green cape, a giant Mexican flag, tied around himself while running the entire Everest Marathon.)

At 5:00 AM we pulled up in front of the domestic terminal of Kathmandu Airport. When the bus stopped we filed out, loaded down with our backpacks and trekking bags, and ran as quickly as possible to get to the shelter of the airport entrance. Rain was pattering loudly on the tin roof.

Our flight was scheduled for 6:15 but the airport was not yet open so we sat outside and nibbled on the boxed breakfast we'd been given from the hotel. The stray dogs occasionally got lucky; from me, they got the piece of cheese wedged between two slices of white bread. Normally I don't eat any meat or dairy products, but prior to travelling to Nepal I began eating some cheese because I knew that a strict vegan diet would not be on offer in the Himalayas. Plus, I did not want to constantly have stomach problems or be worried about what I was eating since taking in those precious calories would be critical to my health in the high mountains.

We were the first group hurried in when the airport doors finally opened. After a quick scan of the bags, we entered the receival hall where Ricky showed us to a group of seats. We all figured we'd be there for a while but before we could get comfortable, a few of our names were called and we were asked to give up our backpacks to be weighed. Apparently our group of twenty-five would be split as each aircraft seated only fifteen. Beatrice and I would be together on the same plane, but Shaun would not. This was not welcome news. Why? Because Shaun had had his palm read the day before while at the Pashupatinath Temple and was told by the wise old sadhu that he would live to be 84 years old. Earlier that morning Shaun had seen my anxiety about the flight but reassured me that nothing bad could happen to us since the sadhu promised he had another 51 years to live. That was under the assumption that we would be on the same plane. Now he would apparently be on a separate flight, either a few minutes in front of or behind mine. So now fate was back in my hands.

I am not normally afraid of flying. So, was there reason to worry? Well, yes.

In 2010, The History Channel aired a program called *Most Extreme Airports*, which rated the airport we were flying into, Lukla, as the most dangerous in the world and it has held that notoriety for over 20 years. The airport was built in 1964 under the supervision of Edmund Hillary. There is only one runway used for both take-off and landing that measures exactly 527 meters (1,729 feet) × 30 m (98 feet) with an 11.7% gradient and it wasn't paved until 2001. It is only accessible to helicopters and small, fixed-wing, short-takeoff-and-landing (STOL) aircraft. There is a ring of hills immediately behind the runway, at the northern end, which essentially eliminates the chance of a go-around on short final. At the southern end of the runway there is a steeply angled drop to the valley below. Almost exactly a year prior, there had been a deadly plane crash at the airport in Lukla, in just the same weather as we were having that day, where the plane came up short and hit the steep embankment just in front of the runway. Ten years previously, there had been a horrifying accident in exactly the same spot—that steep slope—which killed 18 tourists and guides.

I tried to put these thoughts out of my head as we got our tickets and moved into the departure hall. Despite the worry, I was full of anticipation. We found some seats near the gate where we dropped our gear and sat down. And waited. Then waited some more. Then we were told that our flight had been delayed due to bad weather and the new estimated departure time would be 7:04. *Really? 7:04?* That sounded like a pretty random time for a delayed flight. So I had a look around. Anywhere other than in a third world country, that departure hall would certainly be a condemned building. There were broken information screens, loose cables and wiring hanging everywhere, no cafes or food court, just a sad little souvenir shop that also sold a few snacks and coffee.

And still we waited. Apparently there was *one last cloud* that needed to move away from Lukla so that the planes would have a clear view on approach. Ricky had a video clip on his phone from a web cam at the airport in Lukla which showed this stubborn cloud just hanging in there. So the group passed the time by trying to get to know one another.

I had taken a photo of the participant list the day before which was posted in the lobby of the hotel so that I could keep track of everyone's names. There were three groups listed which were lodging groups, as well as a camping group which would be a day behind us. So, there was Lodge Group A (us) with 25 members, Group B with 23, and Group K (Ash's group) which was smaller with only 12 participants. Listed were: name, nationality, date of birth, half or full marathon, and twin sharing or single booking. I scanned the list until my eyes got hung up on a familiar date. Yesterday's date, which was listed next to Shaun's name. His birthday had been yesterday. Beatrice and I had spent half the day wandering around with him in Kathmandu, then had dinner with him and he hadn't said a word. I spread the news to Mark, Jill, and a few others and we began whispering around as to what to plan to surprise him. Serenade him with "Happy Birthday" in the airport? At dinner? We had some time for a bit of brainstorming.

A few in the group got a cup of coffee. A few tried to doze. I was wired. For the first two hours anyway, then I started to get tired. The weather began to clear. Then cloud up again. At one point I took a visit to the ladies' room, which had me almost gagging. It was revolting. I had to wonder if they ever cleaned it. Not that I had much else to do, so after returning to my seat, I pondered that topic for a while. If the domestic terminal was built in 2016 and opened in May of that year and it was now May 2018, then the facilities would be two years old. Considering the state of the floor and the smell in that bathroom, I came to the conclusion that it was definitely reasonable that it had not once been cleaned since it was built two years prior. *Oh, man, is this what happens in the brains of bored people?* I realized we needed to get out of there before I went crazy.

The terminal had been empty when we got there hours before so at the time we had our pick of seats, but by now it was filling up if not full. Every time one of us got up to go to the bathroom, get coffee, or walk a bit, even if we left our backpack just in front of our seat, a Nepali would swoop in and take the free seat. So, after having a whole group of seats for ourselves when we arrived, we were now sharing about three seats and half of a low table that was also completely occupied with passengers using it as a bench. Clearly there was a capacity issue at that facility.

When a man took Beatrice's seat after she stood up to stretch and take a few steps, she commented by saying, "That's all right, he can stay there, I'd rather stand anyway."

Beatrice is a strong believer in karma. She feels that sacrificing for others ensures future rewards and, in contrast, negative thoughts or deeds result in negative effects. As an engineer, I never really considered karma to be relevant since it isn't tangible, until I thought of it as an extrapolation of Newton's third law which states that every action has an equal and opposite reaction. Naturally, he was referring to the physical world and karma is on a spiritual realm which considers energy as the medium, but the philosophy is the same. So maybe there is something to it. Belief in karma is not uncommon, especially in Nepal, where it plays a major role in the country's two main religions. In the Hindu and Buddhist religions, karma is literally defined as actions or deeds and through the course of a lifetime, a person's actions are believed to affect the outcome of the next life. The concept of reincarnation is closely linked to karma, with the belief that one will be continually reborn until achieving enlightenment (in Buddhism), thereby freeing the soul from the cycle of rebirth. I wondered if the guy now sitting in Beatrice's seat had just acquired a good-karma reward, or was dishing out some negative energy by making her stand.

Niki and Carolyn, the two women that I assumed were a couple at the info meetings, sat away from the group by themselves. I'd never seen them apart from each other; they seemed to be inseparable. Niki had a very short haircut and was strong and fit with chiseled facial features, whereas Carolyn had long hair and though in apparently good shape, she was a little heavier than Niki, but had a tough-ass attitude and unbelievably foul language.

*Okay, I'll let you all in on the truth now... No, they were not lesbians—though they told me they were often mistaken for a couple—but they were great friends.*
*Still, they would make a cute couple.*

Whether it was the boredom, jetlag, or the sugar low, eventually my eyes began to close and I drifted off, all the while, not five meters in front of me, construction workers were drilling a new sign into one of the terminal counters. Being able to sleep despite jackhammer-decibel-level noise was a good sign that I was adapting to a way of life whereby taking care of our basic needs (e.g., sleep) is becoming not only a priority, but a way to pass the time. However, I still had some work to do acclimating to the environment on another basic need—using the bathrooms.

Finally at around 11:30 AM we were called to our flight. We were put on busses and brought out to a tiny plane. I was hoping to be able to sit right in the front, just behind the pilots, but I knew I might not be the only one who wanted that spot and I wasn't planning on fighting for it. But Beatrice was. She didn't care where she sat but knew how I felt and so she ran to the front of the bus when we stopped. But it was an abrupt stop that sent her flying, right to the front door. Everyone stood, but then the bus started up again for a short distance, and everyone sat back down. Except for Beatrice. She fiercely maintained her position and stood like she was on the local train, holding onto the overhead railing with conviction. Then, when we were let out, she was the first one onto the plane and secured us the two seats in the front, right behind the cockpit. I owed her one.

We sat on the runway for about 20 minutes waiting to start. It was a 15-seater prop plane. There was a flight assistant on board who offered us a breath mint and cotton balls for the ears to muffle the sound of the engines. That didn't give me a warm, cozy feeling. With the extent of her job completed, she sat in the back row next to Ricky. Once in the air I began to relax, and the ride was surprisingly smooth. Through the cockpit window I got better views compared to the tiny side windows that were badly scratched and fogged. Just out of the city, we flew over the Kathmandu valley, littered with homes settled amongst the rice fields. Then we moved on into the Himalayan foothills where small villages were tucked into the thick vegetation of the hillsides. There were terraced farming plots high above the meandering river below.

As time went by the sky began to darken and clouds moved in. The fog thickened over the mountains. The pilots were looking for gaps in the clouds. Pointing. A few words were exchanged. Then one of the pilots called the flight assistant forward and spoke into her ear. It was so loud in the plane that she took turns coming to each one of us reporting that Lukla airport was closed and we were turning back to Kathmandu. I was not surprised considering what I could see out the window, but I was very upset. All that waiting for nothing. Now we'd have to spend another night in Kathmandu and have one less day and night of acclimatization in the mountains.

But instead of heading back to the terminal after landing, we were told that we would go to the washroom, then restart and give it another try. This "washroom" was a small building located on the side of the runway, and it was (obviously) a restroom. The pilots were the first to jump out of the plane and jog over to use the facilities, then we disembarked, were loaded onto a minibus, driven the 50 meters to the wash room to use the facilities ourselves, before being subsequently bussed back to the plane which was in the process of being refueled. By the pilot himself. Like he was on a Sunday drive with his car and family. We pretended not to notice, hoping that a big professional crew of mechanics would show up any minute. But they didn't. So, once the pilot finished refueling and boarded the plane, we followed suit.

We were then told by Ricky that the other flight with members of our group had made it into Lukla just ten minutes before we were scheduled to land. The plane with Shaun in it. The *safe* plane. *Sigh.* Apparently, the weather changes so quickly and landing there is so critically dangerous that they don't take any chances. Fine with me. I just kept my fingers crossed and hoped that the second shot was a winner, too.

The next attempt started in slightly better weather, but it quickly began to get worse. The pilots were again looking for gaps in the cloud cover, while I was watching the radar for airport codes and distances, as if I had any idea what I was looking at and if it could somehow help. I was a nervous wreck. I turned back to look at Ricky in the rear of the plane and he gave me a reassuring nod and pointed in the distance. There was a village far ahead on the mountainside; it was Lukla, he said, and the landing strip was coming into view. Though I should have been thrilled by the sight of it, what I was looking at was not prana for the eyes, as the runway was a tiny, almost indiscernible, gray strip in the distance. And even as we got closer, it never looked larger than miniscule. It was inconceivable that it was physically possible for an aircraft to land on it.

I closed my eyes and prayed. My palms were sweating. Adrenalin pumping. Pulse racing.

We homed in on the gray strip surrounded by small buildings on both sides that appeared to be just meters from the runway; there was clearly no margin for error. *Are we swaying from side to side? Why is the plane bouncing up and down? Where did the runway go? Oh, there it is again. It was momentarily hidden behind the narrow windshield-wiper resting vertically on the cockpit window.* The droning of the engines kept changing frequency as the pilot reduced speed. The runway was directly in front of us, then suddenly it disappeared below us as we were hovering precisely over that narrow strip of pavement balanced on the edge of a mountain. A couple of skidding sounds, a few bounces, and then... an unexpectedly smooth glide. Some of the group started to clap, the pilots laughed, and at that point I realized it was okay to start breathing again.

We taxied across the landing strip, came to a halt, and were hurried off the plane where we were urged to exit the tarmac as quickly as possible. There was no discernable airport terminal to process its passengers; instead Ricky led us through a chain-link fence and into a constricted stone-stepped alleyway. It was noticeably colder there in the mountains, with an icy wind, and I was still wearing shorts since it had been warm in Kathmandu. We were led into a lodge where we met up with the other members of our group in the dining hall overlooking the runway. A couple more planes landed shortly after we did, then the airport closed for the day. Most of the marathon trekkers had made it in, but two from our group who were on a third plane did not. They would have to wait until the next day and see if the weather cleared; if not, they would have to take a helicopter.

We were all also very hungry as it was 2:30 in the afternoon, and we'd been up since 4:00 AM and had only the slim pickings in that boxed breakfast. The rest of our group who had been waiting there for nearly an hour hadn't eaten yet either; unfortunately, it took another hour on top of that for lunch to be served, but it was worth it when we were treated to a delicious local meal of *dal bhat*. It was perfect, and I thought that if the food continued to be this good I would be in heaven. (Unfortunately, we were to be sorely disappointed with what was to come.)

After lunch, I went in search of the bathroom to change into long pants for the two- to three-hour trek to Phakding. But it was so completely deplorable in there with a disgustingly filthy toilet that I turned right around and just made a speedy change in the hallway where I didn't have to hold my breath. *Is this how it's going to be for the next couple of weeks?* I wondered with dread.

We were then brought down into the ground floor hallway where all our trekking bags were assembled and the porters were sorting out who would carry what. The porter assigned to my bag was named Milan. Beatrice overheard this and was thrilled. "I was born in Milan!" she squealed with delight. She then asked him if he'd ever been there, and I nearly conked her over the head as he shook his head in confusion.

Once organized and all our gear had been distributed, we stepped back out into the cool mountain air. And the trek began.

Lukla was a relatively large village, with lots of lodges, cafes, and trekking shops. Broad flat rocks lined the passageways through the village. Beautiful children dressed in school uniforms passed by us and giggled. Once out of the village center the pathways turned to packed earth, perfect for people and animals. There were no roads as we know them. It was a sustainable civilization without cars, nearly impossible to imagine coming from the Western world.

We came across tiny clusters of homes, shops, and tea houses along the path. I peeked inside the open doors of the homes as we passed by and, though rather dark, they all looked immaculately organized. Shelves piled high with colorful linens. Pots and pans hanging overhead. Cooking smells. Laughter.

After an hour a light rain began to fall, which was about the same time the stomach pains started. The early rise had set my digestive system into rebellion and now after refusing to use the dirty toilets in the airports, my intestines were cramped and angry. I could only hope for a halfway decent bathroom in our lodge that night.

Beatrice then began cursing and sucking the side of her thumb. "Are you all right?" I asked. She was bleeding and had apparently cut herself on a sharp clip on her backpack. So the group stopped on a stone terrace in front of a beautiful green memorial archway spanning the path. Someone quickly found a bandage for Beatrice and in a matter of minutes we were on our way again. Passing underneath the green arch, I noticed it read, *National Luminary Pasang Lhamu Memorial Gate*. The gateway had been dedicated to the Nepalese national hero Pasang Lhamu Sherpa who, in 1993, was the first Sherpa woman to summit Mount Everest; unfortunately, though, she died while on the descent. Monuments to this courageous woman can be seen not only in the Himalayas but also in Kathmandu and throughout Nepal.

We trekked along the scenic Dudh Kosi River, but low-hanging clouds kept our visibility limited to the valley with only brief glimpses of the high mountains that were beginning to appear in the distance. Our first hanging bridge came into view and everyone stopped to take photos.

This might be a good time to mention that I do not like heights. Notice I didn't say I have a fear of heights. I simply prefer to avoid being in the position of being obliterated by potential energy. It makes me uncomfortable. So I knew I had to focus; I had no alternative but to cross. I hesitantly stepped onto it and moved slowly forward, trying to keep balance without having to hold onto the side cables which often had protruding wire edges that could easily cut your hands. The bridge moved in all directions—up and down, side to side—and there was a cross wind to boot. All seemed to be going well until I got about halfway across when suddenly two young porters came running up behind me, making the bridge swing frenetically. They wanted to pass with their heavy loads. But the bridge was very narrow and to let them pass I would have to get up tight to one side, which often had gaps in the fencing. The bridge was bouncing and swinging. I was panicking. I yelled back at them to stop. I considered trying to get by others in front of me, but there was a line of people, so we had to stay single file. Just in front of me were Mark and Jill. I'd find out later that Jill has an even worse fear of heights than I do, and the two of them were trying desperately to keep calm despite the yelling going on behind them.

Finally across that bridge and once my pulse had returned to normal levels, I found myself walking through rhododendron and magnolia forests next to Harry, an introspective Dutch man. He had a very calm manner and soon began to ease my thoughts away from the bridge incident by recalling his own stories of mountain climbing. He told me about winter mountain training that he had done in the Alps. He explained how he was roped together with four others and, as a training exercise for climbing out of crevasses, the first one had to jump into a crevasse that was about 40 meters deep, which usually resulted in pulling the second man on the rope down into the yawing void with the first, while the others were hopefully quick enough to act as a belay and then tasked with getting the others out. I was shocked. "That's crazy! Why would you do that?" I asked. "Well," he said, "if you fall into one you need to be able to get back out again, right?" I just looked at him dumbfounded. Of course it was logical, but I think simply knowing the theory behind such an exercise would have been sufficient enough for me.

The rain had stopped, but we were to see more of it over the course of the trip, as the weather wasn't what I'd hoped it would be. Bright, sunny, clear days were not on the roster and in general the weather could be described as variable: brief periods of sun interspersed with wind, snow, and rain, often with low-hanging clouds in the morning that seemed to hauntingly creep up the valley as the day progressed.

After nearly two and a half hours of hiking, stone edifices began to appear more frequently along the trail which signaled our arrival in Phakding. The village was characterized by terraced agricultural fields, small homes, cafes with outdoor patios, and many lodges. The homes were simple stone structures, but often decorated with a door painted in a brilliant color such as aqua blue or deep green.

It was then that I noticed a dull ache in my right knee. The trek had been mostly downhill, and I was normally accustomed to running rather than a walking gait, so considering the unfamiliar movement plus the additional force on the joints by going downhill, my body wasn't sure what was going on. I was hoping that would change when we began to ascend.

In total we lost about 250 meters of elevation on the trek that day from where we began at the Lukla airport. Though this might sound discouraging, considering that we had nearly 3,000 meters to climb in the next week or so, it was actually a good start, because acclimatization is supposed to work optimally when climbing high and sleeping low. This is a strategy whereby you sleep lower than the highest elevation to which you have ascended that day. Tax the body briefly, then let it adjust. Thus, by flying from Kathmandu to Lukla, we'd already gained 1,400 meters in elevation that day, so the short descent was ideal.

The rhythm for the trip was scheduled as two days trekking then an acclimatization stop, or rest day. During the rest day we were always scheduled to have a hike (or run) up to higher elevations, then return to sleep at our lodge at the lower level. I figured there were numerous trekking routes up to Everest Base Camp (EBC), and various options for the high/low strategy, but since we were a large group we were limited to the main trekking routes in order to stop in villages along the way for lunch and overnight stays. Whether these villages on the main line were optimally located to accommodate this high/low approach was something I'd assumed the guides had figured out and we could only trust their knowledge and experience.

In Phakding we were quartered at the Mountain Resort lodge, a two-story stone structure located high up on a hillside overlooking the river; however, considering it was nearing dark when we got there, we didn't enjoy much of the view. Upon arrival we gathered directly in the dining room for tea and learned there that it would cost us 250 rupees to charge our phones and 500 for WiFi (the exchange rate was about 1 US dollar per 100 Nepal rupee). The dining hall was cold since a fire had not yet been lit, and we would soon find out that the bedrooms were even colder. After tea, we were given the keys to our rooms where our bags had already been delivered. Beatrice and I were upstairs on the second floor in a very small, basic room with two beds, each with an awfully thin mattress and a small pillow. No blanket. I whipped out my sleeping bag and merino wool liner and got everything prepared for the night. Then I went to check out the facilities. There were two bathrooms on each floor, both of which had a toilet and sink, and served about 35 people per floor (there were other trekking groups there). The toilets were surprisingly clean, but they did not flush without manually pouring a bucket of water drawn from a spigot into them. So, other than worrying about 17 people waiting outside the bathroom door when I was on the toilet, the facilities were certainly an upgrade.

By the time we returned to the dining room for dinner, a fire had been lit and it was comfortable (but not cozy). We were all hoping for a delicious dinner of some wonderful local cuisine like the dal bhat that we'd had for lunch, but instead we were served spaghetti, French fries, and cooked vegetables. Hopefully an exception to the rule.

"You think there is any chance of getting a birthday cake?" I whispered to Beatrice.

But somehow Shaun overheard and asked, "Is it your birthday?"

I rolled my eyes at him.

"What?" he asked in confusion.

"You think we don't know." Beatrice chimed in.

Shaun laughed. Apparently it clicked. "Yesterday was not my birthday. That was a mistake on the list. My birthday is the 16th of March, not May. They got those two *M* months mixed up," he said with a beaming grin.

That explains it. Because honestly, I had Shaun pegged for being the type of guy to sing happy birthday to himself and announce it to everyone within earshot.

Then Ricky stood in the middle of the dining hall and yelled, "Rickyyy tiime!" Apparently, it was Ricky Time. We were then introduced to what would be a regular group meeting held every night and led by our leader, Ricky, where he would relay all pertinent information to us for the evening and following day, as well as any interesting stories that he was in the mood to share. And sometimes his stories were no less than enthralling. Ricky Time usually occurred after dinner when we were all gathered together. These briefings would be one of our most treasured pastimes of the entire trip. Ricky was knowledgeable and confident, but very easy-going, tolerant, and above all, patient, which is a critical requirement for someone who has to deal with 25 people from around the world, all with different cultures, habits, wishes, and expectations. On that first night we were also introduced to the sirdar (main guide) assigned to our group. His name was Trijan but we all just called him Boss Man. A sirdar is essentially the leader of the sherpas (assistants to the sirdar) and the porters. He mediates between the climbers, the porters, and the locals, and the title is mainly regional, used for Sherpas in the Himalayas. The sirdar is also normally responsible for the kitchen helpers and cooks of an expedition and regulates the transport of goods and payment as well as the cooperation with local authorities. The sirdar usually speaks fluent English and is typically the most experienced of the group. Trijan appeared to be about 50 years old, whereas the sherpas and porters in our group were between 18 and 40, with the porters being on the younger side of that range. The sirdar is not a mountain guide in the true sense and normally carries only his own equipment and not that of the trekkers. As did our Boss Man.

We also met the other sherpa guides, Pemba, Bibesh, and Dafuri, but one of them wasn't there yet, Tendy, who had remained behind in Kathmandu with the final two trekkers in our group, Pierre and Michael, whose flight did not make it into Lukla that day.

To avoid any misunderstandings with the nomenclature of the word *sherpa*, when written with a capital S, Sherpa is an ethnic group, one of the many pseudo-Tibetan ethnic groups that live at the higher altitudes in Nepal and are most known for inhabiting the Everest region from Namche Bazaar up to Everest Base Camp. The word *sherpa*, when not capitalized, means a trek or expedition worker, someone who carries the trekking bags, gear, and food, puts up and packs tents, and sometimes helps in the kitchen and with serving the meals. In this context it describes a job. This job originally belonged to the Sherpa tribe, but now there are sherpas of other ethnic backgrounds as well; thus, the job title is usually not capitalized. In our group, all the sherpa guides except for Bibesh were of the Sherpa tribe, so they could technically be called Sherpa sherpa, but Bibesh had another ethnic background and would simply be a sherpa. *Whew.*

The responsibilities of the sherpa have also somewhat changed as the tourist trekking industry has evolved. The sherpas in our group were primarily there to look out for our well-being, guiding us on the trails and answering any questions, as well as helping prepare and serve the meals, but they were not tasked with carrying our trekking bags. That job was reserved for the porters (who may or may not be Sherpa), who were simply tasked to transport gear. In our trekking group, each porter carried two marathon runners' trekking bags plus his own gear on his back. The baggage was bundled together with rope and the load balanced by a wide band tied around the load and strung across his forehead. The porter walked severely bent over (how much depended on the weight of the load) and had to strain to look up and forward to navigate the path.

Ricky Time on that first night continued with tips on how to deal with acclimatization. We were told to drink lots of fluids, up to a gallon (three or four liters) per day of water, tea, isotonic drink, juice, soup, etc., but to avoid coffee and alcohol. Eating small but frequent meals of easy-to-digest carbohydrates and some salt was also advised. We were then briefed with a general itinerary for the following day. It would be a long hike with no less than seven hanging bridges. "One will be very high," Ricky said. *Ugh.* He also told us that since running water (when available) shouldn't be drunk or even trusted to brush our teeth, our sherpas would be boiling large pots of water each night, and before we went to bed, we could fill our water bottles with the hot water, tuck them into our sleeping bags for warmth during the night, and then use the cooled water for drinking and brushing our teeth the next day. This would reduce, and almost negate, our need to purchase bottled water, which not only got more expensive the higher we climbed, but our re-usable water bottles reduced the amount of plastic throw-aways in the system. A win-win.

Unfortunately, I did not have a bottle that I could put boiling water into and tuck down into my sleeping bag. I only had a

LifeStraw, which is a 650-ml bottle with a straw filter in it that is supposed to purify and clean water of "bacteria, parasites and microplastics, chlorine and organic chemical matter such as pesticides, herbicides and improve water taste." Promises, promises.

I didn't want to risk damaging the filter with boiling water, and though it was supposed to be leak-proof, it really wasn't, so if I were to put it in my sleeping bag, I'd surely wake up with a puddle in my bed. So, I filled the bottle but left the straw out until the water had cooled, which didn't take long with the temperature in our room, then sealed it tight so that I could drink it during the night and the next day.

Needless to say, it was early to bed after an exceptionally long day and, with visions of high swinging bridges, "Oh, Lord, and Amen" were the last words that I murmured before drifting off into a light slumber that would have to suffice.

# CHAPTER 4

.....................................................

*"The greatest danger in life is not to take the adventure."*

–George Mallory

.....................................................

## Day 5: Trek Phakding to Namche Bazaar (3540 m)

### 0700 0800 0900

First off, let me give a brief description of *0700 0800 0900*. A series of three numbers will appear at the beginning of each trekking chapter. They represent the time of day, where the first number is the time that we were scheduled to wake, the second is breakfast, and the third is departure. This is information that we had been given at our Ricky Time the previous night.

So, that said, let's get down to business.

I did not sleep well that first night in the mountains. I had been very cold. If I was cold here, how was it going to be when I was higher up? And at Base Camp??? I figured I could buy a bottle or two into which I could put boiling water and cuddle up with them at night, or I could purchase a new sleeping bag—expedition grade—in Namche Bazaar, which was supposed to have lots of trekking shops. It would be expensive, but I did not see many alternatives. I couldn't go for the next two weeks without sleep. At breakfast I decided to ask Ricky what he thought and he suggested that I buy a second liner for my sleeping bag, a thicker one. Then with that together with my thin merino wool liner and the water bottles, I should be fine, and be spared the cost of a high-end sleeping bag.

We left at 9:00 AM and began the steep trek up and out of the village, which then leveled off to a nice easy ascent. We were led by Pemba, one of the sherpas, who almost always took the lead of our group. He had a slow, meticulous gait, kept everyone at a healthy pace and was easy to keep in sight because he permanently wore a raccoon-tail hat. He also made regular breaks to keep the group together, give us a chance to take off our packs if we needed to add or take off a layer of clothing, drink something, have a snack, and take photos. When the break was over he would yell, "Jam! Jam!" the command for "Let's get moving!" It's not pronounced like the toast spread, but rather like *pom-pom* but with a soft *J*.

We traveled mostly single file and for a time that morning I walked behind Dave, the New Yorker, who was travelling abroad for the first time. Most of us were hiking in trekking pants or some type of lycra/poly/merino mix of sporting attire, but Dave was wearing jeans. I also noticed that he had brand new hiking boots on that looked as though they hadn't been broken in, but rather just taken out of the box in Kathmandu. I winced at the thought of the blisters that must be forming on his feet after hours of the not un-technical hiking. My maternal heartstrings were getting tugged.

After an hour and a half, we stopped at a tea house for a break. I ordered a large pot of lemon, ginger, and honey tea for Bea, Shaun, and myself. It was so delicious, and I could feel the healthy goodness as it flowed down my throat. We sat on plastic patio furniture and looked at some of the photos we'd taken that morning. Everyone then began mingling around, making small talk, further getting to know the others in the group.

Before leaving, Beatrice disappeared around the back of the café to find the outhouse, and after she returned, shaking her head in disgust, I bit the bullet and went myself. It was a filthy squatter in a small wooden shack with a stench so terrible that I had no choice but to hold my breath, all the while thinking of Cindy who had told me when I first met her that on such occasions a neck warmer really comes in handy. Now I knew what she meant.

Another hour of hiking was in store for us before we stopped for lunch in Monjo, a small village that lies in the Dudh Kosi river valley just south of Jorsale, at an altitude of 2,835 meters. It is situated shortly before the Sagarmatha National Park entrance gate, a UNESCO World Heritage site since 1979. The primary function of the village is to support the tourism industry, as it lies on the major trekking routes, and it has a bunch of guesthouses. We ate at the Jorsalle Guesthouse and Restaurant. Our group was happy to take over the entire outside terrace, as the temperatures were mild and the sun kept peeking out at us. I shared a table with Beatrice, Shaun, Harry, and Raemonde, a robust Canadian woman in her mid 50s. We were served fried rice with warm juice, then black tea. There was also some coleslaw on the side of the rice, but I was careful about not eating that…raw cabbage in some kind of creamy white sauce. I figured it was safer to just stay away from anything and everything that looked suspicious, at least until after the race. We talked about the royal wedding that was taking place that day—Harry and Meghan. Raemonde was telling us stories about how she saw a parade near her home in Edmonton and that Prince Charles was there. She was actually up front in the spectator throng and got to shake hands with him. She emphatically described how he was 'dripping with royalty', which brought Beatrice into hysterics. She loves American and Canadian humor—who doesn't?—but she is a newbie to some of the puns and sayings, and sometimes what we say as routine comes across as ingeniously funny. Well, at least to good-hearted Beatrice.

Raemonde was on the trip alone; she mentioned having a husband or partner at home, but from what I gathered there were no kids in the deal. She told us she worked for Liebherr, but the way she pronounced the company's name was unrecognizable until she said it several times and then added that it was a German company! So once I realized she was saying a German word, it clicked, not just for me, but for everyone else at the table too, since not only do I speak German, but Harry and Beatrice are also fluent. Even Shaun speaks a bit since his wife is Austrian! *Also, gut, Liebherr.* But the same thing often happens when I'm at home in Germany and having a conversation in German; if someone throws an English word with their foreign pronunciation into the mix, I'm also at a loss. So, no hard feelings, Raemonde.

After we finished eating, Bea was distracted by the aqua-colored doors of the guest rooms at the lodge and wanted her photo taken there since she said that Instagram users loved the color aqua and reacted to it. Shaun eagerly took her photo with his iPhone. He loved using it in portrait mode, then tweaking the saturation, lighting, and filter to create a masterpiece. As much as he loved having photos of himself taken, I think he liked taking snapshots of others even more. He'd get a good shot, give a high five, and call out, "Nailed it!"

A quick trip to the bathroom made the previous outhouse at the tea house seem like a luxury powder room in a five-star hotel.

This one will have me scarred with horrific mental visions for life. Again there was no Western-style seat, just a squatter, which we were already getting used to on the trip anyway. But not only was it a squatter, it was a squatter in what seemed to be an old root cellar under the lodge, with an even more atrocious smell than the last one that had my barf button on high alert. (Again I forgot my neck warmer.) Dark-colored stains dominated the floor, there were no windows, no electrical lighting, and a rickety old wooden door that did not fully shut. So, I was in a compromising position. With the door ajar I had light to see what I was doing—well, I knew what I was doing but I wanted to be absolutely sure where I was doing it and what I was touching—but with the door slightly ajar anyone walking by could also see me in the squat. If I shut the door to total darkness, then I might as well just voluntarily commit myself to the Oregon State Hospital with Jack Nicholson. Suffice it to say, I held my breath and took care of business as quickly as I could with an eye on the open door ready to shout out "Just a sec!" had I seen a shadow on the approach.

*Note to self: Beatrice comes as my watchdog to all toilets from here on out.*

Shortly after leaving Monjo we arrived at the entrance to the Sagarmatha National Park where we needed to wait briefly until our permits were all checked. While waiting we were drawn to look at the magnificent Kani gate spanning the path before us. The gate is brightly painted inside and out and lined on the interior walls with dozens of prayer wheels, which are cylinders on a spindle, allowing them to rotate. The prayer wheels are printed with mantras all around, and when spun, the wheels are said to have the same effect as reciting the prayers as many times as they are spun. Flanking the Kani gate are giant rock edifices with inscriptions that are called Mani stones or walls. These stones are positioned singly along the trails and rivers or placed together to form mounds or long walls, as an offering from the passersby to the local spirits. They are inscribed with the six-syllabled mantra of Avalokiteshvara, Om mani padme hum, as a form of prayer in Tibetan Buddhism. Ricky had told us that we should always keep the Mani walls and stupa to our right when passing them, walking around clockwise, the rotational direction in which the earth and the universe revolve in Buddhist beliefs.

Everyone took this seriously.

So, once the wheels were turned and we were through the gate, we found ourselves in the sacred valley of the Sherpa, the major ethnic group living in that region. Gaining National Park status in 1976, Sagarmatha National Park was honored as a UNESCO World Heritage Site in 1979.

A steep descent through a rocky gorge led us back down to the river which we followed for quite a while, until suddenly, more than a hundred meters above our heads, we saw two suspension bridges crossing the gorge. One was really high, and the other was, amazingly, significantly higher, hanging over the first, making the lower one look rather trivial despite its justified greatness. I shot at glance over at Ricky with fear. "Yes, we need to cross that," he said. I was hoping he meant the lower bridge, but it turned out that was the old bridge that wasn't used anymore. We needed to cross the higher one. *Gulp.* At 125 meters (405 feet) over the river—one hundred twenty-five meters; just wanted to make sure no one was sleeping through that statistic—the bridge is only about a meter and a half wide; I could barely touch the cable railings on each side. They are not really railings as we know railings which are traditionally there to help with balance and safety. There is nothing about them that on first glance provides any sense of protection or stability as they seem to be dancing a cosine while the platform is somehow in a sine wave waltz. And with these railings it's not as though you can just glide your hand along them with all those random protruding steel wires pointing in all directions. So I can only assume that they are a structural rather than a safety element on the bridge and, considering the significant traffic of the two- and four-footed creatures that they support each year, they are obviously doing their job just fine.

We hiked up the zig-zag trail on the banks of the gorge to the abutment of the bridge. Jill, with her fear of heights and who'd already had trouble the day before on the small hanging bridge, was now crying while facing her task on the near side. Her husband, Mark, was trying to calm her. I was scared but I also knew I had no choice but to cross it. Or turn around and go home. So with head held high, eyes focused directly forward and walking exactly in the middle of the bridge I bit the bullet and started across. I was doing okay until... no, this time it was not the fun-loving porters, but another woman in the group who caused a scene in front of me. She was being overly expressive about her fear of heights, squawking and squealing the entire crossing, and once she made it over, she sat down on the step on the far end. She made an attention-grabbing exhibition, laughing and crying, but she was essentially blocking the path for the rest of us—Jill, Mark, myself, and half a dozen others—who were trying to get off the bridge. This was pretty upsetting because we wanted nothing more than to get to the safety of the other side, but the rest of us were forced to prolong our agony until she was done with her show and cleared out of the way before we could set foot on safe ground. Which we eventually did.

*Ausatmen.* A sigh of relief.

There was a steep hike after the bridge with very technical terrain, steps made of stones laid into the hard-packed soil, trampled by thousands of trekkers over years. Shortly thereafter we crossed over the 3,000-meter elevation level, which we were informed of by Harry who was wearing a GPS watch, on which he was monitoring our gain. Harry is a pretty reclusive guy, and it wasn't as though he voluntarily gave us this information; the truth is that we were all curious and kept asking—well, Shaun kept asking as our spokesman—until we finally got the answer we wanted (whether it was true or not).

A little apprehensive about the elevation and how I would respond to it, and remembering that Harry was from Holland, I caught up to him and asked him if he'd ever heard of a guy named Wim Hof, also a Dutchman, nicknamed The Iceman, who is known for his daring feats in the extreme cold and at elevation. The man holds multiple world records including one for the longest ice bath (1 hour, 53 minutes, and 42 seconds) and one for climbing to 7,200 meters (23,600 feet) on Mount Everest wearing only shorts. The Iceman has developed breathing techniques which, together with mind power, cause his body to go alkaline, which allows him to withstand the cold. He teaches his method widely and has even brought scantily clad amateur trekkers to the summit of Mt. Kilimanjaro (5,895 meters; 19,341 feet) without supplemental oxygen and showing no signs of altitude sickness. For that reason, I had been considering taking a course on his methods (taught by one of his protégés) prior to my trek to Base Camp. I didn't manage to squeeze it in, but Harry told me that not only had he heard of the guy, a year prior he himself had attended a course taught by one of his protégés! Of course I wanted to know all about it to confirm whether or not I'd missed out on something that may have helped me on this trek. Harry said that what impressed him the most was the ice bath that all participants took after a couple hours of breathing exercises. He said it wasn't that bad, which probably still meant torture for the rest of us mere mortals who don't jump into glacial crevasses for fun. Then I asked him about the breathing techniques for high altitude and whether he thought they could potentially help him on this trip. "Probably not, who knows?" he replied. Hmmm…maybe I didn't miss much after all.

Although there was one thing I was certain that would help me during the trek and I was already reaping the benefits. About a month prior to going on the trip, I texted Beatrice one day saying, "Bring trekking poles." Her response was "NO! I was hoping you would not say that!" Then she went on to say that she had no idea how to use them and does she really, really, really need them? I told her she would later thank me for that advice.

Why was I so sure? Well, the previous summer when trying to conquer the 87 kilometers and 5,000 meters of elevation gain of the Hochkönigman Endurance Trail in the Austrian Alps, I was congratulated by my competitors for taking on the race without trekking poles. What those other runners didn't know at the time was that it was more a question of inexperience and naiveté rather than heroism. After only about 30 kilometers my quads were shredded, and I would have given anything to have even one pole on which to transfer some weight during those steep descents.

It was then I realized that if I wanted to continue running long distance trail races in the mountains I'd need to learn to use trekking poles. So why not do it right the first time and learn from the best?

Thus, on a freezing cold winter day, on the other side of the valley from where I ran the Hochkönigman trail race just six months earlier, I went for a short run with Wolfgang Scholz in the mountains overlooking Lake Zell in Austria.

Who is Wolfgang Scholz, you might ask? Despite being one of the top athletes in the world in his discipline, his name is not well known. This is because until recently his sport was considered more of a recreational rather than a competitive activity. Wolfgang is the European Champion in Nordic walking over the 10-kilometer distance and second in the world in the half marathon. At 44 he is not necessarily in the age group that one typically finds world-ranked athletes, and though in excellent condition for his years, he attributes his success to proper technique rather than physical fitness.

No, I am not taking up Nordic walking. Not yet anyway.

Let's just say that I am not the most coordinated person. So there I was in the middle of winter on a snowy mountainside in the Alps, running alongside Wolfgang, trying my hardest not to trip on my new appendages (the trekking poles), nor slip on the ice and snow. But without him even looking at my stride nor my pole placement he began to talk. He started with the very basics of human kinetics in motion, getting me to focus on what my chest, shoulders, and arms should be doing instead of how to control the poles.

Shoulders back, chest open, breathe.

Keep the arms close to the body and transfer the momentum of the arm swing into the forward motion of the legs.

The principles were very basic, and I soon realized that this was how I should be running whether I had poles in my hands or not. But I was quickly out of breath. Why? Because in addition to the muscles normally used when running, those calves, quads, and hamstrings were now competing with the upper-body muscles for the oxygen they all needed to function. I compared it to how I felt when swimming; when every muscle in the body is working at the same time, you'd better be optimizing your breathing and oxygen consumption or you'll be hanging on the side of the pool (with me).

After a period of running while integrating his tips, Wolfgang evaluated my technique—which he said looked good—and he then took a video so that I could see for myself. And although I'd hoped to find myself resembling a gazelle prancing up the mountainside, what I did see was a middle-aged ultra runner who suddenly appeared to have a smoother, more rhythmic motion in her steps than she did just thirty minutes earlier.

So now, trekking up a steep, rocky hillside along the Dudh Kosi river in Nepal, crossing into the zone where oxygen supply is not what we are used to, Beatrice—in front of me using her trekking poles like a pro—turned to me and said, "I am so glad you talked me into bringing these things!" While there were many in our group that also had them, others purchased some at a trekking shop *en route* (SS)… and were happy they did.

Not only trekkers crowd the trails in Sagarmatha, but also pack animals, because they are the primary means of transporting goods in that region. We wouldn't meet the infamous yak until we were higher up, but in our current location we crossed paths with many horses, donkeys, and of course, dzopkyos. A dzopkyo? Never heard of it? Can you even say it? We couldn't either, which is probably why Ricky told us they were called yokios. They are a crossbreed of yak and cattle, and capable of carrying heavy loads. They are beautiful to watch as they slowly saunter by, and if you stay out of their way and stand still, they ignore you.

But the donkey caravans were unpredictable. You'd get yourself in what you thought was a safe position on the inside of the trail to let them by, and as they were walking past, suddenly one would stop dead in its tracks and stare you down. Like a really freaky donkey stare with those huge brown eyes that sink into oblivion. You didn't know if you should stay frozen or run for your life. Sometimes they get spooked and start a stampede in which case all hell breaks loose and you can only hope that there is a scalable hill behind you where you can climb to safety since an unwanted meeting with a hoof could easily lead to some bad bruises or even broken bones.

The final push for that day was a long steep climb up from the riverbed, the steepest that we would experience on the entire route to Base Camp, but we took it slowly with a much-needed candy-bar break in the middle. We stopped at a trekker's point that had a ring of benches and a great view. It also had two rickety wooden outhouses, each of which had a sign on it. You could choose between a "Pay Toilet" or a "Free Toilet." A woman attendant sat on the dusty ground next to the pay toilet to collect the fee. The difference was most likely a Western toilet versus a squatter, but clearly our group had wizened-up to the fact that these facilities should be steered clear of since no one took the opportunity to use them. (Though you know that during the trek everyone is secretly scanning the sides of the trail for a spot to duck into should the call of nature arise.)

A thick forest surrounded us for most of the climb, but once the trail ascended to a crest, it opened up to provide a break in the trees, and we could see some buildings across the next valley, stunningly high up on the other side of the mountain ridge. It was the monastery at Namche, a breathtaking sight.

Rock-walled yak corrals began to line the trail and then, around the next bend, an entire city unexpectedly appeared before our eyes. I felt like a little girl turning the pages of a fairy tale book, everywhere I looked seeing something new and magical. But I wasn't Dorothy and that wasn't Oz; it was none other than the famed Sherpa capital of Namche Bazaar.

The enchanting city of Namche is set in the form of a natural amphitheater nestled gently into an idyllic U-shaped mountainside. Hundreds of buildings dot the hillside, connected by stone walkways and narrow dirt paths. It has a long history of trading with neighboring villages in the Khumbu valley as well as Tibet and India, and even today has a large traders' market in the middle of town every Saturday. As the staging point for expeditions to not only Everest but other Himalayan peaks, there are many trekking and climbing stores, a visitor's center, cafes, souvenir shops, lodges, and bars. All of us were looking forward to a day of rest to explore this captivating place.

Our arrival was from the lower side of the village near the market square, where there was also a large stupa strung with prayer flags, and a colorfully decorated pavilion, under which we stood as a few raindrops began to fall. Ricky called our attention to himself and another man who he introduced as the record holder of the Everest Marathon, a handsome, young Nepalese, who was beaming from the attention and awe that we bestowed upon him. He said a few words about himself before disappearing back into the streets of Namche, with us following shortly afterwards. We hiked up a wide stone path flanked by large prayer wheels, each housed in its own open cupola. Trekking stores, cafes, mini grocery stores, souvenir shops, and lodges became denser and we found ourselves climbing up a steep staircase that wound its way through the city. There were also homes with small terraced gardens that housed pack animals, chickens and children playing about.

Arriving at our lodge around 3:00 PM, we were promptly served tea in the dining room. The lodge was very nice (everything is now getting relative). Sitting high up on the hillside, the view from our bedroom was breathtaking, with the entire village below us and soaring snow-covered mountain peaks all around. And it felt warmer than the last place. Set up on the hillside it got the blessings of the afternoon sun, whereas the lodge on the day before, though also on a hillside, was hidden by vegetation and on the east side of the mountain, so in the afternoon it lost the warmth of the sun's rays and cooled down quickly. And here we found a warm thick cozy blanket lying on each bed! I was thrilled when I saw this since I'd been so cold the night before and hadn't had a chance yet to buy another sleeping bag liner. I don't think everyone was similarly thrilled since the blankets are probably rarely washed, but I didn't care and reveled in its cuddly warmth. And although we were still sharing the toilet with dozens, it was remarkably clean(er).

A few from the group decided to head to a bar in town with Ricky before dinner. Ricky had a friend there that he wanted to visit. He called him his brother, though they were not related, and he apparently owned The Café Danphe Bar, where they were going to meet up. Beatrice was pretty exhausted, as was most of the rest of the group, so nearly everyone chose to stay at the lodge and relax. And, although the idea of checking out a local bar in Namche was appealing, I was adamant about not drinking alcohol during the trek, at least not before the race, especially after we had been advised by Ricky that, once we got up in elevation, alcohol acted like a catalyst for altitude sickness.

Dinner was planned for 6:30 and those of us who'd stayed behind were milling around the dining room since well before 6:00 since it was warm by the fire. But 6:30 came and went with no sign of the others and no sign of our dinner. The lodge owners held off serving until the group was complete. Most of us didn't mind about the dinner delay, but one woman in our group was upset and said it was disrespectful—which it actually was considering there were about 15 of us waiting in the dining hall—but since we didn't have any time constraints, no one else seemed to be upset about it, or were too tired to care. The rowdy group showed up around 7:00 and Kiki, a young Chinese-American woman who had been among them, couldn't stop giggling when she came into the dining room; she was still working on finishing off an oversized can of beer as she found a spot to sit at a table, eager to eat. Kiki loved food and was always the first to ask for seconds at every meal.

Dinner was finally served and while eating we were relayed tales from the outing to the bar. Apparently there had been a guitar there and Ricky, being a musician who plays and sings in a band in Kathmandu, entertained everyone, playing classic rock tunes and singing, while the rest joined in and had a couple of beers.

But during dinner, there was a stark contrast between the relaxed and sober group who'd stayed behind and the alcohol-laden party-goers. This hung heavy in the air, which led the atmosphere to be very subdued, and after Ricky Time and getting our bottles filled with boiled water, we called it an early night.

While lying in bed the previous night with the light out, I had taken out my compact, foldable, mini-keyboard and linked it up with my iPhone to type up some notes about the day. I had wanted to do the same again, but was afraid I would disturb Beatrice who wanted to sleep. However, before I had a chance to mention it to her, she asked if I would type again that night. She said the dim light of my phone and the light tapping on the keys comforted her, as her husband sometimes worked on his iPad in bed when she was going to sleep.

Ten minutes later, even though Beatrice was almost asleep, I thought of something from the day that I wanted to tell her, and for some reason I decided that I had to do it then. She was dozy but all ears.

During lunch that day, Shaun had asked us what we used as a pillow cover. He said that he had found a bug welcoming him on his pillow as he got into his room in the lodge the previous night so he put the pillow inside one of his clean T-shirts and was pleased with his hygienic solution. I said that I just laid my sleeping bag on top of the pillow and Bea said that she slept with her head on her folded arms. Honestly, even though it was true that I tried to lay my sleeping bag on top of the pillow, of course I was sliding all over the place and my head was directly on the pillow most of the night, but I didn't want Shaun to think I lived in a barn. I mean, I didn't even think of NOT putting my head directly on the pillow. There was a pillowcase on it and since we are used to having clean bed linens everywhere we stay, the thought didn't even cross my mind that they may not be washed regularly, or that they might smell or have bugs living in them! Just the same reasons that a lot of people may not want to use the blankets. But now after Shaun had mentioned it, I began to think. Hmmm… They certainly don't wash the pillowcases after each guest and the blankets are probably never washed, just maybe hung outside to air out once in a while. So, as Bea and I were lying in bed that night, me with my pillow now tucked inside one of my T-shirts, I brought up Shaun's comment and we made up new answers to it since our previous ones that day had been so pathetic.

Shaun: "What do you use as a pillow covering, Holly?"

Holly: "Well, I lay my hair down between my head and my pillow. So, essentially, my hair is the pillowcase."

Shaun: "Brilliant! And you, Beatrice?"

Beatrice: "Well, I have a top-quality germ-and-bug-resistant pillow wrap, specially made by Gucci for third-world trekkers who can't bear to leave the luxuries at home."

Shaun: "Wow, we could all use one of those!"

Maybe it was the low oxygen levels, but this went on ramblingly through our fits of laughter until we both fell asleep, cuddled up under our fluffy, cozy, dirty blankets.

# CHAPTER 5

........................................................................................

*"The real reason for quest is always self-knowledge."*

–Thomas C. Foster

........................................................................................

## Day 6: Rest Day Namche Bazaar (3,540 m)

## 0600 0700 0800

I woke full of excitement for the day ahead. I had gotten a great night's sleep, snug as a bug in a rug. On the agenda for the day was a hike of about five kilometers out of Namche, at which point we would turn around and run back. I was looking forward to some running, being used to doing it almost every day at home. Both my body and mind missed it.

At 8:00 AM we started a hike up the back side and to the top of the village, where we were led to an open area which would be the finish line of the race the following week. A well-groomed trail led us to the outskirts of Namche, and just outside of the village, right on the edge of the trail, we were surprised to see the national bird of Nepal, there called the danphe, but also known as the Himalayan monal or the Impeyan pheasant. It is an amazingly colorful creature—the male, that is—which looked starkly out of place against the monotone-colored rock and gravel landscape. Ricky was surprised to see one this close to the village and assured us it was a good sign.

Ricky by now had received the nickname Ricky-Bobby from Mark, who was a big fan of the movie *Talladega Nights*. I'd never seen it, which is not a big surprise, since I hardly ever go to the movies; watching Hollywood films dubbed into German is more painful than it is entertaining. But as we trekked, the group talked a lot about movies. Mark was a movie fanatic who had seen almost everything, and usually Shaun, Niki, and Carolyn had too, but I hadn't seen any of them. It was definitely sad that since moving abroad I had lost the movie culture in my life. But Jill explained the storyline of *Talladega Nights* to me, and even though our Ricky was about as different from the NASCAR-driving movie character Ricky-Bobby as anyone could possibly get, the name stuck.

The short trek took us mostly uphill on a wide trail. On the flat sections there was a smooth, packed surface, but the climbs were on worn stone steps littered with loose gravel. After about four kilometers we came across an old woman with a collection box. We'd been told about her the night before during Ricky Time. Apparently there is a man, who is quite old now, who has essentially dedicated his life to the upkeep of the trail and is well-regarded by both the Nepalese and international trekkers. Considering that his efforts and those of his supporters take time and money to accomplish their goals, this checkpoint was set up on the route that all trekkers pass in the hopes that donations will be given to continue the work. A book was there for us to sign our names and countries of origin, and although it was by no means obligatory, we all tossed something into the pot.

Finally, we reached a tea house where we could take a break and get a drink, which meant more ginger-lemon tea with Bea, Shaun, and the rest of the troop while enjoying the view and chatting with some Australian trekkers who were in another group. They couldn't believe that we were planning on running a marathon on those trails and at that altitude. They said they were having enough trouble walking. But one should keep in mind that the trekkers in our group were all of above-average fitness level. They were there to run a marathon, which meant they have trained their aerobic systems comprehensively prior to arrival. Shaun had even done some high-altitude chamber training. We weren't huffing and puffing and struggling along the trails (too badly), but for many trekkers visiting the area, that is far from reality as many are testing their physical limits.

Suddenly we were distracted by a loud commotion. A giant yak had slipped off the edge of the trail and was hanging by only his forefeet from the path, trying desperately to get back up. He was holding himself up with his front legs while frantically trying to catch a firm spot with his back legs to propel himself back up. The pure physics of it looked like the animal had no chance, he had so much weight already hanging over the side and I knew that if he fell, he would be badly hurt, but amazingly he managed to climb back up onto the trail. I was stunned, and relieved.

From Namche on upwards we would soon get used to the clang of yak bells along the trails. The yak is a highly valued animal to the people that live there as they supply transport, milk, protein, fur, hoof, dung, bone, and skin. Tea is made with yak milk and is a staple of the diet of yak herders and inhabitants of the higher villages. The animals graze in the highlands and convert the sparse grass into clothing, butter, fuel for the stove, and meat for the fire. Herding yaks has essentially enabled the Sherpa to live in this land of rock, ice, and snow for centuries. The long shaggy hair of the animals is their most notable feature, and it helps them withstand temperatures to forty degrees below zero; they are so well insulated that several inches of snow can accumulate on their backs without melting. Their hoofs are round and have sharp edges which help them secure footing in ice and snow.

From the tea house we were then free to run the trail back to Namche. Those few kilometers would be the final ones heading into the finish in the race the following week, and it is always a mental bonus when you know what to expect: the gift of no surprises when you are at your physical limits.

We took off our jackets and gave them to the sherpas to carry back to our lodge so that we could run without ballast. And since we were on our own, everyone at their own pace, there was no group start. We were all just milling about when, suddenly and without warning, Shaun took off. I saw him go and raced after him. I caught him on the first steep descent but then he powered ahead on the next incline. How could he be so fast going uphill with all that muscle mass in tow? We were alone for a few minutes, me right on his heels, and I thought it would stay that way all the way back to Namche until on the next descent I heard footsteps from behind and Henni came flying by us. He is a great trail runner with really quick, short steps. I overtook Shaun but couldn't catch Henni running downhill; it was there we gained some distance over Shaun. However, once the route flattened, Shaun caught me, then we both caught Henni, but on the next ascent Shaun nosed ahead again. He was just like one of those yaks! We taunted him by shouting that we'd see him again shortly... and we did on the next descent. The trail was fairly technical and the downhill sections were a tricky stone-jumping game. Henni obviously had some experience with those techniques and I tried to stay right behind him and follow his line. The London streets were no training ground for technical descents so we'd shaken Shaun again, but I was starting to feel winded. This was no surprise since we were over 3,500 meters (11,500 feet) above sea level. At the next steep ascent I had to walk briefly to catch my breath, but by that point Henni did the same, and I'm assuming Shaun did too because he didn't catch up with us. Back to running, the hikers, sherpas, and porters cleared the way for us and cheered us on. Sooner than I expected we passed the large flagpole up on the hillside promontory, signaling the entrance to the village. Henni had gained about 200 meters on me, but he missed the cutoff down a narrow alley to the finish. He realized it after about ten steps, and had to double back. Just enough time for me to get right back on his tail and in a flash we were at the future finishing line after about 24 minutes on the run. Shaun came in 30 seconds later with no one else in sight. He looked at his watch with a huge grin and yelled "Nailed it!"

It definitely had been exhilarating to run again despite the difficulty with the altitude.

To kill time and keep moving while waiting for the rest of the crew, Shaun and I started shooting some photos in the maze of stone walls in an adjacent small park. After about ten minutes of trying to capture the essence of where we were, we headed back to the finish and found Beatrice was there. I was so happy and surprised to see her as I had been pretty sure she would walk the route back, but she had decided to run and she looked rejuvenated. It had done us all some good.

While I was talking to Bea, I noticed that Shaun was chatting with a group of men from another group. Then the other group started to walk off and Shaun strolled over to us, mentioning something about his buddy Ash. *What?!? That's Ash? Your buddy from London?* Shaun had talked about him quite a lot and I'd wanted to put a face to a name so I dashed over to meet him myself. He had a warm smile, and I liked him from the first moment. I'd later find out that the Everest Marathon was only a small part of a major fundraiser he was working on called *Run7.global* to raise funds in support of global sustainable business practices. His group was also in Namche at the moment, doing the same exact trek up to Base Camp but staying in different lodges. They had arrived in the mountains a day ahead of us, but were now essentially on the same trekking schedule. Beatrice then joined us and we chatted for a minute before his group took off.

"Mamma mia!" Beatrice exclaimed once Ash was out of earshot. "That guy is a hunk!"

She had a point there; he was definitely a good-looking guy, to top off his charming personality, not unlike his buddy Shaun. What do they have in the water in Merry Olde England?

We started to cool down fast so we headed back to the lodge to change into warm clothes and have lunch; then it was time for some shopping! Bea and Shaun joined me as we went to discover what we could find on offer in the shops of Namche. Our first stop was The North Face store where I bought a black, expedition-weight base-layer long-sleeved half-zip shirt. Shaun tried on some cool relaxed-fitting, tapered-legged sweatpants, which Bea and I thought looked great on him, but he thought they were too short and he left them in the shop. Then to the Sherpa store where we had fun trying on just about everything and I ended up leaving with a winter hat, sunglasses neck strap, T-shirt and a 1-liter Nalgene water bottle, plus a Vapur soft plastic bottle, both of which could hold boiling water and I could tuck into my sleeping bag to keep me warm at night.

Obviously I was a bit obsessed with the cold.

Next up, a café for herbal tea and cake with WiFi, all for 100 rupees, which also included free phone charging! We stayed there for a couple of hours, sipping tea, taste-testing the cake selection, and uploading photos and videos. Then to one final shop for the day where I found a fleece sleeping bag liner (still not warm enough) and some mountaineering socks.

Out on the street, we met up with a few others from our group who were headed into the bar that Ricky and the crew had visited the night before, so we popped in too. Our two-man camera crew, Aayush and Anuj, were there as well (there was a third, Manish, but he was much more reserved and didn't mingle with the group as much as the other two). Anuj was the leader of the photo team, a few years older than the others and more experienced. (Anuj took the amazing photo which adorns the cover of this book.) Aayush, nicknamed D3vil (pronounced devil), has two very unique physical characteristics. He has amazingly gorgeous, long, dark wavy hair, which he usually wore tied up in a knot somehow, and he also had scars from a cleft lip that had long since been operated on. These guys would follow us during the course of the entire three weeks of our trip, and even though they were technically working while they were there with us in that café/bar, even if they had been off-duty, they would have still joined us there. They were game for everything.

Several people had ordered tea or water, but no one drank any alcohol that afternoon. Ricky had gotten hold of the guitar again and the entertainment began. We all gave it our best shot and together we belted out *Wish You Were Here*, a couple of Beatles tunes, and some Stones, but mostly we just laughed at ourselves and the slightly misunderstood humor of a hodge-podge of cultures.

Suddenly I felt really warm; the place wasn't heated, but I felt flushed. I asked Beatrice if she thought it was hot in there. She shook her head, then pointed out my reddened face; apparently I had a sunburn. I'd been so careful all week about putting on sunscreen, but that morning I'd forgotten it amidst getting the right walking clothes plus running gear ready for our short run. Argh! I'd have to be more careful, especially about something so basic and important!

Bea and I made it back to the lodge around 5:00 PM to give us enough time for a shower before dinner, which brings us to a very interesting topic. Let's talk about showers in the Himalayan lodges for a minute. Showers were not located with the toilets, nor were they free to use at any time. Usually there was only one single shower in the entire lodge, there was an extra fee involved, and sometimes there was a waiting list to use it. And, since it was so cold there, with no heating in the building except in the main dining room from a wood-burning stove—and that stove was only lit once a day at 5:00 PM to keep the trekkers from freezing while eating their dinners—it was nothing less than torture to get undressed in the ice cold air in the shower shack only to stand under a weak stream of lukewarm water. Therefore, if I wanted to wash my hair, I had to be sure to shower around 5:00 PM, coinciding with the lighting of the fire, then sit in front of the stove to let my hair dry, because of course there were no hairdryers and even if I'd brought one, we had no access to electrical outlets anyway!

You may be wondering whether a shower was even necessary. Quite honestly, probably not, since at those cool temperatures we didn't do much sweating. Not everyone in our group showered when given the opportunity. It is certainly a luxury that we have gotten very used to in our daily lives. While I was in the desert during the Marathon des Sables, though I took a couple of makeshift showers, I didn't wash my hair for 9 days. And I survived. So, like I said, showering is an indulgence, just like WiFi and cozy dirty blankets, but one that I personally decided was worth enduring a little suffering in the form of chilly goose bumps as a trade-off for that wonderful feeling of cleanliness.

The shower at the lodge in Namche was actually relatively nice. Relatively. And in order to be relative, you have to have a comparison, which I would eventually have after I saw the showers at some of the other places. In Namche, the shower was in a small room on the ground floor across from a toilet and sink cubbyhole. The floor was tiled with some sort of plastic mat which strangely enough made it super slippery since the mat itself wouldn't stay in place. In the corner was a stool and behind that was an opening in the wall which served as a shelf where I could keep my clothes. The room was about six feet wide by ten long. I reluctantly took off my clothes and turned on the water, hopping up and down with my arms folded tightly across my chest to keep warm. I had initially laid my towel on the stool, but once the water was on and spraying everywhere, I tucked the towel up into the hole in the wall to keep it dry too. Naturally I was hoping for a nice powerful stream of steaming hot water, but what I got was a slightly warmer than lukewarm cascade which was doing nothing to warm me up. It seemed a losing battle, so I began scrubbing and lathering as fast as I could to get it over with and get back into my layers of clothes.

Beatrice had showered just before me and when I got back in the room she asked me if I had any of those sticks with the cotton balls on the ends.

*What???*

"The ones that you can dry your ears with," she added.

*Q-tips? Oh, man, Beatrice!* She really wasn't sure what they were called. Cotton swabs is the generic name, but I've always referred to them by the brand name of Q-tips. In German they are called *Wattestäbchen*. She could have simply said that but we rarely speak German with each other except when we don't want others to know what we are saying. But we still had to be careful since you never know who speaks what language. One day while trekking, Bea and I were talking about who speaks German in the group and a Vietnamese man in front of me said that his wife also speaks it fluently! She and I then started up a conversation in the *deutsche Sprache* about how she worked for a German telecommunications company and lived for a while in Frankfurt. We were an American and a Vietnamese woman chatting away for nearly an hour in German while trekking in the Himalayas. There has to be a first for everything I suppose.

Once Beatrice and I finished with our *Wattestäbchen* and got dressed, we headed down to the dining room where we pulled chairs up next to the wood stove to dry our hair. Most everyone was hanging out there since it was the warmest place around. Plus, before dinner we were all required to have a quick check-up by our group's doctor, Prajwal, who was camped out in a corner. Pulse and blood oxygen levels would be taken and we would also have the chance to ask about any other general concerns such as digestion problems, headaches, or sleep troubles. When I first met the doc the day before while trekking, I thought he was one of us runners. He was a young guy that looked to be in good shape. He had dark skin and hair, but dressed in Western trekking clothes, it wasn't immediately clear to me that he was part of the Nepali guide team nor that his backpack wasn't filled with snacks, cameras, and a change of clothes like the rest of us, but rather medical supplies. He was humble and shy and appeared to be almost embarrassed to admit he was our group's doctor when I met him trekking. But once he got into his role of medical provider, he was nothing less than professional and competent.

The doc put a clip on my pointer finger and the digital numbers on the screen came to life. My blood oxygen was at 87%. That sounded low to me. He told me that it is normal to be constantly changing and that if I took slow deep breaths it would increase, so I did, but instead it began to decrease! Then it slowly began to rise up to 96 percent and I suggested seeing if I could get it to 100 but he said that was also dangerous! But considering it was low—technically anything below 90% is considered hypoxemia—he advised me to go to the pharmacy and buy a particular isotonic drink that helps absorb fluids, which would aid my body in adjusting to less available oxygen.

So, because altitude sickness is a really important topic and not exactly one that gets a considerable amount of attention when hearing tales of adventures in the Himalayas, I am going to spend some time on it here.

(Do not skip this part.)

What exactly is altitude sickness anyway? Even non-mountain climbers probably know that it is the negative effects caused by rapid exposure to the low amounts of available oxygen at higher altitudes. Rapid here roughly means climbing more than 300 meters (1,000 feet) per day at an elevation of more than 2,500 meters. The concentration of oxygen at sea level is about 21% and the barometric pressure averages 760 mmHg. As altitude increases, the oxygen concentration remains the same but the number of oxygen molecules per breath is reduced due to the reduction in pressure. For example, at 3,500 meters the barometric pressure is only about 490 mmHg, so there are roughly 40% fewer oxygen molecules per breath. Thus, at altitude, in order to properly oxygenate the body, your breathing rate (even while at rest) has to increase, which isn't so easy. Symptoms of high-altitude sickness are widespread but the most common are headache; gastrointestinal issues (vomiting, diarrhea, constipation, loss of appetite); fatigue; insomnia; swelling of hands, feet, and face; nose bleeds; and of course, shortness of breath upon exertion. Level of physical fitness *apparently* has no influence on the risk of suffering from its effects and for mild cases drinking fluids and descending to a lower altitude is normally sufficient. If left untreated, altitude sickness can progress to high altitude pulmonary edema (HAPE) or high-altitude cerebral edema (HACE), both severely life-threatening. Unfortunately, we would encounter victims of that later in the trek.

With my blood oxygen level at 87%, I was technically hypoxemic. Hypoxemia is the condition of low oxygen in the blood, and that can lead to hypoxia which is low oxygen in the tissues. When the blood doesn't carry enough oxygen to your tissues to meet your body's needs, you can get into trouble (i.e., organ failure and even death). To put it in perspective, if I were at home and my general practitioner were to measure my blood oxygen level and find it to be at 87%, she would likely call an ambulance and have me rushed to the hospital. It can be that dangerous.

But in the Himalayas, the world is a different place and more risks are wagered. Some 40,000 tourists trek through those trails each year; many get sick and some even die, but most survive to tell the tale. A tale that normally doesn't include severe altitude sickness as a highlight.

That said, there would be bumps in the road for some of us ahead and in fact several in our group were already experiencing minor symptoms of high-altitude sickness including diarrhea, nausea, loss of appetite, headaches, and sleep problems. Thankfully, I had none, but we were nevertheless all encouraged by Prajwal to take Diamox, a medicine used to treat altitude sickness. Actually, Diamox is the brand name for the active ingredient acetazolamide. Those in our group without symptoms or only minor ones were to take a low dose of 250 mg per day, which was half a tablet in the morning and half at night, while those showing some symptoms took a regular dose (500 mg/ day). Some in the group had already started taking Diamox as a prophylactic long before we arrived in Namche. Both Niki and Carolyn had started in Kathmandu.

I was worried that the side effects of the drug would be worse than any mild symptoms caused by the altitude. I was wrong. There was only one side effect of the drug and it was marvelous: tingling toes and fingertips brought on by temperature change. So, upon gripping that hot mug of tea in the morning, I soon felt a tickling tingle build up in my hands until I felt like Harry Potter ready to send lightning bolts from my magic fingertips!

But I digress. Leaving Hogwarts and returning to Namche…

After the medical check-up, dinner was served. We were beginning to see a pattern. The three meals a day were dominated by carbohydrates. Pasta, rice, potatoes, French fries, toast, and oatmeal. Not necessarily in that order. There was always some form of eggs for breakfast, which would immediately jump from my plate to Shaun's. There were also occasionally some specks of green mixed in with the carbs, but essentially there were no vegetables, which makes up the majority of my diet at home. Sometimes we were served veggie dumplings, but no real good local food like we were hoping to get. I guess it is tough satisfying such a large group of people from all around the world, and nothing is safer in that respect than pasta and fries.

Following dinner it was Ricky Time, after which we waited by the wood stove for the water to boil, then cool a bit, before filling up our bottles. Now I had three! And even though the water was boiled, I still had my doubts that it was completely safe to drink. What about the pots that it was boiled in and poured out of? And the hands of the men boiling the water and handling my bottles, opening and closing the lids? So, just to be safe, I had water purifying tables with me and tossed one into each bottle. Yes, it tasted like chlorine, but as far as I was concerned that minor unpleasantry was worth avoiding dysentery.

At around 9:30 we trudged up to our room and, first things first, I tucked my two new leak-proof bottles down into my sleeping bag so that it would be all warm and cozy when I climbed in. Brush the teeth, wash up, take that half tablet of Diamox followed by a few minutes of writing before futilely setting my alarm that I knew I would not need with those paper-thin walls through which I could hear the neighbor's as well as the neighbor's neighbor's alarms, then lights out and the end to another unforgettable day.

# CHAPTER 6

*"You don't have to be a hero to accomplish great things—to compete. You can just be an ordinary chap, sufficiently motivated to reach challenging goals."*

–Edmund Hillary

## Day 7: Namche Bazaar to Khumjung (3,780 m) Over Hotel Everest View

### 0700 0800 0900

I did not sleep well. After waking to the sounds of Beatrice opening the lock on our door around 3:00 in the morning to go to the bathroom, I lay awake for a couple of hours. Was this a symptom of the altitude? Probably not, I figured, since I often have the same problem at home.

Most were awake by 6:00 and roaming around the halls. Having a room right across from the bathroom and at the head of the stairs was not the most ideal location for peace and quiet. First things first, we took our half tablet of Diamox, as instructed, like good little girls.

At 7:15, with our bags packed and handed over to the porters, Beatrice and I quickly headed out to the pharmacy before breakfast to get those isotonic drink mixes that the doc had recommended the night before. Prajwal had said that those mixes had "saved Nepal", by which I assume he meant it was used to treat stomach ailments for a variety of illnesses since it is supposed to help with liquid absorption in the stomach.

After stocking up on the wonder drug, the cafe from the previous day was our next stop. Our WiFi password was good for 24 hours and the server speed was much better there than in our lodge where the WiFi was completely overloaded by our group. We ordered a cup of tea, charged our phones, and checked and sent messages. A busy morning at the office.

We were back to the hotel by 8:30 for a quick breakfast and by 9 we were on the road, taking a different route than the day before. Right from the start, the trail up and out of the city was very steep. We passed a schoolyard full of playing children, who soon began military-style drills. Their chants accompanied us as we walked, echoes carrying all the way up the hillside. Once out of the city, the terrain quickly changed. Compared to the thick forest on our way into Namche, we were now on barren hillsides with scrub brush and spindly low trees. Ground-cover flowers were strewn about. Helicopters kept flying in and out of the two landing pads over Namche. The clouds were constantly shifting, and we sporadically enjoyed views of some of the high peaks.

The climb was steep and arduous, most people had stripped off their outer layer of clothing and were in T-shirts and tanks. A determined Nepalese woman hurried past us just before we passed Syangboche Airport, an unpaved airstrip not licensed for commercial flights and only used for chartering high-paying tourists heading to the Hotel Everest View. Ricky told us that the woman we saw was a local politician, who had just returned from Kathmandu via helicopter. He went on to explain that many of the village leaders are women, who hold strong positions in the Sherpa culture.

Lots of people in our group now had chronic coughing. Ricky called this the Khumbu cough, which is apparently common among the Western trekkers and is referred to in almost all the literature on Everest treks. The combination of low humidity and cold at high altitudes dries out the lungs, which causes them to be irritated and inflamed, resulting in a dry hacking cough. Many in our group wore neck warmers up over their mouths and noses to keep the dust at bay and to warm the air before it enters the lungs (and like Cindy, to protect their sensory glands from the stinking toilets). But I found it too difficult to breathe with something covering my mouth and nose, and despite having days where the donkeys, yaks, and our large group were tossing up the dust, simply letting my body do the filtering was (thankfully) good enough for me.

Soon the cloud cover was thicker, the tree coverage was thinner, and the wind began to pick up. Everyone began frantically putting their jackets back on. We traced a ridgeline up to the Hotel Everest View. There, on a large stone terrace overlooking the valley, while Beatrice was flirting with Jesper, I shared a pot of ginger-honey-lemon tea with Niki and Carolyn. Niki pulled out her stash of protein bars, emptied it onto the table, and my mouth started watering. She had peanut butter–chocolate chip Lara Bars. When she saw the look on my face she said, "Go ahead! I've got another box of them in my trekking bag." That PB and chocolate combo was heavenly. Peanut butter wasn't even sold in Germany when I moved there in 2000, and as an

American, that is a no-go. I always had to stock up when I visited home, and nearly overdose on it when I was there to keep me satisfied until the next trip. It goes without saying, I didn't waste a single crumb of that Lara Bar.

Carolyn was just finally starting to feel better after being really sick in Kathmandu. She'd caught some kind of stomach virus just after their arrival and spent most of the first couple of days in the hotel hugging the porcelain goddess. That was also one of the reasons that Niki had faithfully stayed so close to her everywhere I saw them; she was taking care of her best friend.

I then wandered into the lobby of the Hotel Everest View where there was a 3D model of the Khumbu region, a relief map upon which Ricky showed me our entire trekking tour, the glacier path, all the names of the mountains in the area and where the villages were located that we would be staying. All at a bird's-eye view. It was fascinating.

After about a 45-minute break we exited around the back of the hotel and descended a hillside through an amazingly beautiful forest of rhododendron, the national flower of Nepal. They weren't bushes as we know them in Europe and North America, but trees! Six-meter-tall fragrant flowering walls! It was like being in a magical fantasy world. Disney has nothing on that place. We were barely making any forward progress since everyone was constantly taking photos.

And as if it couldn't get any better, when the trees opened up, we were blessed with a breathtaking view of the enchanted village of Khumjung, tucked into a valley and guarded by Mount Khumbila (5,761 meters/18,900 feet). Ricky told us that if you look at the village and the neighboring one on a satellite map, it looked like a horse with the princess spirit of the mountain riding it. Though a relatively small peak compared to some of its neighbors, Mt. Khumbila has never been climbed, or at least not

to its summit. An attempt decades ago ended in tragedy as all of
the climbers were killed by an avalanche. Considered home to the
local patron God, most of the local Sherpa people believe it is too
sacred to climb.

It was a dreamlike walk into the village; there were people
busy in their gardens but along the paths it was eerily quiet.
Peaceful old women were ritually burning juniper branches as a
sacrifice on stone altars in their yards. The feeling of being in a
sacred place was overwhelming. I thought this could possibly be
my favorite place on earth.

In the center of the village the town was alive with people of
all ages. A group of teenagers were playing volleyball in a large
open space. We walked to a school and very young children were
standing in the courtyard, some being greeted by their parents and
others already starting on their walk home. One precious little
boy stole my heart: he had the distinctive Mongolian features
and stood there without emotion, just looking around. He had a
North Face jacket on and a cute little Paul Frank backpack (both
certainly knock-offs). He held a small piece of paper or plastic in
his hand. I had tears in my eyes and had to tear myself away from
him for fear of wanting to scoop him up and take him home with
me.

We then arrived at our lodge, the Amadablam View Lodge,
which had no view of Ama Dablam on that cloud-covered
afternoon. There we were served a lunch of fried noodles, French
fries, and a slice of yak cheese. I ate the carbs and tried a small
bite of the cheese, but it had a really strong gamey taste, so I left
the rest on my plate. There were no other willing takers for it.

We were then shown to our rooms and I was shocked. The
conditions were very poor, borderline inhospitable. We were in
the dungeon, a row of six rooms underneath the main building.
The room we were given was very cold and gray and dark. There

was a window, but it faced north and was so low to the ground overlooking a stone-walled dirt field that it received very little light. I couldn't bear to begin to unpack my things just yet so I went in search of the bathroom.

Of course, the bathrooms were even worse. *Bathroom*, as you know by now, is a misnomer, as there was no bath and usually not even a sink; from now on I'll just say the toilet so we are all on the same page. The toilet adjacent to our rooms was behind a heavy metal door (maybe it had a different function at one time but it reminded me of a bomb shelter or maybe even a torture chamber) and it was a squatter, with no natural light—not that one wants much light at all in any dirty old squatter toilet, but this one was not an option for me—so I set out looking for another toilet. I soon found a Western one in a cubby-hole under the stairs leading to the dungeon, but it stunk so badly that I had to hold my breath while hovering over the bowl. Then I made the mistake of looking straight ahead and found there was a window, right at waist level, not facing outside into the courtyard but looking into the hallway in front of me! Anyone walking along the hall would have a perfect face-on view of the occupant perched on the throne. I quickly pulled up my pants. Oh, good god. Could this get any worse? So much for my favorite place on earth.

Since going to my dreary dungeon room was not an option, I returned to the community dining room for the free hour until we were to visit the local monastery. Several people had paid for WiFi but there was apparently no service. The lodge owner said it would come, be patient. Is that even possible for a Westerner?

The skies were gray, and it was chilly as we walked the ten minutes across the village to the monastery. We were allowed inside without even taking off our shoes and we marveled at the brightly colored fabrics on the walls and benches, the golden Buddha up on the altar and the other golden Hindu-Buddhist deities flanking him. But the *pièce de résistance* was a purported Yeti scalp in a glass showcase in the middle of the room. It was truly a mass of long, dark-black, rough hair bound together in what may or may not be a scalp. Personally, I've never seen a Yeti, but if others swear that they have, then that's good enough for me to believe that this just may be the remains of one.

For some reason, I did not feel comfortable inside the main prayer room as we were given a short tour and explanation of the statues. There was an eeriness to it, so I snuck outside to be alone and sat on a wall overlooking the village.

Out of the frying pan and into the fire.

A local man came and sat beside me, a man who looked about my age but was probably half that. I said hello and immediately noticed that he was mentally handicapped. He said nothing, but was watching me; I saw it out of the corner of my eye. He looked like he wanted to move closer to me. I wondered if he might try to push me off the wall, which had a pretty good drop-off. I got up casually and walked towards an impressive collection of Mani stones, pretending to be fascinated by them but all the while watching my friend on the wall, who was watching me, so I eventually went back into the monastery, to the safety of a known discomfort.

By now the tour had moved upstairs into an open community room where young men were busy painting the walls in bright colors. They played music and were in good spirits. That helped a bit to lift my mood, but once we left, the disposition of the entire group took a downturn, as it was a cold, dour walk back to the lodge in a light drizzle of rain.

Once back we were less than thrilled to learn that there was still no WiFi. Not even sporadic reception; there was no connection whatsoever. Of all the places that I could have used a familial diversion, this would be it, but it was not to be.

Beatrice and I were then scheduled to go to a hostel for young girls to distribute some children's jewelry that I had brought from home. I have three daughters and they had loads of barrettes, hair elastics, bracelets, head bands, toy rings, and all kinds of ribbons and things that they no longer used so my youngest daughter and I packaged them up in bags with ribbons for me to give away. We had done the same thing when we made our family trip to Nepal three years earlier and my own children would never forget those moments of interaction with the young girls. They insisted I do it again.

Beatrice, Ricky, Anuj, D3vil, and I soon headed back out to the local hostel to give away the gifts to the girls. But it was a bit awkward. It seemed staged and completely disingenuous with the cameras there. Not like my experience in 2015. We were brought into a room with mothers and their children where music was being played and we were asked to dance. Beatrice obliged, but I was frozen. I smiled and tried to busy myself with the children, but I was really feeling very uncomfortable and longing to find some place of comfort and security. Some of the mothers of boys wanted the little packages for their sons too, but as the gifts were just jewelry, intended for girls, it was disheartening to try to explain why we had nothing for them.

Returning to our lodge, we unwillingly went to our room and prepared our beds for the evening, then to the dining hall where the fire had just been lit. WiFi was working very sporadically we were told, but at that point I had resigned to go without for a day.

Since most of us were simply making small talk or staring into space, I figured it was a good time to fish out the two decks of cards I'd brought with me and we played a game that Shaun taught us called *Bullshit*. Soon everyone was laughing and somehow the name of the game got changed to *Yakshit*, which was considerably more appropriate in the Khumbu valley.

Dinner was potatoes, half-moon-shaped fried spring rolls, and a red sauce. It was surprisingly good. Our sherpa guides always joined the staff at the lodges to prepare and serve the food. Occasionally, we ate buffet-style, but most of the time the food was put on the plate and served to us as we took our seats. The sherpas then cleaned up after us, served tea, and only when all of us were through, did they themselves get to sit down and eat. This was usually after 8:00 PM. They worked long hard days and, even though working as a sherpa guide for a trekking group was a very good job for a Nepalese, their standard of living was far from what we know.

So, that night, while the sherpas ate dinner in one corner of the dining room, the trekking crew, with full bellies, happily started playing *Yakshit* again. See what the lack of WiFi does?

We retired early to bed but I woke at 2:00 AM and was freezing cold. I was in my sleeping bag and the new merino wool liner, but the top blanket had slipped off. Again I was worried. Even with the new liner, I'd have no chance of being warm while sleeping on a glacier at Base Camp. I only had the other thin fleece liner that I could add, and relying on getting hot water bottles before bed was far from guaranteed.

Somehow, I fell back to sleep until about 6:00 AM when I awoke to the sounds of the early risers wandering the halls.

# CHAPTER 7

.....................................................................

*"Why do we travel to remote locations? To prove our adventurous spirit or to tell stories about incredible things? We do it to be alone amongst friends and to find ourselves in a land without man."*

–George Leigh Mallory

.....................................................................

## Day 8: Trek From Khumjung to Deboche (3,780 m)

### 0700 0800 0900

Breakfast was muesli with yak milk, but instead of yak milk I used hot water, which made the cereal soggy and gross. There were also pancakes and two boiled eggs, but four were too many eggs for even Shaun that morning, so mine went back to the kitchen.

As we walked outside to greet the day, we were blessed with beautiful sunshine revealing amazing views of the high snow-covered peaks. And we finally got that view of Ama Dablam.

Ama Dablam, rising 6,812 meters (22,349 feet) above sea level, is optically a very unique mountain peak visible during much of the trek to Base Camp. The name itself means "Mother's necklace," which refers to the hanging glacier on the southwest face that is reminiscent of the traditional double-pendant necklace (*dablam*) worn by Sherpa women. The long ridges on each side of the peak are said to represent the arms of a mother (*ama*) protecting her child. True to its name, the mountain emanates a sense of familiarity and comfort. She is unmistakable. Distinctive. Beautiful. Watching over us. Just like a mother.

Trekking that day was, strangely enough, mostly downhill, and we met the marathon course after a short time. I was disappointed to find it very technical with lots of rocks, high steps, and loose sand on steep grades. The marathon would be difficult.

Now that we had been trekking for several days, I recognized that there were people in our group that were much easier to walk behind than others. I had come to realize that I had trouble walking behind Jill; though a good runner and overall a strong woman, she was not used to the trails and was very unbalanced, probably due to both her inexperience on that terrain and her fear of heights. She walked with her arms out for balance like a marionette. This in turn made me feel out of equilibrium. Several others were also difficult to follow, including Dave, the New York City dweller. Niki was pretty easy to walk behind and Shaun too, but the best were, for obvious reasons, those with years of hiking experience. There are some trekkers that have a very rhythmic, confident gait. Pemba, our leader. Harry, with lots of hiking experience. So after a few days I had a feel for who to follow, and I would search them out and tuck in right behind them on the hike.

For lunch we stopped at a place with lots of trekkers, an entire group of young Americans. We had fried potatoes and a grilled sandwich that had some sort of shredded veggies in it. Plus lots of black tea. Beatrice and I chatted with a few from the other group, who practically wanted to adopt Shaun. Most of them were amazed that we were planning on running a marathon from Base Camp; just as we'd heard from others, most trekkers were having trouble enough with the hike.

For the most part we had the trail to ourselves during the entire trip, occasionally we would pass small groups, and hardly a café would be free at lunchtime, but I had imagined that it would be much worse. I'd heard that in the high season, the trails are like overcrowded highways, and that it was nearly impossible to find a room in a lodge if you hadn't booked months in advance. But we were at the very tail end of the season and were able to enjoy some isolation from the masses that at times dominate the region.

Another hour of trekking brought us to the village of Tengboche, home to the infamous Tengboche Monastery, also known as Dawa Choling Gompa. It is a Tibetan–Buddhist monastery and the largest gompa in the Khumbu region. A gompa is what they call the main meditation room where the monks listen to teachings. You could compare it to a church or temple. Surrounding the gompa are living quarters, storerooms, a large courtyard, temples, chortens, and a Mani wall, as well as homes, cafes, and lodges. Tenzing Norgay was born in a village near Tengboche and actually lived there at the monastery for a time, studying as a monk. In fact, it is said, that at 4:00 AM on the morning of May 29, 1953, when Edmund Hillary stuck his head out of a tent perched high on a ledge at Camp IX on Mount Everest at about 27,900 feet above sea level to admire the breathtaking view beneath him, Tenzing Norgay looked over his shoulder, pointed downwards, and in the frigid morning air grunted a single word: Tengboche.

Upon entering the village, we took a short break to enjoy the surroundings before being led inside the gompa. We were allowed to sit on mats at the perimeter of the room as the monks chanted out of their prayer books. The shrine was brilliantly painted in the Hindu colors of blue, green, red, and yellow, similar to what we'd seen in Khumjung. A large statue of Buddha was deified in the sanctum flanked by Manjushri, the deity of wisdom, and Maitreya, the future Buddha.

There must have been at least 30 monks sitting on the wooden benches positioned perpendicular to the sanctum. The benches were wide, covered with cushions and colorful squares of cloth, and each had a small wooden table in front to hold cups of tea. All the monks had shaved heads and burgundy robes. They appeared to range in age by at least half a century. The head monk sat on an altar up front wrapped in a golden robe; he wasn't the lead chanter but had slips of paper in his hand as though he were reading along, and occasionally he took out two bells and rang them. The chanting varied from individual muttering to group singing to drums and cymbals. A younger monk came around to the others at one point and served what looked like masala tea. The chanting was hypnotic, meditative, and before we knew it, an hour had gone by. We then tiptoed out and collected our shoes in the entry hall. Descending the stairs of the monastery we were blessed with a brief glimpse of Everest through the clouds.

An overwhelming percentage of Nepalese are Hindu, but in the northern Tibetan-influenced regions, Buddhism dominates. More often than not, however, Buddhist and Hindu temples are shared places of worship and thus reflect an amalgamation of the two religions, living together with tolerance, understanding, and peace.

Before leaving Tengboche a few of us stopped by a small café and drank rhododendron tea before making the twenty-minute walk downhill to our lodge through a beautiful forest of birch, fir, juniper, and most spectacularly, rhododendron. I talked to Ricky for most of the walk. He told me about how the rhododendron trees speak to one another in one particular enclosed valley that we walked through. Frost forms on the leaves during the night, and in the early morning, as the sun begins to creep into the valley, the ice crystals melt and a soft crackling noise is heard which some believe is the trees communicating with each other, recounting stories of the past.

Ricky also told me about his family, his wife, his parents, and his upbringing traveling around the world since his father was in the military. But it was the influence of his grandfather that set his life in motion. A naturalist. A musician. His grandfather showed him the wonders of the outdoors and inspired his fascination for music. No, I'm not talking about the classics here. Bob Dylan was his idol. And thus it was his grandfather that inspired Ricky both to pick up the guitar and to go out into the mountains.

Soon after we arrived in Deboche. The lodge was wonderful in comparison to the night before. A robust stone building with lots of light. There was a really cozy dining hall with an entire wall of windows where the view, when clear, promised to be of several high peaks including Everest. The fire was already lit and warm when we arrived. I paid 600 rupees for an Internet card for 200 MB. That was pricey, but I wanted to get in touch with my family after a day of silence. Then I indulged myself with a hot shower, which was located in another makeshift closet, but was spacious, bright, and clean. Back in the dining hall to dry my hair by the fire, I charged my phone, power bank, and watch for another 500 rupees each. Meanwhile, the group joined up for a few hands of *Yakshit*.

We'd saved a spot for Harry at our table, but he was somehow wrangled by the guides to sit at the far end, so Jesper entertained us with stories of his island home in Denmark and how he and his wife were married by the local mayor at the airport while standing on the rolling staircase descending from a plane.

Dinner was a veggie broth, then dumplings, with noodles and tomato sauce, and fried rice with veggies. A little of everything so that there is something for everyone, I suppose, but it wasn't particularly good and I was still keeping my fingers crossed that we'd get some of the local cuisine. Dessert was pumpkin pudding with canned apples. Sounds fancy but it was unfortunately very basic and bland. I really think they just wanted to play it safe with us, so as not to compound the stomach problems that many face as a symptom of altitude sickness.

As always, Ricky Time concluded the evening and then everyone dispersed. By 9:00 PM we were bone tired and in bed, but just as I lay my head down on the pillow I heard something scurrying across the roof. My eyes shot open and I was wide awake. And I listened. At first all I could hear was Beatrice snoring. How could she have fallen asleep so fast? And then, there it was again. Whatever it was, its claws were scratching against the corrugated tin roof as it scurried along. And it was moving fast. Scampering back and forth. Then again silence, and suddenly it was right at my head. Okay, not in the room, but running through the walls just behind my head. Yikes! I was praying its next move would not be running across my pillow. I popped in the earplugs, pulled the sleeping bag up behind my head, the zipper up to my chin, said a short prayer and hoped to get some shut-eye without a close encounter from a four-footed critter.

# CHAPTER 8

........................................................................

*"In the mountains, worldly attachments are left
behind, and in the absence of material distractions,
we are opened up to spiritual thought. We should be
attempting to carry the spiritual experience of the
mountains with us everywhere."*

–Tenzing Norgay

........................................................................

## Day 9: Trek From Deboche to Dingboche [4,400 m]

### 0600 0700 0800

I finally fell asleep at some point, but when Beatrice woke around 2:00 to go to the toilet, she was having trouble getting the slide-lock on the room door open and I woke up, probably worried that a giant rat was trying to break in. I had been in such a deep sleep. From then I tossed and turned until probably about 4:00, then slept deeply until the alarm woke me at 6:00. I immediately popped up and looked out the window, hoping for a glimpse of Everest. But it was cloudy! Darn it! But they weren't thick clouds, so there was potential for the clouds breaking up as the sun rose higher in the sky.

A horse and her foal were just outside my window. The foal was whinnying and prancing around. I opened the window wide and leaned out; she came towards me, bobbing her head up and down, as though inviting me to come outside to play. She then ducked her head down and trotted off in the opposite direction for a bit before turning around to see if I was still there, or perhaps following her, giving her chase across the courtyard. I would have loved to, but I'm not sure if mama horse would have liked that.

Breakfast was porridge, a fried egg (here you go, Shaun) and more fried potatoes with a piece of very, very lightly toasted white bread. Or maybe it was just stale. When did I last have fresh fruit? I'd forgotten. I never imagined it would be possible to live without it.

Spirits were high due to the sun appearing during breakfast, revealing Ama Dablam, Lohtse, and yes, Everest! We couldn't wait to get outside and start the trek.

The sun was warm and most of us were in short sleeves or tank tops. Carolyn was wearing the same shirt she'd had on for the past three days. No one else probably would have noticed, but she was pretty proud of the fact and announced it to the group. "It's merino wool! That stuff just doesn't fuckin' stink!" she exclaimed. She had an unbelievable talent for cursing and somehow it suited her perfectly. She was crass and abrasive, but regardless, she was entertaining and fun to be around. And that would be far from the last time we'd see her in that shirt.

We took some videos and group photos outside before starting off on a steady climb. The terrain was better than the day before, which isn't to say that it was good. It would still be a challenge during the race, and we also spent a lot of time traversing very narrow ridges that fell off to the river hundreds of meters below. I kept thinking how I never could have brought my kids on that trek; doing it myself was one thing, but worrying every moment about my children slipping away into those river valleys would have been a nightmare.

On that section of the trek I talked for a long time with Niki. She was a couple of years younger than me, so essentially the same generation, and since the culture of Canada is similar to that of the US, it was really enjoyable to talk to her. It felt like being at home. Well, except when we were dodging yak trains and crossing scary hanging bridges. Even after having resided for nearly 20 years in Germany, speaking the language fluently, and having plenty of good friends there, I still find chatting in my mother tongue to someone with similar ideals and of my native culture to be somewhat of a luxury. I listened a lot as Niki talked about having a tough time at home: a family business which was stirring up a familial crisis. The trip to Everest was supposed to get her mind off it, but she was having trouble letting it go. We also talked about our kids, races and training, our work, and future plans. A former competitive diver, adventure racer, long distance trail runner, and fitness instructor, she could brag right up with the best, but she didn't. She was very humble and almost hesitant when talking about her achievements. Carolyn, on the other hand, bragged about Niki all the time. Two extremes. Rightly so. I guess that's part of what makes them good friends; they complement each other. Carolyn had even told me she would never go on trips like this one if Niki weren't there to coax her into it. I saw that same kind of character polarity in the other pairs on that trip too: Cindy and Henni, Jill and Mark. One was the driver and the other needed a nudge.

We had to cross another very high hanging bridge that morning, but I was getting used to them and took it with relative ease. As was becoming our standard daily rhythm, we trekked about 1.5 hours and then stopped for tea.

We came across more trekkers than normal on the trail that day, and we kept crossing paths with the two other groups from our organization. There were several groups of runners from other organizations as well, but obviously, for logistical reasons, we were traveling separately. There was also a group of students from Boston College. They were not there for the marathon, but would trek to Base Camp and back out on the same day. All trekkers are welcome to go to Base Camp and look around, but then return to one of the lower villages to sleep. The honor of camping at Everest's South Base Camp is reserved only for the high mountain expedition climbers with an exception made for the runners of our race, which was what really drew me to it. A chance to sleep at Base Camp! Considering I had no intentions of ever climbing Everest or any other one of the high peaks in the area, the marathon was my only chance for that. I couldn't pass it up… and I got to run a marathon too! What a deal!

We then walked another hour and a half until our lunch break at a basic café in a small village. There were several small cafes, mostly with outside seating, but today every place was full outside, so we were brought inside to a nice large room. There was a wood stove in the middle and tables in a ring around the outside with benches along the windows for seating. Together with Bea, Shaun, and Harry, we ate veggie noodle soup and half a piece of pita bread, then a cup of weak black tea. It wasn't much, but for some reason it was more than enough. Our bodies were getting adapted to the routine, the food, the monotony. Several in the group bought candy bars in the small shops after lunch, and tucked them away for a snack later on in the afternoon but, like the price of water, showers, and battery charging, the price of candy bars was also increasing as we ascended.

After lunch we continued to head uphill and soon emerged from the tree line. The wind picked up and it got cooler. Eventually I had to put on my light windproof jacket that I had in my backpack. Everyone wore a backpack of varying size and contents, except for Mark and Jill who shared one. He almost always had it on despite Jill offering to carry it. Mark was a really social guy and seemed to enjoy talking to most anyone whereas Jill was somewhat more reserved and quiet, but the two of them were nearly inseparable. He called her Mama Bear, and you'd often see them standing very close to one another in quiet conversation, Mark checking to see if she was doing alright; he seemed overly concerned. Maybe he had reasons I wasn't aware of, but my feeling was that there was a strong woman behind the gentle façade. *We'd later find that to be true when Mark got sick and Jill took over the reins without a blink.*

During one of our brief pauses, Pemba told us that one of our group members, Kiki, had shown some signs of altitude sickness and had to stay behind where we had lunch, for observation. Ricky was with her, so she was in good hands.

Niki was also having some side effects from the altitude in the form of constipation (or maybe it was the lack of vegetables), but regardless she hadn't been able to, you know, *go* for several days. She looked pregnant with a bulging belly on her otherwise petite body. It was especially hard for all of us women to use a toilet that is not very clean and shared by 20 or more people. That was a persistent topic of conversation. So along the way that day we were joking about how our next lodge would be *en suite* to solve at least the privacy issue, one of the basic elements of our problems.

Our destination of Dingboche finally came into view, another large village in the middle of nowhere, only accessible by pathways. It is another popular stop for trekkers and climbers heading to Everest, Ama Dablam, or Imja Tse (Island Peak). There are several lodges and camping areas, as well as bakeries and small shops, so many visitors spend two nights there for acclimatization.

Dingboche is characterized by its kilometers of stone walls, which were built from stones removed from the soil for farming. The walls are sometimes quite high, easily up to my shoulders, and the stones are not fixed in place with cement, but just laying on top of each other (and readily toppled, as I would later experience).

At our hotel, the Bright Star Lodge, we were served tea when we arrived but the fire in the dining hall was not yet lit and it was very cold. We had to wait for our room assignment because all the bags still weren't there. Everyone in the group had the same red and black, heavy-duty canvas trekking bag, with the Mount Everest Marathon logo on it, and they were only differentiated by a number printed on each of the long ends. The number was simultaneously our start number for the race; mine was 32. This is how they maintained track of us and kept us organized. Each pair was randomly (or not so randomly as we would soon find out) assigned a room and the two trekking bags were placed there. When all bags were assigned, then we were given our keys and could go to our rooms. Apparently, the bags from the porters had all arrived, but those on the yaks were still in transit.

Once the porters had deposited their baggage, they were free to find a porter house in the village to spend the night. Although their lodging fee was essentially included in their wages, the lodging standards for tourists was still not affordable for them and thus porter houses were available along the trekking routes for them to have a meal and a place to stay. The guides, on the other hand, all stayed in the lodges with us, ready to wait on our beck and call.

The yaks were stubborn and kept us waiting for what seemed an eternity. It was so cold in that lodge. After drinking our tea, we didn't know what to do, so some of us bought WiFi access. Beatrice and I kept adding layers of clothing.

Then to all of our surprise, Kiki had arrived! She seemed to have recovered quickly and since we were to spend two nights in Dingboche, she would have time to acclimatize there before climbing higher. The fact that we had a doctor accompanying our group was also a huge comfort for a lot of us. We were all checked regularly for signs of altitude sickness, but he was available for any other maladies as well and seemed to be constantly handing out medicine and advice for stomach problems, respiratory troubles, headaches, and twisted ankles.

Finally we were given our room assignments where our bags had already been placed. As I opened the door to our room and looked inside, I caught sight of another door in the back going into another small room. As my eyes adjusted to the light, I realized that the back room was none other than... a bathroom! It was as though I was experiencing nirvana. A private bathroom! Beatrice and I giggled and shouted with joy. There was even a sink, a shower and an electrical outlet!! Ok, the water was ice cold in the sink and shower, and the electrical socket didn't work, but we had our OWN TOILET!!!! *En suite*! The gods were looking out for us. Maybe Beatrice had been right about her good karma. Her words rang in my head, "All the things that I do, it will come back to me."

Then Trijan came over to us with a big smile since he knew why we were so excited, but he said we should be quiet because not everyone had a bathroom, only us and Mark and Jill next door, so we needed to keep it to ourselves. But it was too late for that as the guys across the hall had heard our jubilations and tried to have a look in our room, but we shut the door and continued our rejoicing semi-quietly behind closed doors. A few minutes later, when I tried to open our bedroom door, it wouldn't budge. It took a moment to realize that we were locked in. Padlocked. Locked from the outside with someone else's padlock, since I had ours along with our key in the room with us. *Hmmm... who could be so devious?* Only one person came to mind. Shaun. It must have been him. We were both sure of it, so I sent him a photo of a Twix bar and said that we would pay that as ransom if he would let us out. After a few minutes, we heard some chuckling out in the hall and someone began fiddling with the lock. We opened the door and there in front of us stood Ray, Harry, and Dave...all pointing the finger at Shaun who wasn't anywhere around. Gullible as I was, I believed them and set off to find the culprit.

I located Shaun in the dining room. He was talking to his wife on the phone. So I waited, biding my time. When he got off and saw me hovering over him he gave me a confused look, showed me my Twix photo and asked unknowingly what the meaning was. I could tell from his reaction that he really didn't know. He was actually innocent! I told him about the lock-in and he loved it, said he would have definitely done something like that, but unfortunately, this time, no, it wasn't him.

So it was the others. Harry and Ray, maybe Dave was in on it too. We'd have to remember that and see what kind of opportunities for revenge would arise. Or, we'd go with Beatrice's standard approach and just let karma play out its role.

Soon afterwards, the fire was finally lit and the mood changed completely. More and more from our group made their way into the dining room where we gathered talking, laughing, and making jokes. By 6:30 the dining hall was full, the room was warm, and everyone was in good spirits over dinner.

During Ricky Time we were told that we'd have the chance for another short run again the next day. We'd make an acclimatization hike together and then be free to run back to town, just like we'd done outside of Namche. This was good news. Most of us were runners, not hikers, and we craved that functional motion of running that had become a part of our make-up. It's what we love to do.

By 10:00 PM the lodge was quiet and another remarkable day in the Himalayas was behind us.

# CHAPTER 9

*"Polypro wicks away the sweat. Cotton absorbs it. Ergo, cotton is for suckers."*

–Sir Edmund Hillary

## Day 10: Acclimatization Rest Day in Dingboche (4,410 m)

### 0700 0800 0900

I slept well enough, but was frustratingly cold again. I had placed two hot-water bottles in my sleeping bag but once they cooled down I woke up sometime during the night and had to grab my winter jacket and lay it over the top of me to keep me warm enough to fall back to sleep. This had me worried. If I was cold here, how would I be at Base Camp? *Is this not the same damn thought that I had almost every night?!?*

I thought that maybe I could buy a wool blanket from one of the local shops. At breakfast in the morning I asked Ricky what

I should do and he said that I could rent an expedition-grade sleeping bag from the lodge. Trekkers sometimes rent from them and go straight out to Island Peak. Ricky would get it back from me in Namche Bazaar after the marathon and have it returned to the lodge. I was thrilled with this solution. And it would only cost me 1,000 rupees, about 10 Euro.

The plan for the day was to hike the Bibre Loop, which is a 3-kilometer out-and-back loop that would also be part of the marathon course. It was added on to the marathon in order to make it a full 42.2 kilometers (26.2 miles) from Base Camp to Namche, and it was slightly uphill on the out loop alongside the Imja River, with about a 200-meter gain. The terrain was strewn with various-sized rocks and other times there were barren swaths which were crisscrossed with footpaths. The area was occasionally intersected by small streams. We took it slowly as the altitude was affecting us all, and my legs were tired from trekking over the past couple of days.

At one point we saw a local woman with a large basket strapped onto her back like a backpack. She kept stooping over to the ground, picking something up, and tossing it into her basket. When we got closer we realized what she was collecting, yak dung, which she would use in her stove at home for heating and cooking. We were above the tree line, so that was the choice of fuel. The waste product is already relatively dry when she collects it, but then at home she would leave it out in the sun, then stack it up for the winter, like we do with our wood piles.

It took us about 50 minutes to get out to the far end of the Bibre Loop, which was marked by a collection of stones that spelled out, smartly enough, BIBRE LOOP. Most of us had our running gear on, just as we'd done on our fun-run from the tea house to Namche a couple of days before. Ricky briefed us quickly about what would happen there during the marathon.

We were all required to run the loop, and to be sure that we all complied, there would be a check point at the turn where we would be given a green wrist band to wear for the remainder of the race to show we'd been there. Shaun joked about offering Ricky $1,000 to get a green band *beforehand.* That would effectively shorten the marathon by those six kilometers. Ricky played along, said he wouldn't budge, though he knew that Shaun was joking. In reality, no one would have cheated themselves out of the full distance at any price.

I had my eye on Shaun who was standing at the back of the group. I knew he was itching to bust out again as he had the other day for our run to Namche. And true to form, as soon as Ricky had finished with our briefing about the turn-around point, Shaun was off and running.

I gave chase and soon found a chance to cut in front. Not a moment later we were again steamrolled by Henni. We zig-zagged across the terrain, looking for the paths that weaved back and forth the least, in effect, the shortest distance between two points. I tried to stay right behind Henni, with Shaun on my heels. Then, somehow, we went the wrong way, and instead of the upper trail leading directly into the village, Shaun and I were headed down towards the river. Shaun, one way or another, snuck in front of me again and I followed right behind with the hopes of him finding us a way out of there. Then suddenly he was behind me again and we got separated! I was stuck behind some massive stone walls that were nearly as tall as I was, those infamous yak corrals! I saw Henni on the upper trail. No time to spare looking for a way around the walls. I decided to climb over and cross directly through the corral; a straight shot to where I was supposed to be. But unfortunately the walls were not very stable and the stones just tumbled down as I tried to get over! I contemplated building it back together, but my rock-wall repair skills are just not what they should be, so I left the damage and trudged as quickly as possible through the deep sandy soil. On the other side was the same fiasco with a destroyed stone wall which led me out onto the trail where I caught a glimpse of Henni before he darted around a corner ahead! But where was Shaun? No time to worry about that as I was sure he somewhere ahead, so I picked up the pace over the path which then wove through the outskirts of the village. There were giggling children as well as complacent pack animals as spectators as I skirted around stones and jumped across pools of water collected from the mountain run-off. Soon I was on the final several hundred meters, still without Shaun in sight, and got back to our lodge to find the only one on the terrace was Henni, heavily out of breath. Panting myself, there was no chance to even say a word before I heard a gallop and Shaun jumped up to join us. It was invigorating to run like that. It had been tough though. I felt winded right from the start and my pulse was high. My bronchia and lungs were raw and I was coughing, like when running in below-freezing weather. But despite those minor discomforts, it had been worth it.

Beatrice showed up a few minutes later and had unfortunately stumbled and twisted her ankle. This led her to be kind of down in spirits for a few hours, but I knew she would bounce back soon enough. She's not one to brood and she enjoys life too much to worry about things she cannot influence.

We sat on the terrace, waiting for the rest of the group to finish. The sun was shining and we noticed other trekkers as well as local inhabitants laying their laundry out on the rocks across from our lodge, so once most of the troop had returned I went back to my room and washed a few pieces of clothing in the sink and lay them out on the rocks to dry. It was completely full of fresh laundry. Beatrice had done the same but since her ankle was hurting, I climbed out on the rocks for her and lay out her clothes, including her tiny thong panties, in the warm late-morning sun.

The short run had been great but after the long slow hiking over the past week I still sensed that I was getting stiffer and stiffer. I felt like I needed to do some stretching. But it was tough to find a spot to do it. It was too cold outside, our rooms had always been too small, and in the dining hall with the rest of the crew was not an option, but in the lodge where we were now, the rooms were larger and there was finally enough space. I mentioned it to Shaun and he said he was game, so I joined him in his room where he had a lacrosse ball and some other exercise gadgets. The lacrosse ball was awesome on the knots in my back, I leaned against the wall and rolled it all around to deep satisfaction; but I needed to stretch my glutes and hip flexors too, so Shaun, being a fitness guru, showed me how he usually does it. After basic instructions, I ended up in some kind of a pretzel position which gave me exactly that deep stretch I was looking for. I felt like a new woman.

Then it was time for lunch! For the first time we were actually given the option to order our lunch from the menu in the morning before our run and it was then all brought out between 11:30 and 12:00 (Nepal time = plus/minus an eternity). I had ordered vegetable Sherpa stew! A rich stew with potatoes, large flat noodles, carrots, and cabbage. Yummy. It was one of the best meals that I was served the entire week. Then black tea, of course, which at that point I don't think I could have gotten through a day without.

At lunch, we talked about the thin walls in the lodge and how you can hear your neighbor's conversations, snoring, and even farting. Which brings me back to Niki, who I mentioned was having trouble with constipation. Well, a day later, still with no action nor progress, and her stomach swelling fast, even though she wasn't having luck on the toilet, she was still able to get rid of some excess gas. Yes, you know where this is going. Carolyn told us about how, when they woke that morning, Niki crawled up to the top of her bed, to reach over and open the window drapes, and in that bent over squatted position she let out a loud fart. The two of them giggled and Carolyn commented that it was so loud that Shaun probably heard it on the other side of the wall. To which there was a prompt knock in confirmation from Shaun who was just on the other side of that paper-thin separation and had indeed heard it all.

After lunch we were all required to get another check-up with the doc. My blood oxygen level was even less, only 75%. This did not make me happy, but Prajwal still maintained that it was fine. I had my doubts. I felt just fine, my blood pressure at 110/70 was normal, and I had no other symptoms of altitude sickness, but still.

I wasn't the only one with low morale, everyone was obsessed with the threat of altitude sickness. It was a constant topic of conversation. That and going to the bathroom.

Cameraman Anuj then told Beatrice, Shaun, and me that we would be doing a photo shoot at 2:00 PM with both the video and camera crew and that we should dress in our race clothes. We would walk to the stupa near the entrance of the village which was situated on a hill; it would make a great backdrop with its strings of prayer flags and hopefully some clear mountain peaks in the background. They were planning on making a documentary of the whole race event and they needed some footage. Cool!

But before we got there the afternoon clouds had moved in and it became cold and windy. I wore two jackets on the ten-minute walk down to the stupa and unfortunately had to strip down to my short-sleeved race shirt for the photos. It was freezing; we were all shivering and although running up the steep slope on which the stupa stood was tough work at that elevation, it didn't do much to warm us up. But after running in circles—clockwise, of course—around the stupa and then taking some shots with goofy poses, we packed up as fast as we could and rushed back to our lodge to warm up.

Beatrice was having some stomach troubles and asked to have a few minutes of privacy in our room, so I sat out on the terrace in the sun that had briefly decided to peek out and chatted with Harry about the giant solar parabolic heaters which had been placed there and were being used to boil water. The heaters are about a meter-and-a-half in diameter and are simply a hollow half sphere of a reflective material which focuses the solar rays to a cooking surface positioned in the center. We had started seeing these more and more at higher elevations, often at the hotels but also in people's gardens. They were not only used for boiling water for washing and cleaning, but also for cooking food.

A lone hiker was sitting there, too, and was apparently just hanging out there for a while (his words) even though he was staying at another lodge. In about his mid thirties, the hiker told us how he'd been in that region many times, first as a kid with his father, and now alone. He told us that he'd just seen a Chinese hiker who was suffering from altitude sickness and would have to be evacuated. Apparently Ricky had seen the hiker being helped along by another man, and that the Chinese hiker wasn't capable of carrying his own weight for even a single step. Ricky watched them for a moment and then urged them to sit down while he went to get the doctor. After being examined and finding that the man's blood oxygen was dangerously low, he was treated with some medicine, and a horse was arranged to bring him to a lower elevation once he was stabilized. The doc said that Ricky may just as well have saved the man's life.

The dangers of altitude sickness really should not be underestimated. Just the previous year a Singaporean woman who was there to run the Everest Marathon died from high altitude sickness before she made it to Base Camp. She had been an avid ultra runner, and had even trekked to EBC five years previously, so she was likely well aware of altitude sickness, its symptoms, and warning signs. But it still claimed her. (Note: She had not been travelling with the organization that we were trekking with.)

Next up on the agenda was a hot shower, especially after all that running on the Bibre Loop and at the stupa. I wasn't sure when I would have the chance for the next one (turns out it wouldn't be until after the marathon). I paid the 500 rupees at the bar and was shown to a funny little utility room that had a washer and dryer and a shower head in the back corner with a large tin bowl on the floor. I laid the bowl under the stream of water and let it fill to keep my feet warm. Although it was a utility room, the roof was corrugated plastic and partially covered with clear plastic tarp, so it was ice cold in there, not to mention that is was large, about six square meters (~60 square feet), so it never got warm even with a steamy shower running!

After the shower we all gathered in the dining room, drank tea, ate biscuits, played cards, uploaded photos, and waited for the wood stove to be lit. Beatrice was still at a low point due to her twisted ankle. I asked her if she wanted me to massage her feet. She said yes but she didn't think I was serious. So when I finished uploading some photos to my family, I took her foot onto my lap and she was very surprised and über happy that I started to gently massage her injured appendage. I knew she needed some kind of a pick-me-up and was hoping that this small gesture of affection and attention would do just that. Of course, it did.

Dinner was at 6:30 as usual, but we were served something new: veggie burgers! With a side of fries. Then they brought out cake and black tea, but hardly anyone touched the cake. It had an oddly artificial peachy color and some kind of cream filling, and considering half the group was by now suffering from stomach problems, most everyone steered clear. Whether the intestinal troubles were from the food, the water, or the altitude, no one could be sure, but better to be safe than sorry.

After Ricky Time I collected my extra-thick expedition-grade sleeping bag and trotted off to our room where I felt like I was in a luxury hotel with our own private bathroom and a warm bed to rest. I was so looking forward to crawling into that cozy warmth and resting my happy but tired body.

# CHAPTER 10

........................................................................................

*"The last word always belongs to the mountain."*

–Anatoli Boukreev

........................................................................................

## Day 11: Trek Dingboche to Lobuche (4,900 m)

## 0630 0730 0830

*Yes!* I slept fabulously in my borrowed super-duper expedition sleeping bag. It was so comfy and warm even without socks and a hat! Breakfast was at 7:30 and we were served porridge and toast along with some kind of omelet for an interesting twist on the egg.

Trekking started at 8:30, but not with the entire group. Kiki would not be advancing with us. She had been advised to spend another night acclimatizing in Dingboche and then head up with the camping group on the following day. There was no point in taking any risks.

Out of the hotel and around the backside, the trail wove along the edge of the village as it curved up the adjacent mountainside. It began to get very steep until we reached the top of the ridge and had a magnificent view in all directions. The landscape then turned to raw plains with low shrubs and large boulders. Stone-walled yak corrals and small stone shelters for the herders were scattered randomly about. There were some wild dogs running around and Cindy pulled out her bag of leftovers to feed them. After every meal, she collected uneaten food in plastic zip-locked bags and fed the many dogs that we came across.

We were walking on a ridgeline high up above the Tsola River and below we could see the tiny village of Pheriche, where a small hospital is located, open during the main climbing months of March–May and November–December. The hospital is staffed by volunteer physicians from around the world as well as Nepalese. During the busy trekking season, helicopters are continuously taking off and landing from there, transporting patients from Gorakshep and EBC.

When the sun came out and the skies briefly cleared, we stopped for some photos with the high peaks in the background. That's where the cover photo of this book was taken. But the weather changes quickly and soon thereafter the heavy clouds were back, it was cold, and a light rain had moved in. The landscape also began to match the weather as it turned gray and monotone.

Down a rocky embankment and across a rickety wooden-plank bridge that I thought would certainly break, we came across the tiny village of Thukla which, at 4,620 meters elevation, was little more than a few buildings and corrugated-steel shacks huddled together. That was where we ate lunch in the Yak Lodge & Restaurant, one of only two in the village. The noodle soup with pita bread had little flavor; it was basic but satisfying.

The mood was very subdued and there was hardly any conversation among the group, so we gazed out the window as a large caravan of yaks slowly sauntered down the rocky trail and the magnificent animals stopped to drink from the river.

Those who went to the toilet commented that it was the worst seen so far with excrement all over the place. I abstained. Then Shaun livened things up a bit by taking photos of a sexually excited horse.

After lunch and back on the trail heading up to the Thukla Pass, the rain was very light, but the higher we got, the stronger the rain and wind became and everyone began hastily pulling on rain gear and gloves. It turned into a very steep climb, everyone was winded from the elevation, and even though it was strenuous, it was so cold that we weren't warmed by the effort. Then it began to snow. We made a brief stop on an exposed section to let the slower trekkers catch up, but everyone began complaining about the cold and blasting wind so we continued on until we reached the relative shelter of a large boulder where we waited for the rest of the group to join us. But even behind the boulder, we were all cold, wet and miserable. A mood that was perfectly suitable for what we were about to encounter.

When we got to the top of the climb, we reached the memorial to those who had lost their lives climbing in the Khumbu valley. An eerie mist was hanging over the surrounding ridges and dipping into the hollows. As far as the eye could see, there were stone and mortar cairns, some with engraved plaques, built as shrines to the lost climbers. I felt as though I were in a traditional graveyard, the cairns were literally everywhere. There were so many of them. *Had that many people really lost their lives here?* There was a large shrine to Scott Fischer decorated with what appeared to be hundreds of prayer flags. Then I read a plaque about a Sherpa who was the youngest summiter of Everest and had climbed it several times, attaining many records until he lost his life one day on a descent by falling into a crevasse. It was so emotional I spent most of the time there by myself, fighting back tears, as did most of the others. I bumped into Ash, whose group was also there, near one of the cairns and I mentioned how wonderful the place was, but he was so moved that he could hardly speak a word in response.

It was without question a holy place.

Eventually the snow turned back into rain which then also subsided and shortly afterward the sun tried to peek its way through the clouds. But the mist hung low and the light played strange paranormal games around us. Prayer flags were flapping in the wind from most of the shrines. I found a small torn piece of a prayer flag that was blowing around on the ground. I picked it up and felt its energy. I placed a few small stones in it and tucked it into my pocket as we gathered to leave.

Nepal is famous for its idyllic prayer flags which are seen everywhere along mountain ridges and peaks in the Himalayan landscape and even extending into Kathmandu. The flags are square or rectangular in shape and appear in a sequence of five colors connected along their top edges to a long string. They are often seen hung on a diagonal line from high to low between two objects such as from the top of a stupa or over a mountain pass.

The five colors of the flags are arranged from left to right in a specific order—blue, white, red, green, and yellow—and represent the five elements. Blue symbolizes the sky and space, white symbolizes the air and wind, red symbolizes fire, green symbolizes water, and yellow symbolizes earth. The center of each typically depicts a horse with three flaming jewels on its back: each of which represent one of the three cornerstones of Tibetan philosophical teachings: the Buddha, the Dharma (Buddhist teachings), and the Sangha (Buddhist community). Surrounding the figure are writings of various traditional mantras or prayers for a long life or good fortune.

Additionally, images or the names of four animals appear in each corner of a flag: the dragon, the garuda (a legendary bird-like creature), the tiger, and the snow lion; these are also known as the Four Dignities. Unlike prayer wheels, the flags are not intended to carry prayers to gods, rather, it is believed the prayers and mantras will be blown by the wind to spread the good will and compassion to all.

I wondered, is that why I continually felt blessed while trekking in those beautiful mountains?

Leaving the memorial, we strode along a relatively flat plain and into the glacial moraines. We were passed by many yak trains coming in the opposite direction, religiously moving out of the way when they came by and sometimes even jumping up onto the ridge to safe ground. But once, as Beatrice and I were standing a step above the trail to let a yak by, another decided to come up behind us. We could not jump down because another was right behind him. We stood nervously still until the beast on the path sauntered by, then we jumped down and ran away from the yak standing right behind us on the hillside. That was a close call.

At first glance the topography appeared inhospitable, but looking more closely there was plenty to see. There were small pools of glacial melt. Tiny purple flowers decorated the barren landscape. And everyone stopped short to ooh and aah when we came across a baby yak with its mother.

Around 2:00 PM, we arrived at Lobuche, a small settlement with a limited number of very rudimentary rooms for trekkers. Ushered into the dining hall of our lodge, we were served tea with some simple cookies before getting our room assignments. Most everyone was in the same building where the main dining room was, but for some reason Bea and I were in a building out back with the sherpas and a group of guys from California who were there to do some trekking and take photos. The leader of the group was a professional photographer and the others were under his tutorial. One of them was an actor, Michel Gill. Shaun recognized him from the TV series *House of Cards*. But just like all the recent movies, I'd never seen it. Of course Shaun asked him if it was really him, and the actor confirmed it. All the while Beatrice and I were busy chatting with the photographer who talked about his trip, which was essentially paid for by the fee from the others, and he got to get some photography in himself. He was pleased with the deal. Who wouldn't be?

Around 3:30 in the afternoon we went for a hike up to a ridge over the village, again to help with our acclimatization. The village was at 4,900 meters and the ridge was over 5,000. We were winded on the way up but on top the view was spectacular. In the distance was Kala Patthar, the black rock, and Pumori, the unwed daughter, the spirit mountain that can only be conquered by someone with superpowers (or so we were told). But most impressive was the Lobuche Peak towering over us. The mountain was just over 6,000 meters high, but looked immense and daunting, with razor-sharp ice ridges and a rock face that seemed so sheer that it would be impossible to climb.

It is easy to lose yourself in those surroundings, to just stare at a particular mountain and imagine what it is like up there, which routes may be possible to climb, who had successfully reached the summit and what they went through to get there. Not that I have any aspirations to be a climber, but when there you can surely identify with what draws them to it.

We took photos and enjoyed the view for some time in order to acclimatize. The Californians were up there too, testing out their photography skills. Then we hiked back down to the lodge in the hopes that the wood stove would be lit. Unfortunately, as we were becoming accustomed to, it was not. It was freezing in the dining room, or at least it always felt that way after coming in from the cold and hoping that the ambient environment indoors would be more comfortable than that outdoors, but here in the Khumbu valley, both were usually the same. Finally, after half an hour or so and several requests, the fire was lit and a bunch of us huddled around it for its scant warmth. Most dining rooms in the lodges were set up the same: A stove in the middle and a ring of tables encircling it, benches at the perimeter of the room covered with thin cushions and pillows, with chairs on the inside of the tables facing towards the walls.

Once the fire was lit, we began to come to life again and when our bodies reached comfortable temperatures, we found places to sit and the card games started up. I played rummy with Harry while another group including D3vil, Anuj, Shaun, and several others were back at *Yakshit*. Unfortunately Kiki wasn't there. She and D3vil were the biggest fans of *Yakshit* and usually rounded everybody up.

Dinner was served at 6:30 and everyone was thrilled to see we were getting dal bhat! Unfortunately, though, it didn't hold a candle to that first meal in Lukla. For dessert, there were canned pineapple rings and then, as always, black tea. Ricky Time signaled the end of the evening and even though it was only 8:00 PM most everyone was ready for bed.

Before retiring, Bea and I needed to use the toilet, but it was *really* gross (even on a sliding scale we're way down here); we did not want to touch anything, and the smell was again teasing the gagger. So, we adapted a strategy: I pushed open the door with my foot, Beatrice ran in and let the door swing close behind her, and then when she was finished, she called for me to kick open the door again from the outside so she did not have to touch it; she then repeated the whole procedure for me. I know what some of you are thinking. That we are being ridiculous. But all I can say is just keep on reading. Once you get through Gorakshep and Base Camp, you'll be singing another tune. I promise.

We bundled up for the short walk to our building out back. Of course there was no outside lighting and there were no stars that night due to the cloud cover, so it was very dark as we carefully ascended the steps. After fumbling around to find the light switch near the entrance door and flicking the switch, we realized there was no electricity. It was pitch dark. One of our guides came up behind us and then returned to the main building to ask to have the electricity turned on, at least for a few minutes, otherwise, without our phones or flashlights, it would have been tricky to find our room, and nearly impossible to open the padlock. Once inside, we hurried to get changed and into our warm sleeping bags because that night it was well below freezing. We'd have to wear hats to sleep.

Last thing before bed was to take that half of a Diamox tablet, but with ice-cold hands we couldn't break the pill in half, so a water bottle came in handy to smash it to smithereens. And then we gobbled up the crumbs.

Time to rest.

# CHAPTER 11

........................................................................

*"One comes to bless the absolute bareness, feeling that here is a pure beauty of form, a kind of ultimate harmony."*

–George Leigh Mallory

........................................................................

## Day 12: Trek From Lobuche to Gorakshep (5,180 m)

### 0630 0730 0830

Dogs had been barking all through the night and there seemed to be guys continually stomping back and forth in the hallways making their way to the toilet. Oh, and Beatrice snores. Not very loud, more like a cat's purr, but still loud enough to wake me. Plus, for some reason, I just did not feel comfortable or safe there. I was in and out of a restless slumber until 5:15 AM when we were woken by a wake-up call of banging on the door of the room next to ours. The guides were sleeping there and were woken earlier than us in order to prepare breakfast. After that I never fell back to sleep so I lay still until Beatrice woke. Unfortunately, she was having a tough time too, as her stomach troubles had reappeared during the night. We were both cold and feeling pretty miserable and had no desire to get out of our sleeping bags, but the thought of moving on to another location was appealing enough to get us going and pack our bags.

Once we were in the dining room and got our hands around a hot cup of tea things began to look up. The tingling-finger side effect of Diamox seemed to hit us at the same time, which lightened the mood. Sometimes the toes began tingling too and, if you were lucky, it ran all the way up to the knees.

That day we had some pretty steep climbs. My legs felt over-tired, as if I'd just had a tough leg day in the weight room; it was probably a combination of both the altitude and sleep deficiency. The terrain had become very rocky. At some points we had to pick and climb our way over boulders. It was impossible to imagine running that track on marathon day.

Beatrice then had a semi-nervous breakdown. She began crying and thought maybe she was having a hot flash. Niki and Carolyn were with her but I was already 50 meters ahead up a steep climb when we all stopped to take a short rest. Then, when we began again, I stayed with her, but at the next stop she was still struggling and appeared very weak. She sat down on a rock and another woman in our group from the United States, nicknamed Bluesky, gave her a head and back massage. I gave her a hug. And just before we were about to leave again, without her noticing, I picked up her backpack and put it on my back then strapped mine onto my chest, but then when she realized what I had planned, I saw the devil in her eyes and the fight came back because there was no way she was going to let me carry two bags! Had I known what an effect that would have on her I would have done it earlier! From then on, amazingly, she was back to being herself again.

We kept having to yield the right-of-way to porters and yak caravans coming in the opposite direction carrying huge loads out of Base Camp. Their backs were laden with tables, doors, four-by-fours and bright green rolls of artificial grass. *Why do they need fake grass there?* Some of their cargo was so lengthy that it nearly reached to the ground behind them and kept knocking against rocks as they passed by on the winding, jagged trail.

We were at the end of the climbing season. Actually, the marathon extended the tourist season for the entire Khumbu valley, bringing in not only 200 runners, but guides, porters, and other support crew. We occupied the lodges, tea houses, and cafes along the major trekking route for an additional week in what is in truth a very short season, especially for the higher villages approaching Base Camp, which is not only functional for expeditions to Everest but also on the neighboring mountains, including Nuptse and Pumori. The window for attempts on all those peaks is limited by the weather, which follows a typical pattern. In early May the monsoon pushes up from the Bay of Bengal and forces the jet stream winds as far north as Tibet. This effectively forces a time-out between the hurricane-force winds of the winter and the tremendous snowfall that the monsoon brings. The window is short, two or three weeks at most, which has to suffice, not only for peak attempts, but also advanced preparation of the camps and the fixed ropes on the routes to the peaks. The tourist season is short, and bringing an international marathon in at the tail end of that window is a smart move to keep the cash and employment opportunities coming in for many of the locals.

There was no stopping for tea that morning, for the simple reason that there were no more tea houses or cafes along the route. The only thing left between us and Base Camp was our next destination, the tiny settlement of Gorakshep. Our arrival there was marked by passing a stone edifice serving as a helicopter pad on the ridge separating the glacier from the village; that pad would be in constant use during our stay. Although it was only 11:00 AM when we arrived, it felt like we'd been trekking all day. At our lodge, as usual upon arrival, we were promptly served tea. That was followed by a lunch of spaghetti with tomato sauce that tasted like canned tomato soup. There were also fried potatoes and a plate of some kind of salami, all served buffet style.

Then we were given our rooms where we only had a few minutes to get settled before we were to meet for an acclimatization hike up an adjacent embankment, the initial slope up to Kala Patthar, which we would climb the next day.

We then had a drama with the toilet.

One guy in our group (not naming names), whose room was on the first floor, headed into the single toilet on our floor with a fat roll of toilet paper in one hand and a package of wet wipes in the other. *Uh-oh.* I had just wanted to go in there for a quick pee before the walk. (We were on the second floor and each floor had only one toilet, which was to be shared by about 40 people, though we'd later find out that the toilet on the first floor was only a squatter.) Soon there were four women waiting to get in there and ten minutes later the guy was still not out. We began to knock. Finally he came out and Beatrice went in to check out the situation. He had not flushed and the bowl was full of shit. She gave him hell and told him to clean it and he said he did the best he could which was little more than nothing, so Bea cleaned it herself, to the horror of us all. We were all pretty upset because the sanitary conditions were appalling as it was, so the least we could do was to clean up after ourselves, which is only fair when travelling in a large group and for everyone's sake it should be without question that we all play by the rules. As we trekked higher the conditions got progressively worse, as was anticipated, and since this was our last lodge before Base Camp, it was expected to be the worst. There was no running water in any of the bathrooms nor anywhere else. Near the latrines on the ground floor, there was a bucket of water raised on a ledge over a basin. There was a spigot on it so that water could run out as if from a tap. I squirmed at the thought of the biotope living in that bucket of water, and instead reverted to using massive amounts of antibacterial fluid and wet wipes to clean myself from then on out. No running water also meant no flush toilets, and although the toilet on our floor was a Western-style that you could sit on, it did not flush. For that action there was a huge plastic barrel of water in the corner of the room in which floated a large tin can. We were to fill the can with water and pour it into the toilet for the flush action. Fine. Pretty straight forward, except that that water was certainly no cleaner than the bucket on the ground floor, and probably much worse considering the dirty hands that were dipping the can in and out of it. Topping that off with no clean water to wash our hands after the deed was done ranks this place right on top of my 'so unbelievably gross' list.

After Beatrice finished cleaning up, we ladies quickly emptied our bladders and then headed outside for the short walk up towards Kala Patthar. We were told by our guides to only climb the first steep switch-backs which would take us to a somewhat level place after about 45 minutes. We should stay there for half an hour or so and then climb down. The plan for the next day would be to climb all the way up to the top of Kala Patthar as a more intense hike to get used to the altitude, then return to the same lodge for a second night. Both treks were under the climbing principle of climb high, sleep low.

Kala Patthar is not exactly a mountain in itself but a prominence on the south ridge of Pumori. It would be the highest point of our entire trek in the region because Base Camp, though about 200 meters higher than Gorakshep, is actually slightly lower than the Kala Patthar peak. Our itinerary stated that Kala Patthar has an elevation of 5,545 meters, although Wikipedia actually states it is 100 meters higher at 5,644.5 meters. I tend to side with Wikipedia after making the jaunt and because, of course, higher is cooler.

So on that first afternoon we went on the hike with Niki, Carolyn, Harry, Raemonde, and the doc. Niki was leading the pack, practicing pacing our group since she was hoping to someday do that kind of guide work for kids. The climb was so steep and, since we were starting at 5,180 meters and increasing rapidly, the going was tough. We had to stop very often; usually after taking about 20 steps I had the feeling that I was going anaerobic. My legs were heavy, as though I'd just hit the wall in a marathon.

But the view even just partially up the mountain was majestic. We took photos of Everest, Nuptse, and Changste and whatever other gorgeous peaks fell into our scopes.

The sun had been shining most of the day so the ground was warm and we sat up on the hillside for about 20 minutes, mesmerized by the view and watching the rescue helicopters flying back and forth, in and out of Base Camp, before we headed back down the mountain.

Once reaching the valley, a few in the group headed over to a large boulder next to a rusted and rickety sign that had a large arrow on it over which was written "Way to Everest BC." We took some photos and Shaun got his bare-chested Popeye shots.

Cindy, who had not joined us on the hike, was crouched there under the boulder where a couple of dogs were napping in the shade. She had apparently just fed them from the leftover scraps that she always had on hand. With full bellies, the dogs lay contentedly and dozed as Cindy was lovingly petting them.

Returning to our lodge, we bought WiFi cards (700 rupees for 200 MB) and got in touch with our families. We then had some free time, so I sat outside on a shaky stool in a quiet place in the sun. The village name, Gorakshep, actually means "dead ravens" due to the complete lack of any vegetation in the area, and it was the original Base Camp for Mount Everest, only about 5 kilometers from where today's current Base Camp is located. The village sits on a narrow ledge between the Khumbu glacier and a frozen lakebed covered in sand. There is a helipad, on the highest point of the ridge, and a few lodges, and that's about it. Not surprisingly, the settlement remains uninhabited in winter.

Bea soon joined me and we meditated and philosophized while overlooking that wide open space that had once been a lake, but was now full of roaming yaks, horses, and dogs. The area was nicknamed the beach, and through it traversed all foot traffic to and from Base Camp. Since the climbing season had just ended, the gear from not just Base Camp, but all the upper camps was on its way down, so we sat contentedly and were entertained as the porters and yak trains slowly passed by. One particularly heroic porter stood out that afternoon. He was carrying foam sleeping mattresses on his back; they were each only about 2 inches thick but of normal bed length and width, and he didn't just have a few on his back: there must have been at least twenty! The main stack piled high lengthwise along his back and then on each side of the load there were more tied up perpendicularly with ropes. The guy was miniscule underneath his load. It was probably not an overly heavy pile in itself, but to balance it must have required superhuman powers! Other impressive feats that we witnessed were men carrying wooden doors on their backs upon which everything and anything would be balanced and piled high. Some of the porters were carrying loads almost the size of a compact car. It was hard to tell how they could see, as they were so bent over, facing the ground and only taking a quick peek up at random intervals. Some would use a wooden stick as a cane, but a very, very short stick of max two feet in length… giving them the effect of having a front leg, like any other four-legged animal, or in this case, a three-legged one.

As the sun began to sink in the sky, I went back to the room and stretched a bit before dinner. Then Bea came to tell me that they had lit the fire in the dining room (the yak dung fire) and that I should come down and warm up. The dining hall was packed as there was also a group of students from Boston College which we had seen many times on the trek over the past week. Some of them seemed to want to adopt Shaun into their group. *Who doesn't love Shaun?* Shaun actually told me they were from Boston University, but considering that I saw one of them with a Boston College bag, which I cannot imagine a BU student would carry, and vice versa, I think I can safely say they were BC Eagles.

Shaun had been really down that afternoon. He'd consistently had bad luck with his room placement, getting a view of a back alley instead of the majestic mountains, or a tiny room that was half the size of the rest of ours, and this lodge was no different. So, he was kind of in a slump, and that afternoon he wanted to make himself feel good by giving himself a shave. But since he couldn't find a sink in the whole lodge (the details of which you are now all aware of), he went to just brush his teeth in the bathroom on his floor, bringing his own bottled water and intending to spit in the toilet. His bathroom on the first floor (no, he was not the culprit from the toilet fiasco) was located under the bathroom on our floor and apparently, while brushing his teeth, as he leaned over to spit into the toilet, he felt drops of what he hoped was water landing on the back of his head from above. Dripping through the floor from the bathroom above. Needless to say, this brought him to an even lower point than he was before and he became completely reclusive. Everyone noticed. Or at least Bea and I noticed. We went to talk to him and he said he just needed some time to be alone.

Shaun was the heart and soul of our group. He was like our unofficial team leader in charge of motivation. He was always there when someone needed help, or a laugh, and he made everyone feel like his buddy. And despite him being someone who has a relatively high profile in his business and is extremely popular on social media, there is nothing superficial about him, he is absolutely genuine.

We respected his wishes and left him alone but by dinnertime he was still down, so our mission was clear: Cheer up Shaun. This was a job that we took seriously.

The dining room was overfilled as the college kids were there as well as another trekking group, so the tables assigned to our group were in the back of the room along a dark wall. Most were occupied since many people had spent a good part of the day there, not having gone outside after we returned from our short hike. Others had just stayed put simply because it was very dusty outside and they were having trouble breathing at the altitude as it was. Hopefully they were experiencing the Khumbu cough and not something contagious. In any case, there were only scattered single seats still free at our group tables when we got there, so we ended up grabbing four spots together in the middle row of tables that were typically used by the sherpas. Bea and I corralled Shaun to our table, collected Harry, and got to work.

We were first served baskets of popcorn and we began tossing pieces up in the air and catching them in our mouths. Then I asked Bea, who was sitting across from me, to hold her mouth wide open. I took aim and sent the fluffy white kernel into the air in a perfect arc which hit its target on the mark. She was delightfully surprised and let out a squeal which began to turn the mood at the table. The conversation then turned to bowel movements, or lack thereof, which was now by far the most talked about subject over the entire trek, but once our food was placed in front of us that topic became taboo.

Dinner was momos (dumplings) and fried potatoes, with mixed canned fruit for dessert. The pear and pineapple in the dessert bowl were edible, but then came my first bite of a peach with such a horrible consistency that I had to spit it out. Shaun raised an eyebrow, dubious of my extreme reaction, though now hesitant to try his fruit at all. He then courageously began eating it and said it was all right, though I noticed that he hadn't tried the peaches yet, so I pointed out a particularly large chunk of peach in his bowl. He popped it in his mouth and began to chew, then in an instant grabbed a napkin and spit it out. I laughed. We all laughed, but we weren't done with him yet.

Beatrice likes to ask people questions about their preferences and favorite things, so she asked us all where we would have vacation homes if we had no financial limit and could choose anywhere in the world. Harry said Scotland, since he loves the green rolling hills and cold weather. "Preferably Skye or the Isle of Lewis," he added. Then Beatrice chirped in, "Hidden away with your lover, right Harry?" He chuckled and shook his head. I wasn't quite decisive on my choice, probably a beach house in Rhode Island. But Shaun knew exactly where he'd want his vacation home and said, "Right here in Gorakshep, so I could walk over there now and have a hot shower." We all laughed until the tears were flowing.

Mission accomplished. Shaun was back.

Brushing our teeth that night involved a bit of creativity. Of course we would use bottled water as we have the entire trip, but where were we to spit since there was no sink in sight? In the toilet? Preferably not; they are bad enough when used for their main function. So, Bea and I decided that we would brush our teeth in our room and just open the window quickly (to avoid that arctic cold) when we were ready to spit. We thought we were so smart as the toothpaste frothed and filled our mouths with the thorough brushing. Then, when we were both ready, I turned the latch on the window, pulled and …nothing. I wiggled the handle around, trying to pry the window open, but it didn't budge, then I noticed that it was actually TAPED SHUT. I don't know how we didn't see the clear duct tape before but we had no time to spare as dribble was now seeping out of the corners of our mouths and we both bolted towards the bathroom, hoping to find it empty— which it wasn't but thank goodness it was one of the Mexican women who was also brushing away. We busted open the window in there and spit out into the night. For subsequent brushings I used the trash can in the hall which was already full of trash so I figured a little *Spucke* on top wouldn't be a sin, but then I found another window in our hallway which opened up easily and that sufficed for the rest of our stay.

After tucking into bed that night I listened to the sounds from outside our window and down the hallway, not necessarily because I wanted to, but because the walls were so thin that even my earplugs couldn't block everything out. Then out of the blue I heard a familiar voice shout at the top of her lungs, "This place is a fucking shithole!" It was Raemonde, and something had obviously gotten her upset. Like pushed-to-her-limits upset. I could then hear some confrontational discussion between her and a man and then again, "This place is a fucking shithole!" At that point I couldn't help but burst into hysterics and although Beatrice was almost asleep she was immediately alert and asked what happened. I told her about what was going on and what Raemonde was yelling through the halls and we tried to listen in, wondering if we should go out and help, but the voices quickly faded as they slowly departed through those fucking-shithole hallways.

# CHAPTER 12

*"Gradually, very gradually, we saw the great mountain sides and glaciers and arêtes, now one fragment and now another through the floating rifts, until far higher in the sky than imagination had dared to suggest the white summit of Everest appeared."*

–George Leigh Mallory

## Day 13: Acclimatization Rest Day at Gorakshep; Hike Up Kala Patthar (5,644.5 m)

**0430 1000 0500**

It was to be a rest day in Gorakshep, our last acclimatization stop before reaching Base Camp. The plan was to get up early and hike up to the peak of Kala Patthar. Our alarm was set for 4:30 with an intended departure at 5:00, but since the group from BC was planning the same trek starting at 4:30 with a wake-up call at 4:00, we were wide awake half an hour earlier than intended due to what sounded like a disco out in the hall. The college students were so loud, fumbling around in the dark, but instead of being irritated, Beatrice and I just lay contentedly tucked in our warm sleeping bags and giggled while listening to their half-hearted complaints about the early rise.

The trek actually seemed easier than the day before. Were we acclimatizing so quickly? But it was not great for all of us. After only about ten minutes Harry began to have a nose bleed; he was exhausted and he decided to turn around. He'd been suffering stomach troubles for a few days and was feeling generally weak. Though he was not a newcomer to altitude and had done some impressive treks, he told us that he was sometimes sensitive to the height, other times not. A roll of the dice.

The hike started with that same series of steep switchbacks which we had done the previous day, and then the path leveled out a bit before becoming very steep once again until we were at the summit ridge, where we finally got a view of the peak. We took it slow and stopped occasionally to catch our breath as well as take in the incredible views surrounding us that were getting better with each step. The last hurdle was a difficult scramble over a football-field-sized stretch of large boulders to finally reach the large outcropping of the granite peak. It had taken us about 1 hour and 45 minutes to reach the top, which was unmistakable from the prayer flags strung in every direction off a metal flagpole that also held a web cam.

The pinnacle resembled a pyramid and when I reached it the doc was standing at the very peak of the steepest rock. He looked like a pharaoh. King of the World. I crawled up there too, not fully aware of the expanse of the summit until someone said to me, "Not too close to the edge. It's a long drop." At that moment I froze. I hadn't seen the drop off the back side. I sat down, peered over the edge and saw a barren riverbed hundreds of feet below. A sheer drop to an abyss. So I didn't climb the two or three meters higher to the very top; the spot where I was sitting was good enough for me. I waited for Beatrice since I knew that she wanted to take photos of us together, but the longer I waited, the more uncomfortable I became with that precipice just a breath away. More people were arriving and it was getting crowded. Beatrice finally arrived and was so excited, but I was at my limit. "Sorry, Bea," I said, "but I have to go down a few steps." Just to the next ledge of rocks. I found a sheltered area there where I could relax and enjoy the moment. It was magical. The sun had risen above the horizon shortly before we reached the peak, giving us amazing views of the surrounding mountains in the early morning light. Although we had caught glimpses of Everest during the trek, this would be the best view that we would get of the tallest mountain on earth during the entire trip, as it is not visible from Base Camp due to its enormous neighbors. Everest actually looked smaller than Nuptse from where we were since it was further away, but there was still no denying her majesty. And as if confirming her own righteousness, she wore a wispy swath of clouds as a crown. Not only did we have a magnificent view of the mountain peaks, the glacier, and the valley but we also got our first glimpse of Everest Base Camp, a sea of tiny yellow tents at the foot of the Khumbu Icefall. Behind us was Pumori, or daughter peak in the Sherpa language, which was named by George Mallory, who sometimes referred to it as Clare Peak after his own daughter. Pumori is a picture-perfect mountain in form and, bathed in the morning light, it was difficult to draw my eyes away from it.

There was a river of clouds moving up the valley, crawling over the glacier like a cunning serpent. Far above we sat in the sunshine, but we knew down below it would be cold in the village underneath that cloud cover.

After a brief stay above, we descended about 100 meters and found a spot to rest and drink hot tea which Pemba had lugged up the mountain for us to enjoy. The simplest pleasures in life are the most wonderful and memorable. As we sat there in paradise sipping black tea, some of our group passed by, still on their way up. Dave was the last to arrive. Everyone was happy to see him pushing through since, apart from Kiki, he was one of the ones who'd been having some of the most severe altitude sickness and also had to remain at a lower elevation one night. The fact that he was so determined to get up that mountain was impressive.

The descent was quick and we were back at the lodge around 9:00 where we sat in the cold dining room, dreary and gray from the thickly clouded sky. On each of the tables was placed a plastic peanut butter jar. Other than the remnants of the PB labels, there was no peanut butter in sight. Rather they were filled with reddish jelly of a bizarrely unnatural color. But we had to wait as we wouldn't be served breakfast for another hour, once the majority of the group had trickled back in.

A young woman who worked in the lodge was busy cleaning up the dining room after the first round of breakfast, wiping down the tables with a filthy cloth that looked remarkably similar to the one she was using to clean the bathroom the previous afternoon. This was also the same woman who had been loading the fire with yak dung, bare-handed, the night before.

Just let me throw this back out there as a friendly reminder.... No running water.

After breakfast we all wondered what we could possibly do all day to amuse ourselves. Until then, our only form of recreation had been a couple of decks of cards and a rowdy game of *Yakshit*. We had not had an entire day without something on the agenda and since Gorakshep was not a permanent settlement it had no homes, no schools, and no shops, other than the few necessary items sold at reception in the scant handful of lodges. Thus, sitting out on the beach and watching foot traffic looked like it was going to top the list for the day.

Beatrice had brought a solar pack and battery charger with her on the trip that, until then, she had forgotten about. "How could you have paid every day for phone charging when all along you had a charger in your trekking bag?" I asked. "Oh, I don't know," she answered, "so many things that I packed, so I just forgot." Typical Beatrice. Then she added, "But it does not work very well, it is almost fully charged now, but it takes a long time to recharge in the sun." Her phone was still nearly fully charged from the night before, so upon bringing the solar charger into the dining hall and setting it on the window ledge in the sun to top up, Raemonde caught sight of it and asked if she could use it to charge her phone. "Yes, of course!" Beatrice said. But two hours later, with Raemonde's phone fully charged and the charger completely drained I asked why she let Raemonde use it when she knew that it would then be of no use to her for at least a day or more, if at all.

"Karma," she replied. "It will come back to me."

We sat with Niki and Carolyn, making small talk to kill the time, while the Mexicans occupied a cozy table in the corner.

"Is that racist that we call them the Mexicans?" Carolyn asked.

"We sometimes call you guys the Canadians," I answered.

"And the guys in Lobuche were the Californians," Bea added.

Carolyn hesitated for a moment before shouting, "I can't fucking believe you call us the Canadians! That is so fuckin' racist!!"

She is crude but somehow hilarious.

But then I started to get a headache and I was really tired. We were advised not to sleep during the day. Taking naps was counterproductive to acclimatization because when sleeping the rate of breathing slows, thus the concentration of oxygen in the blood decreases. But I was so tired so I thought just lying down for a bit and resting couldn't do any harm. After all, we were up at 4:00 AM that morning for a massive hike. Of course I should be tired! So I went and curled up on my cozy sleeping bag, where I ended up relaxing for an hour and a half. During that time I also drank a lot of water. And despite giving my best effort to combat the heavy eyelids, I did fall asleep briefly, but only for about ten minutes. Afterwards, I felt worlds better and my headache was gone.

Then wouldn't you know it, already time for lunch! We were served fried potatoes and an incredible garlic soup. It was made purely of garlic. Tons of it…pressed, mashed, chopped and boiled up into what turned out to be an amazing bowl of goodness. Garlic was supposed to help the body deal with the high altitude. Not sure about that, but it definitely endowed us all with the same perfume, which wouldn't help matters as we were all slowly getting a bit ripe anyway.

In the meantime, Raemonde told me about what had happened in the hallway the night before. Apparently the lock on her door was broken and she explained this to the only person she could find working there who, of course, said he was the manager, which was probably only one of his several job titles. He took a look, and tried to fix it, but couldn't. He told her that she did not need to lock it, that there was nothing to worry about. But Raemonde had no roommate and just did not feel comfortable sleeping in a room that did not lock, on a floor with dozens of people, all essentially strangers, in a lodge that had its front and back doors open at all hours so that anyone and everyone could just walk right in. (Although, they'd have to trek for days just to get to our remote location.) For some reason he made her feel that her request was unreasonable and tensions escalated which led her to get everything off her chest. She was offered another room but she did not want to move all of her gear that late at night. But eventually, with no other option, she was moved to a 'luxury room with a private bath'. She told me there were four of these luxury rooms set out separately in a courtyard of the lodge and they were kind of like two duplexes, each of which shared a bathroom. Since the bathrooms were shared, albeit only with one other room, they were not locked, and actually, anyone could walk in there and use it, you just had to know where to find the rooms, but at least she had a secure lock on her bedroom door and with that and her earplugs intact, she could finally get some sleep.

And so, at her mention of earplugs, she had my full attention. I told her that I wore earplugs every night, but even with them in I could still hear just about everything, including her incident in the hall. She then told me about her own super-duper industrial earplugs that she used at *Liebherr* and said she had some extras. (Later on she handed me a small plastic package with those amazing little polyurethane wedges and she was right, they were great, so from then on my old earplugs were garbage.)

After that it was time to separate our bags. Only one trekking bag per each two persons was allowed to go further on to Base Camp, the other would be sent down to Namche. This had a dual purpose. We obviously needed our sleeping bags, mattresses, warm clothing and race gear with us at Base Camp, but after running the marathon to Namche we would want to have warm dry clothes waiting for us there as well. Thus the split. The yaks were headed down, whereas the porters would join us at Base Camp, then carry our single bag down on the day of the marathon (amazingly enough, most porters could make the trek down with a 20-kilogram load on their back in about the same time that the average foreign runner could run down).

By mid-afternoon, the sun had made a reappearance with no trace of that thick cloud cover from the morning, so I did some wandering around outside, checking out the helicopter pad, the yaks, and the dogs. And as I headed back inside, I ran into Kyaron. Literally. In the hallway. What an amazing reunion. For those of you who have read my first book, you may remember him as my Nepali guide from that incredible trail run in the Himalayan foothills near Dhulikhel three years previously, and we have maintained contact ever since. Kyaron lives with his family about 30 kilometers east of Kathmandu, in Nagarkot, where they run a small hotel. He is very environmentally active in Nepal and always involved with projects to support the development of his country. Ten days after I left Nepal in 2015, a series of horrific earthquakes struck, destroying city infrastructure, temples, roads and even causing an avalanche on Pumori that swept into Everest Base Camp, killing 19 people. After the earthquake, Kyaron was involved in raising private donations to fund a small group of helpers who delivered fresh water and rudimentary water purifiers as well as other essential goods to remote villages in the Kathmandu Valley that had been cut off from supplies.

I had told Kyaron that I was going to be back in Nepal for the marathon and we were going to try to meet up in Kathmandu. Then about a week before my arrival, he told me that he was trying to get a spot in the marathon himself! As his messages were always vague, I was hoping to run into him, but was by no means sure where I would see him along the way, if at all. Obviously, this was a great surprise. He is such a terrific guy, and a huge warm smile never leaves his face. I introduced him to all my buddies. They loved him too. He then told me that he was not yet officially registered for the race, but was hoping that it would happen that day although that was dependent on his group leader.

I didn't quite understand this scenario, but had gotten used to understanding very little about the Nepalese way of doing things.

When Kyaron was pulled away from our conversation by a couple of his friends, his group leader, who was from Denmark, approached me after having seen me talk to Kyaron. He asked if I was a friend of his, so I relayed our history in brief. He subsequently told me that he was sponsoring some young Nepalese runners and asked me if Kyaron would be able to finish the marathon. I was slightly taken aback. What a bizarre question... Why would he have him in his group, schlepped all the way to Base Camp, if he wasn't sure if he could complete a marathon? And what did I know? I ran once with Kyaron years before and only about 20 kilometers, not a marathon. But of course I replied very optimistically that of course he could run it! He was young and tough and had a very strong mind. *That* I was sure of.

Later that afternoon Kyaron told me that his group was comprised of some very promising young Nepali athletes; Kyaron didn't really fit into that niveau, but it was too late for the group leader to judge that, a conclusion that he had likely come to by himself, since Kyaron also informed me with that huge smile that he was now officially registered for the marathon.

There would be no battery charging or WiFi for the two days at Base Camp, so I wanted to get my phone fully charged before going there in order to be able to take plenty of photos. Charging at the lodge was only available at the reception, which was little more than a cubby hole behind a half wall where a man was always staked out (I think he slept there too). There you could buy phone cards, candy bars, water, and, if you had your own charging cable, you could also leave your electronics for charging. But at the moment all the outlets were being used. This was an electrician's nightmare. A ten-port electrical extension bank that was piggy-backed all over the place. I cringed at the thought of an electrical fire in that wooden tinderbox of a lodge. But, I still wanted to charge, so I had to wait. Finally, just before dinner there was free space and mine was plugged in, but normally it took about three hours to fully charge.

After dinner I had time to spare, and I sat and played Rummy with Harry while waiting for my phone. I was so tired. At one point, he laid down a 5 and said to me, "You already have two fives, don't you?" I looked at my cards and said no and played further, then after discarding I realized that I did in fact have two 5s. How did I not see them? I was so over-tired that I really needed to go to bed, charged phone or no phone. We finished our hands; I obviously got slaughtered even though Harry had never played Rummy before that trip. I asked at the desk if my phone was charged and it was only at 74%; so I asked to leave it overnight but the man said they turn the generators off and, so, *there is no power during the night*, he explained with precision. Tired or not I would have been able to come to this same conclusion on my own. And so I took my phone with the promise to return it first thing in the morning for completion of the full-charge deal, and I wearily found my resting place upstairs.

# CHAPTER 13

................................................................

*"If you only do what others have already done, you will only feel what others have already felt. However, if you choose to achieve something that no one has ever done, then you will have a satisfaction that no one else has ever had."*

–Sir Edmund Hillary

................................................................

## Day 14: Trek From Gorakshep to South Base Camp Mount Everest (5,364 m)

**0700 0800 0900**

The sound of clanging yak bells could be heard throughout the night, but they were somehow calming and always paused for moments into silence to let me fall back to sleep; that is, until 6:00 AM when we were woken by the women cleaning the bathroom. They were having an animated conversation, yelling up and down the length of the hall. After that awakening we were at least hoping that the toilet room would be clean, but on inspection we found that they had only wiped down the floor. The water barrel that was to be used for flushing was completely empty and the garbage can had not been emptied.

Now I know I've gotten into some detail about the facilities before, but there is actually more juicy information that I would now like to share. We were asked not to throw anything into the toilets at all the lodges, and I don't just mean women's hygiene products. I mean, specifically, toilet paper. That means that every wipe, of every bottom, of every person in that lodge is stuffed there in that open waste basket. Which was now overflowing.

*Yes, I am aware that this book often goes immediately from the topic of toilets to meals, but that's unfortunately exactly how it was, two activities with high priority. So continuing with tradition...*

On to breakfast.

That morning we were served oatmeal and toast. Surprise, surprise. In addition to the peanut butter jars filled with red mystery gel, there were also sticky jars of honey on the table, which leads to sticky hands, which is difficult to remedy without...yes, you guessed it... running water.

By 9:00 AM we were ready to go and you could feel the excitement in the air. Today we would arrive at Base Camp Mount Everest! Until now I could only dream of being there and finally it was actually going to become a reality. Being able to stay overnight there had been a main driver for me to take part in the race. You hear stories throughout your life about Mount Everest, the tallest mountain on earth, and the famous mountaineers who climb there, all of whom have an interlude at Base Camp. News stories, movies, documentaries, tragedies, and triumphs. It's all happened there. I felt like a kid on Christmas morning brimming with anticipation.

The beginning of the trek that day was flat and easy going, but quickly the terrain became very rocky, with some short steep scrambles and lots of boulders to maneuver around. Porters were constantly coming through in the opposite direction with their massive loads and they always had the right of way. So when they were spotted coming towards us, a call would be made from someone in the front of the group that would travel back amongst us, "Porter!", and we would get off to one side of the trail to make room for him (and sometimes her) and the colossal cargos on their backs. Yak trains were also on their way through and they were similarly announced in the group, but as opposed to the porters for whom we moved out of the way out of politeness, for the yaks, we moved out of the way for our own personal safety.

The last kilometer before reaching Base Camp was on the glacier itself. I had always pictured Base Camp as a snowy wonderland, but it is not, or at least it wasn't when we were there. The ice was covered with glacial debris that terminated in a moraine field. There were rocks ranging in size from large boulders to sand. Most of the trail, which was difficult to discern, was covered in a thin layer of sand under which there was ice, so it was slippery, the stones were not stable and you had to concentrate with each step. *How am I going to RUN on this during the marathon?*

We reached Base Camp by midday and before even having a chance to look around, tent selection was first on the agenda. Unlike at the lodges where our rooms were assigned to us and already contained our trekking bags when we got our keys, here at camp we were allowed to choose our tent. I immediately went out to search for one, which required a high degree of coordination just to get around as the entire area was strewn with football-sized ankle-twisting stones. I was afraid I'd sprain an ankle even before I made it to the starting line. But soon I found a tent that was in a relatively sheltered area (some were very exposed) and it additionally met my second requirement that it was to lay flat, as some were on a slight slope and I didn't want Beatrice and I sliding into each other all night long. The tents were each numbered with a laminated double-digit number sign attached with a zip tie. Then I saw it. Our tent. It was perfect. Number 29. My age. Wishful thinking. The tent next to us was grabbed by Niki and Carolyn, the one next to them by two of the Mexican women. We were sheltered next to an altar on which burned some offerings. Good karma. There was one more tent available in our little cloister and I went to hunt down Shaun to get him to move in, but he had found another tent which had a monster view of the glacier and icefall in front of him. Shortly afterwards, Jianqi, the Chinese girl (well, she wasn't exactly a girl; she looked like she was about 20 but I think she was pushing 40 years old) moved in next door and we were a big group of women surrounding the altar. We then scavenged for a few chairs and made camp. We joked with others who tried to pass through our area that they needed a password for access. "What's the password?" Niki asked. As I contemplated something meaningful, such as summit searchers or mountain girls, Carolyn was the first to respond with "Titties." And so it was settled.

Shortly after our arrival and tent selection we were served warm juice and shown around, which entailed Ricky pointing towards the dining tent. Then he pointed to the toilets. Tour over.

But he did continue on with some important information that all visitors to the Base Camp, as well as anyone visiting the entire area, must abide by. Nudity (and even shirtless-ness) is acceptable only in private and intimacy only with your committed spouse or partner. Ricky told us about how the previous year there had been a couple who had met while making the trek up to EBC and were getting quickly involved. He had to warn them against any physical intimacy while at Base Camp in order not to upset the spirits. The same went for defecating outside the constructed toilets, although this rule may have been piggy-backed onto the original nudity and intimacy warning in order to keep the place clean. If it works, then we all win, mountain spirits and trekkers alike.

So there I was sipping warm juice and sitting in the sun at Mount Everest Base Camp. I started to relax and take in the remarkable surroundings. We were essentially on the glacier, or actually the moraine field, so there was a lot of exposed ice, sand, and rocks covering the ice and lots of flowing water, really fast flowing streams all over the place from the glacial ice melt. Everywhere I looked was a natural wonder. There were huge boulders being held in place by columns of ice, a ton of rock balanced by a delicate arm of frozen water. These sculptures looked like they could topple at any moment and eventually they would, but hopefully once we were long gone. Despite the entire environment being just ice and rock, no green as far as the eye could see, it was amazingly beautiful and beyond my wildest expectations. And as picturesque and perfect as that entire landscape of Mother Nature's artwork was, the next year, after the monsoon rains, it wouldn't be at all the same. She would create another masterpiece. It would still be beautiful, but upon returning one may not recognize a thing, since the glacier is always moving and changing. As if alive.

From where I was sitting I could look up and see the Khumbu Icefall directly in front of me. Some call it the Popcorn Field, and I could actually see five climbers coming down off of it. They were hardly discernable, just tiny specks. It is optically deceiving, the glacier; it looks so close and not very expansive—it appears to be crossable in a short time, and it certainly does not look steep at all—but that is all a fallacy. Climbers usually need four to five hours to get up or down, depending on the conditions, and it is supposed to be one of the most difficult and dangerous parts of the Everest ascent.

Actually, the Icefall is just a part of the entire Khumbu Glacier which is a 10-mile (16-km) river of ice that begins high on the Lhotse Face at about 25,000 feet. Once it leaves Lhotse, the glacier carves out the Western Cwm for about 2 miles before dropping precipitously to create the Khumbu Icefall which extends for 2.5 miles and varies in width from about a third of a mile to over half a mile. Around Everest Base Camp (EBC), the glacier makes a sharp turn to the south and continues another 6 miles (10 km), descending to an elevation of 16,000 feet (4,900 meters). That is the section we had just been trekking alongside of for the past couple of days.

In the early 1920s, as George Mallory was searching for a route to climb to the summit of Everest, he was said to have sighted the Icefall and remarked that it was "terribly steep and broken … all in all the approach to the mountain from Tibet is easier." Not that they had much choice at the time since Nepal chose to remain isolated from the rest of the world with its borders firmly closed to all foreigners. In the late 1940s these restrictions were loosened slightly, welcoming a few scientists. And then finally in 1949 the first trekkers were allowed inside the country, but only if they were accompanied by scientists.

Thus, it wasn't until 1950 when Charlie Houston and Bill Tilman led a British reconnaissance team into the Himalayas in order to search for a possible route up Everest from the Nepal side that the Khumbu Icefall was considered feasible.

In 1951, another British team led by Eric Shipton, who was renowned for his Himalayan expeditions in the 1930s, climbed through the Icefall but stopped just short of the top due to a wide crevasse. During that time, it was common for expeditions to use long tree trunks brought up from the tree line far below to cross the crevasses after they ran out of ladders. By the time Shipton and his crew reached that crevasse they were all out of trees or couldn't bring one to that location; either way, it brought that particular expedition to an end. But a year later, a Swiss team overcame that final obstacle by climbing into the crevasse and crossing a dangerous snow bridge. They reached 8,500 meters of elevation using today's southeast ridge route but were still unable to summit.

Then finally, a year later in 1953, John Hunt's British expedition made the first summit using that same route. And as we all know, Edmund Hillary and Tenzing Norgay summited during that expedition on May 29, the day of which is commemorated yearly by the Mount Everest Marathon along with many other events in the entire Khumbu valley.

Naturally, all of these thoughts about past Everest treks were *not* running through my head as I sat there captivated and completely in awe of the Khumbu Icefall. With all its beauty, the warm sun shining, and the glacier sparkling, it was easy to understand the fascination with this area and these mountains. Needless to say, she had claimed another victim. I was hopelessly in love with the Khumbu valley.

Shortly thereafter I was having a chat with Ricky when Shaun approached us with a problem. He realized that he had left his laminated race bib—number 45—in the trekking bag that was sent down to Namche Bazaar. He confided this with some embarrassment. I said to Ricky, "Well, that must happen a lot, right? In all the confusion?" No, he shook his head while smirking. This is the first time. Shaun asked if Ricky had any extra race numbers. Or some paper and markers??? Double no. I laughed and said, "Shaun, just go find tent number 45 and you've got yourself a laminated start number." His eyes widened. Ricky laughed. Shaun went off on a mission.

That first day for lunch at Base Camp we were spoiled with an awesome vegetable soup. Spicy and...did I mention it was VEGETABLE soup? Cauliflower and greens. Finally. Hallelujah. Base Camp rocks!

The dining tent was large enough to fit about 20 of us inside at one time. The tables were neatly set with large plastic oatmeal containers filled with sugar for our tea, salt and pepper, as well as tubs of honey, which was frozen in the morning, so we couldn't use it on our oatmeal or toast, but by afternoon it had thawed... just in time for pasta and potatoes. There was no artificially colored red jelly in sight but to the sheer joy of just about everyone, there were jars of peanut butter! Freshly unopened jars at that! And loaves of white bread! Heaven! Peanut butter on white bread has been a stranger to my palate since I was a kid, but after what we'd had to eat over the past two weeks, it was a luxury, savoring the flavor that brought me back to Wonder Bread and Jif and that feeling of *Geborgenheit* as a child in my mom's kitchen.

Next up was settling into our tent and trying to get organized. We had multiple sleeping bags and mattresses and sleeping bag liners; our stuff was scattered all about and it was so perfectly cozy and homey! I liked it more than any of the lodge rooms we shared.

Then Beatrice confided that she'd never been camping before. *What? Yes, you have Beatrice!* She looked at me confused. *Two years ago with me at the MdS!* Oh, yes, that's true, she giggled. Hard to believe that the only two times that she had camped in her life have been with me! I used to go camping for vacation with my family as a kid. But it wasn't really roughing it in the outback; it was always at family campgrounds that had lots of entertainment for us kids so that my parents could chill with their friends. But even later, just after college, I'd go with friends and a few tents out in the deep woods in Pennsylvania, mostly to party around a campfire rather than enjoy the natural surroundings. Eventually my husband and I would take our kids camping, but a giant eight-man tent with gear for a family of six is more work than vacation so we didn't do it all that often. And now my current experience with camping is limited to adventure races. So I guess I'm on a progression, and maybe someday I'll set out on my own in the wilderness and make camp.

Or not.

Then we decided it was time to check out the toilets. There were two toilet tents set up to serve several of our runners' groups plus the guides, porters, and kitchen staff, which totaled about 100 people for just those two toilets. There were a few other toilets located elsewhere to serve similar-sized groups. (Just setting the stage here.) The toilet tents were about a square meter in area and about 2 meters tall, and blue, as opposed to our sleeping tents that were yellow and the dining tent which was green, not that we would get them mixed up anyhow even if they weren't color-coded. Inside the toilet tent was simply a 10-gallon blue barrel with a plastic liner that had been set down into the rocks, flush with the ground surface, with two relatively flat rocks on either side to stand on. So, essentially a squatter. Into a bucket. They had been set up by our organization specifically for our groups; thus, on that first day, before most of the people had arrived, the toilet was remarkably clean. But, as the day progressed, and those trekkers who were afflicted with diarrhea (and there were many) had made several hurried trips to relieve themselves before they made a mess of their own clothing, well, they made a mess of the tent instead. There was excrement everywhere, in front of and on the sides of the bucket and directly on the standing rocks, and notably (and surprisingly) a considerable amount on the rear wall of the tent. Apparently projectile diarrhea was flagrant amongst the trekkers, otherwise I can't imagine how it is physically possible for shit to travel from A to B on a horizontal path.

The front of the blue canvas tents had flaps with Velcro that theoretically should be able to close up for some privacy, but the tents were strung so tightly with guy ropes that the form was stretched and misshapen enough so that the Velcro didn't match up. Thus, Beatrice and I always travelled together and took turns being the watch dog.

Of the two tents, one of them I only used once, and was too frightened to use it again. It was perched on a ledge with a 3-meter drop directly behind it, just centimeters from where I was doing the balancing act. And there was a gap in the tent so that you could look dizzyingly down between your legs and behind you into an abyss. What would be worse? A 3-meter fall with my pants around me ankles or a slip into the poo pot?

I think I'll be forever haunted by these visions.

Back in the safety of our tent following a delicious dinner of veggie dumplings and after filling our water bottles with lukewarm water, we got organized and changed up for the night ahead. I had brought two blue glow sticks with me, the kind you snap and they emit a dull light that lasts eight hours or more, and I hung them from the center top of our tent; one to snap each night. Then we lay back, staring mesmerizingly at its luminescence, and Beatrice started with her questions again. "Name your three favorite designers," she said. Beatrice is a fanatical fashionista, runs one of the most popular fashion blogs in Switzerland, and knows all the labels in the industry. I am not completely ignorant on the topic, but this situation was like attempting to play religious trivia against the Pope. Thankfully, my first answer came quickly: Salvatore Ferragamo, whose grandson James is an acquaintance of mine. Whew. Next, Michael Kors. I have a small collection of their handbags. Bea nodded, though it was

Hotel Shanker.
*Photo courtesy of Hotel Shanker.*

Funerals at the Pashupatinath Temple of Shiva.

Bea and me, sightseeing in Kathmandu.
*Photo courtesy of Shaun Stafford.*

Our group in the small plane headed to Lukla.

Safely arrived in Lukla at the "Most Dangerous Airport in the World." *Photo courtesy of Shaun Stafford.*

Peeking into a private home in Phakding.

Porters ready to go in Phakding; Ricky tossing something from the upper window down to Trijan.

Lodge Group A having lunch in Jorsalle.

Mark and I photo-bomb Shaun standing before the infamous double-hanging bridges.

Niki (right) with Carolyn, wearing her favorite shirt.

Dining hall in Namche lodge.

Children at a school in Namche.

Collection for preservation of the trail.
*Photo courtesy of Harry Hilberdink.*

Jill facing her fear of heights.
*Photo courtesy of Shaun Stafford.*

Emerging from the rhododendron forest with the first view of the village of Khumjung.

This little cutie stole my heart.

One of the many hanging bridges.

Yokios laden with our trekking bags and some provisions in Khumjung.

Playful pony outside my window in Deboche.

Approaching Dingboche.
*Photo courtesy of Harry Hilberdink.*

Woman collecting dung along the Bibre Loop to be used for heating and cooking.

One of the many cairns at the memorial to those who have died climbing in the Khumbu region.

Photoshoot on a frigid afternoon in Dingboche.

With Kyaron in Gorakshep after our surprise reunion.

Tea after climbing Kala Patthar with a view of Mt. Everest and Nupse.

Porter carrying an immense load just outside of Base Camp.

Those amazing yaks.

View of the Khumbu glacier "popcorn field" from Everest Base Camp.

Everest Base Camp latrine in *pristine* condition upon arrival.

Everest Base Camp kitchen tent and happy cooks.

Ray and Shaun, enjoying the ride in the Base Camp dining tent.

With a Sherpa who has summitted Mt. Everest a whopping six times!

Harry in Dutch orange at Base Camp.
*Photo courtesy of Harry Hilberdink.*

Raemonde in her gorilla costume.
*Photo courtesy of Anuj Adhikary.*

Lodge Group A: Ricky (lying in front). Back row (from left to right): Pemba (Sherpa), Ray, Shaun, Carolyn, Vero, Harry, Raemonde, Dave, Henni, Cindy, Jill, Mark, Pierre, Sherpa, porter, Bibesh (Sherpa), porter, Sherpa. Front row (from left to right): Holly, Beatrice, Trijan (sirdar), Pedro, Gris, Tendi (Sherpa), Bluesky, Niki, Dafuri (Sherpa), Kiki, porter, Milan (porter), porter, porter. Absent: Jesper, Clara, Michael, Thuan Na, Thi Thu Ha, Jianqi.
*Photo courtesy of Anuj Adhikary.*

Start of the Mount Everest Marathon.
*Photo courtesy of Anja Kaiser.*

Helicopter pad on the ridge over Namche.
*Photo courtesy of Harry Hilberdink.*

The beautiful prayer flags of
Z-street.
*Photo courtesy of Beatrice Lessi.*

Beatrice, in her skin-tight red
dress, and me, just before the final
night celebration in Hotel Shanker,
Kathmandu.

Mark.
*Photo courtesy of Beatrice Lessi.*

Sightseeing at Swayambhunath on final full day in KTM.

unclear if she was in agreement or simply happy that I could come up with a second response. One more. *Think. Think. Who was that designer that my aunt worked with in Florence???* Roberto Cavalli! *Yes!* She nodded again and then whipped out her three favorites as though they were, and always are, on the tip of her tongue. "Gucci, of course," she said. *How could I have forgotten that one?* "Dolce & Gabbana because they are very, very Italian." (She admits that she is biased.) She said they do some fabulous things for Melania Trump from time to time, which is why she nearly boycotted them, but just couldn't. "The third," she said, "is Versace because of their beautiful Oscar dresses." She joyfully went on and on about designers for a few minutes, but I was more or less tuned out, due to both ignorance and impartiality, so I just occasionally retorted in acquiescence.

Next question: "Name three famous men who you'd love to get in your bed." Okay...this is easier. Number one, a younger Sean Connery, in the James Bond years. Two, Mats Hummels. And three, David Beckham. Whipped 'em out, just like that! Yep, I like soccer players; not only that, but Beckham's tattoos are just so irresistible.

Beatrice said that she has a long, long, long, long list but, reducing it to three, she selected Elon Musk, Richard Branson, and Ben Affleck, in that order, but only Ben Affleck when he was in the movie with the beard... "There is a movie where he is a nice spyyyyy," she said in her throaty voice.

So, as in everything else, the two of us also have very different tastes in men. She thinks I am useless because I like the good-looking manly men, whereas she tends for the more interesting powerful intellectuals. But the question was for a fantasy roll in the sheets and as far as I'm concerned conversation can be left out altogether there.

Anyway, I'm married to an intellectual.

At about minus 15 degrees Celsius (5°F), it was especially cold during that first night. (*Do I have to even say that anymore?*) I had hunkered down in everything I had: a merino wool sleeping bag liner inside a mid-weight sleeping bag inside an expedition-grade bag on top of one foam mattress and a thermal air mattress, and on top of me I piled my jackets. With a hat, gloves, and a buff. And I was just barely warm.

During the night we could hear the glacier creaking and cracking right beneath our tent. I imagined a giant crevasse opening up underneath and swallowing us whole. We also heard numerous avalanches in the distance. I would hold my breath and listen, waiting and hoping the rumbling sound would fade before it got louder. Thankfully, it always did.

Though never really warm, I was comfortable enough so that I could get some much-needed sleep. And considering that we were in bed by 7:00, asleep maybe around 8:30 and awake around 6:00, there is a lot of time to rest during that period. By that point, we didn't need an alarm anymore, our bodies were adjusted to the schedule and simply took the sleep they needed. Though not always asleep during the night, just laying and resting was also regenerative for the body and soul; I spent lots of time counting my blessings and being grateful that everything was good with me and Beatrice. We were healthy and, despite being together 24/7 over the past two weeks, which could tax any relationship, our friendship was strong.

# CHAPTER 14

......................................................................

*"Just to lie here in the sun with great white peaks all around me and the biggest glacier (...) at my feet, to eat from time to time, to sleep a little and dream a great deal - it is a heavenly existence."*

–George Leigh Mallory

......................................................................

## Day 15: Rest Day and Mock Race Start at Mount Everest Base Camp

### 0730 0830 0930

Poor Niki had stumbled into a really dangerous situation during the night. Literally stumbled. She went out to use the toilet and on her return, crossing what she thought was firm ground, she broke through some ice into a glacial melt pool and was up to her mid calves in ice-cold water, with shoes and socks on. Everything was soaking wet and obviously at those temperatures that can be really dangerous for hypothermia. She rushed back to her tent and took off all the wet things, put on dry clothes and jumped into her sleeping bag. She assured us all that she was okay in the morning, and thankfully the sun was shining so her shoes would be able to dry out quickly.

Mark also had a tough evening. He was apparently vomiting and had diarrhea all night long and was very weak in the morning. At least he would have a full day to rest and recuperate before the race. But he also had another reason to get well quickly. Not only was the 29th of May race day, annually marking the first ascent of Everest, but it was also Mark and Jill's 11th wedding anniversary. Both Everest fans, once they realized that they shared this memorable occasion of their anniversary with the first ascent, they felt compelled to come to Everest Base Camp, and why not top it off by running a marathon together on that day too? They could only hope the day would bless him with a tremendous recovery in his health so that the two of them could fulfill that dream, instead of being evacuated by helicopter.

On the agenda for that day was a mock start of the race. Everyone was to meet at the starting line and wear their running gear with the race jerseys; many even had their start numbers on. The plan was that the photographers and cameramen would take lots of photos and videos and after the mock start they would take individual photos of any runners that wanted to them. Lots of people were carrying their country's flag. Some people were even wearing costumes as we had all been asked to bring them for a special photo which was to be used as advertisement for a fundraiser for talented Nepalese runners to travel to foreign races. Raemonde was there in her gorilla suit. There was a British knight, and a man in a Scottish kilt, though that may not have been a costume. It was all very chaotic. Two rivers of glacial melt ran through it. It was icy and stony and nearly impossible to walk there, let alone start a race! But the sun was shining and glistening off the glacial 8,000m+ peaks surrounding us. The atmosphere was amazing, and hundreds of adults were running around like five-years-olds, having the time of their lives.

We were lined up behind an imaginary starting line on a pile of stones bordered on one side by a stream and the other by in ice wall. Someone was trying to give us all instructions, but it was impossible to understand a single word; there may have been a countdown though no one was sure of anything, and suddenly it was, *GO!* The first few people in the front ran about 10 or 15 meters, but the others behind them just carefully stumbled over the rubble and were completely clogged together. Apparently it didn't have much cinematic quality since they called us all back to do it again. But this time the people from the back got to be in the front, so Bea and I pushed our way forward. On the initial run we kind of hid in the back since it was all so crazy, but then on the second go-around, we thought, hey, why not get in the photo? We positioned ourselves in the front row and held our ground. On the signal we did our best in front of the rolling cameras to try to look as if we were actually running, or at least not look too ridiculous as we tiptoed over the loose stones, gravel and ice.

Afterwards there was a hodge-podge of filming going on. Runners of each nationality were asked to group together and say a few words in front of the camera, either in English or their native language. Most also gave some kind of pumped-up cheer like, *Ready to rumble!*, or *Let's rock this!*

Then we were asked to put on our costumes. Beatrice had a unicorn outfit and I had a Viking hat with braids. We looked absurd, which is probably why lots of people wanted photos with us. I was embarrassed but Beatrice was in heaven, dancing around like a ballerina since her costume had a little tutu on it. Then some of us climbed up onto a ledge on the glacier and there we found some treasures buried in the snow. Old pieces of rope and fabric.

I was amazed, wondering how old the relics may be, wondering if I'd stumble upon the next Ötzi. But Beatrice burst my bubble and said she was certain it was just trash left behind from the current climbing season. I also found some beautiful rocks that I wanted to bring home as souvenirs. One that was particularly fabulous I had earmarked for my son, a charcoal grey with lime green layers. But it wasn't all that small, it covered my palm. Should I make the porters schlepp it down? Hmmm...

People finally began to trickle back to their tents and we followed suit, actually pretty exhausted after all the excitement. But then again, any activity at 5,364 meters above sea level can be quite draining! We rested for a while then were asked by the cameramen to come out again and do an interview and some running shots. Running? Where do they propose that we run? But they found a strip about three meters long but so narrow that you could only put one foot directly in front of each other. I think that was the longest stretch that was relatively flat within two square miles. But there was no room to get up to any speed so we borrowed a move from Shaun, otherwise known as super-hero slow-mo running.

Lunch was bok choy with chickpeas and white beans! So delicious! That was served with some fried bread that was sweetened with sugar on top like donuts. The best food we had the whole trek was here at Base Camp! As we were sitting there enjoying the meal, we suddenly heard a loud rumbling in the distance. A couple of the people at the entrance of the tent went out to look and called out, "Avalanche!" A bunch of us followed to watch a huge white plume fall off the northwest side of Nuptse. One of the guides said it was lucky that the avalanche was not on the eastern side or it would have taken out the climbers that were currently making their way down the Icefall. What a frightening thought! But day to day it was becoming increasingly clear just how dangerous it was there, as though the gap between life and death is much narrower in those mountains.

After lunch several of us headed up to the toilets and were shocked at the state of them. The buckets were overflowing. Niki and Carolyn approached Ricky and asked if the buckets could be emptied or replaced. At the time we weren't really sure what they did with those full buckets, but I've since found out. The buckets are removed from the ground and sealed. Then they are transported by porter or yak back to Gorakshep where the plastic bag is removed and left in a landfill. Where, in the extremely harsh environment, it eventually (sooner rather than later) begins to leak, and after the monsoon rains, the human excrement makes its way into the soil, rivers and ground water.

And we thought that the altitude was causing the stomach problems (*yes, said with sarcasm*). I was glad I used those water purifying tablets, even in the boiled water.

But solutions are being sought after and a project is now in the planning stages in cooperation with the Sagarmatha Pollution Control Committee (SPCC) and the Mount Everest Biogas Project to build a facility in Gorakshep which can treat and process the 28,000 pounds of human waste that is transported there each year out of Base Camp. The facility will be completely solar-powered and will convert waste into methane, a renewable natural gas fuel that will be made available to the local community to be used as a power source.

Once we were reassured that the toilet buckets would be replaced, we returned to the ladies' den and were just relaxing when some strangers started making their way through the camp. They were getting a lot of attention and so we wanted to know what was going on. We ended up talking to them and learning that they had just summited Everest seven days before and both were going to run the marathon the next day! One was an older man, probably in his mid 60s and of Asian descent, and the other was a Sherpa who'd already summited six times! Six! I got my photo taken with that super-human!

It had actually been the most successful climbing season ever on Everest that year. Over 700 ascents in 11 days. Usually the climbing window is much shorter. But even with the success rate, there were unfortunately the accompanying deaths of six climbers and Sherpas. It was a stark reminder of the dangers and risks involved, because when you are sitting below and look up onto that mountain, full of respect and awe, barely grasping how such a staggeringly beautiful land mass can even exist, it is nearly impossible to comprehend a connection with human death. It seemed almost inconceivable that such horrific tragedy could be possible in a place of such peace and beauty. It reminds me of when I stood at the finish line of the Boston Marathon in 2013, on top of the world and enjoying a moment of exhilaration with thousands of other runners after just having completed the fabled race, when the last thing we expected was that two bombs would go off right in front of our eyes. Happiness and horror cannot coexist.

Other latecomers were also trickling into Base Camp including a group that had just climbed Island Peak. There were 14 people in that group, all of whom looked pretty exhausted. One of the women was clearly not doing well; whether she was sick or injured we weren't sure, but she looked as though she wasn't going to be running the next day and may have to be evacuated via helicopter. And then Kiki showed up! She said she was feeling good and she joined Jianqi in the tent next to us. Our Lodge Group A was now complete. We'd all made it there. Ricky was thrilled.

Then Shaun joined Bea and me in our cozy tent for a while to chill. Well, chillin' was actually the opposite of the temperature change in there with Shaun around. He is like a boiler plate! It was cold when we got in there but within 20 minutes we needed to open up the zipped entrance to let some cool air in and avoid suffocating. After Shaun left and we could breathe again, we all had some work to do in terms of sorting through our gear in preparation for the last night and the following day—race day. We needed to get our running backpacks ready and sort away into the trekking bag all the things we wouldn't be taking with us during the marathon.

That night at dinner we were again spoiled with vegetables! Deep-fried cauliflower! It was so delicious. I ate so much. Every time the serving plate went by I grabbed for more! But... Monday morning quarterback. No real veggies for 10 days and then masses of cauliflower?!? My stomach rebelled. Later on, I was so bloated. Ugh. The evening before the marathon. Not good timing.

In the tent that night we made our final preparations for the next morning, separating out what would come with us and what would go with the porters. Beatrice put on her race clothes, saying that she didn't want to have to get changed into them in the morning. Not a bad idea. I put on my first running layer and tights, but laid the mid-layer and race shirts next to me in my sleeping bag to keep them warm, while I slept in the merino wool mid-layer top that I'd been using all week. The temperature had suddenly dropped when the sun went down. The "hot" water that they had given us for our bottles was not really hot and my body temperature was not rising, even after climbing into my triple-bag set-up.

At that very moment, sitting shivering in a tent on top of the glacier at Everest Base Camp, I made a solemn promise to myself that I would never let myself be that cold again. Ever. Cross my heart and hope to die, stick a needle... You get the picture.

The last thing I muttered to Beatrice before falling asleep that night was, "If I ever mention the word *Antarctica* to you in context with a marathon, then you have my permission to hit me over the head."

# CHAPTER 15

*"Toeing the starting line of a marathon, regardless of the language you speak, the God you worship or the color of your skin, we all stand as equal. Perhaps the world would be a better place if more people ran."*

–Dean Karnazes

## Day 16: May 29 and 65 Years to the Day After the First Ascent of Mount Everest

### Race Day: Marathon Base Camp to Namche Bazaar

### 0430 0530 0630

An early start.

I snuck out of the tent and collected some tea for me and Beatrice at about 5:00. Raemonde was there outside the dining tent, already eating breakfast. She was running the 60-kilometer ultra. I was hoping that I would get to see her, but had been worried that I might miss her before she started her race which began one hour earlier than the marathon. She was happy to have some company and I was happy to be there with her; she was so positive, just radiating joy and thankfulness.

This place is truly the best medicine.

My toes were already ice cold. I was hoping that moving around would warm them up, but they just got worse as I packed my gear. The porters were perched outside our tent, ready to take our trekking bag. They wanted to get an early start so that they could also get to the finish as soon as possible. It was difficult to part with my warm winter jacket, but I had to make the break.

Then I tried to use the toilet. But could not. Uh, oh. *Was it nerves or that damn cauliflower?* Oh, well, can't force it, especially not on a squatter, and it's not as though I'd been eating very much anyway, so in effect, less in equals less out. Thus, I wouldn't be carrying much ballast to slow me down.

By the time we headed to the starting line my toes were even worse and it felt like there were stones stuffed into the front of my shoes. I'd experienced that once before at a race, the Polar Circle Marathon in Greenland. That day, they never warmed up, not even after a post-race hot shower; it wasn't until late that night that I finally got some sensation back in them. I was hoping that the same would not be true that day.

Most runners had a small backpack on; well, I think all the international runners did, although the fast Nepalese did not. I had my Camelback filled with about a liter and a half of water, an extra-light rain jacket, gels, protein bars, isotonic and salt tabs, a heat-sheet blanket, and basic first aid.

Everyone was nervous. Milling around. No one was quite sure what would happen. And then from the crowd emerged the happy couple! Mark and Jill! We all wished them a happy anniversary.

Though still weak, Mark was feeling better and they planned to take it easy, stick together, and run or walk as needed to get them back to Namche on foot.

People had been contemplating how long we would need to finish. It was really hard to estimate due to the elevation, a factor that none of us had had to deal with before to that extreme in a race. But I roughly estimated, due to the terrain and the altitude, that I would need about twice the time it takes me to run a road marathon, so my goal was about 7 ½ hours, maybe a little less. Although that was really a shot-in-the-dark.

Just like the mock race the day before, the atmosphere at the start was ridiculously chaotic. A starting line rope was drawn between two organizers across a giant pile of stones and ice upon which we were all cautiously trying to balance. The ice-melt river flowed on one side, a steep icy wall on the other. There was no visible path to follow ahead of us, but a few marker flags were seen randomly protruding from between the rocks which I assumed was our route.

We all wished each other luck and promised to celebrate that evening. Then I tried to place myself as much towards the front as possible, of course still behind the fast-footed Nepalese, but right behind them so as not to get caught in a single-file slog over the first several hundred meters. As we stood waiting for the last ten minutes, the sun thankfully came out and began to warm us up. A good sign. One last look up to the highest place on the planet, and before we knew it, we were sent off like homing pigeons on a journey. Finally set loose to do what we came here for ... RUN!

It seemed that all the worry that I'd had about running over the terrain was a waste of energy, because it was easier than I'd anticipated. Of course there was lots of jumping and careful foot placement, but at least it was runnable. And now in motion, with the sun smiling down, it was only a matter of minutes until I realized that my toes had thawed.

The trail was narrow, so occasionally when a runner came up behind me and was following closely I asked if he wanted to pass, sometimes they did, but others were content to follow my line. It seemed that the field thinned out quickly and, once off the moraines, I soon got into that trance-like rhythm of a long-distance runner when you know you have a long day ahead of you, and you are simply doing what you love. There was nothing I'd rather be doing.

The trekkers on route that day were fabulously uplifting. Any time they would see runners coming through, they would clear off the trail. There was a large group in Gorakshep; they looked at me with wide eyes when I passed by surrounded by men; they shouted every possible encouragement imaginable. Whether they knew it or not, their cheers give us runners so much strength and bolstering. You can't help but push yourself just that little bit more.

The first official checkpoint was in Lobuche where a table was set up with three men seated behind it. We were required to stop and report our race number which they recorded on paper, and then they would send the information via cell phone to the time-keepers at the finish so that we could be tracked on the Internet. There was also water in cups on the table. I drank one cup and realized that I was really out of breath, so I bent over with my hands on my knees and tried to slow my breathing. It did not work. So, with no other options, I took off again.

I was wondering how the altitude would affect me when running. Ascents are difficult at any altitude so when climbing I paced myself according to how I felt. But strangely enough, the altitude was not as significant as I'd expected, at least not while I was in motion. It wasn't until at that first aid station, gasping for air, that I realized something was very different.

At around kilometer 9 a sherpa passed me going the opposite direction and he said to me, *"Erste Frau."* First woman. Seriously. He spoke to me in German, telling me that I was the first woman. First international woman, of course. Wow. Cool. I hadn't seen other women around me, but you can never be sure who pulled out ahead at the start. And I had no idea how many Nepalese women were in front of me, but I knew we were essentially running different races. There was no way I could compete with them.

Shortly afterward a familiar face snuck up on me. It was Ash. *Hey!* He stayed behind me for a few minutes then I let him pass but I kept right on his heels. He was a solid runner, but apologized for not making a good line, which is essentially the path that you choose when running rough terrain. You certainly can't run straight on rocky trails, so you need to try to choose the shortest route possible where you have sure footing. His line was fine by me, considering we weren't at a sprint pace anyway and so I simply tried to stay right on him, using his line so I wouldn't have to contemplate one myself.

Just before the memorial to the Khumbu valley's lost climbers, I saw another familiar face, or actually, I recognized her not from her face, but from the black fur covering her body. It was Raemonde, in her gorilla suit, of course, minus the headpiece. She had started an hour before us on the 60-kilometer course and was planning on power walking it instead of running, but I was still surprised to see her so early into the race. I yelled out to her as I approached, and she gave me a big wave. She was standing there and talking to two men, who appeared to be sherpas from another group, but as I got closer I noticed that she had a cut on her nose from which she was bleeding. I asked if she was okay and she said she was fine. She still had a long day ahead of her. I hoped she'd be okay.

On the plains high over Pheriche was where Ash slowly began to gain ground on me. I hesitantly let him go, since I knew I had to pace myself, run my own tempo, and by the time we approached the descent into Dingboche, he was out of sight.

It was there in Dingboche, at kilometer 17, that we began the Bibre Loop, the out-and-back 6-km loop which we had run during our acclimization stay a week before. The loop gave us the opportunity to see where we were in the field, as well as to greet our friends. But just as I started into it, I had to stop and take off my long-sleeve thermal top. It was getting too warm. I stuffed it into my backpack. I still had a first-layer T-shirt on under my race jersey. That should be enough as long as the weather held. The Bibre Loop was traditionally known to be one of the Everest marathon runner's least favorite sections of the course. That was because we gained elevation there in a gradual climb and, though not steep, it was noticeably tiring. Even though I knew the trail, it was still hard to follow, dodging scrub brush, rocks, and washed out stream beds. There were actually several footpaths so you were constantly scanning to see which one was the most worn and the most direct. It seemed to take forever, but finally I saw the checkpoint at the far end and was relieved to make the turn. At that point they again recorded our bib number and we also received that infamous green armband, as confirmation that we'd completed the loop.

On the back side of the Bibre Loop was my first chance to see where others stood in the field. I noticed that I was about one kilometer ahead of the next international woman, a buffer but not safety, since we still had a long way to go. The first person that I saw from our group was Pierre and just after him I saw Niki! She is a very strong runner, but she was taking it cautiously since she was still recovering from a recent sprained ankle. Then came Harry and Shaun who had decided to run the whole course together. A good match, especially for Shaun who had never run a marathon before. He would definitely benefit from an experienced runner who could pace him. As I saw them approach with big smiles, Shaun opened up his arms for a hug and puckered up for a kiss. Just as I reached him I was jumping off a rock, landed briefly in his arms and got a fat smooch on my cheek before he set me down in one fell swoop and I continued on without missing a step. I was also relieved to see Beatrice just before I finished the loop. Although she is a tough runner, I still felt as though I needed to look out for her and make sure she was all right, so it was an enormous relief to see her. She looked good. Thus, uplifted at having seen my gang, I felt great heading into the second half.

The trail remained technical. Lots of steep rocky climbs and descents. I ran where I could, and used the mountain-climbers hike where I was forced to slow down. At the first several checkpoints I had always stopped to drink a cup of water, bent over with my hands on my knees to try to catch my breath. But it never helped. So I never stopped anymore, except for the quick number check or if my water needed refilling.

That's not completely true. Sometimes I didn't have a choice and was forced to slow to a walk, that is, when I got behind the yaks. If there were only a couple of them, you could usually get by relatively quickly if the trail widened or, if there was an adjacent path on the ridge which wasn't sheer rock or overgrown with scrub brush, you could jump up onto it and sprint by the animals, then jump back down onto the trail. Usually the tactic of using an adjacent path up on the inside ridge was the best, although the effort required to jump or climb up there and sprint by was taxing. But at least it was a safe bet. These animals were not to be messed with. They were really dangerous. We were told at the beginning of the trek to always pass them on the mountain side of the trail, since they'd been known to simply push trekkers over the edge. That wasn't the only danger they posed. During the race a guy I was with got gored in the hand. He was trying to pass but must have spooked one of them which thrust his head and mighty horns at the passing runner who reached out his hand for protection and got a bloody jab in return.

I counted eight herds that I had to get by during the race. Normally they were just short delays, but a couple of kilometers before the Tengboche Monastery I got caught behind a herd of about fifteen animals. Initially I was with one male runner, but we found no opportunity to get by and the longer we walked the more and more runners started gathering in our group. Although we were constantly looking for an opportunity, there was no chance, not even for single runners to pass. This was really frustrating since I knew I was losing precious time in this slow walk. After nearly ten minutes (which felt like a lifetime), we saw our chance as there was a stone-walled yak corral adjacent to the trail. All of us dodged behind the stone wall and picked up the pace, struggling through the soft sandy soil. Thankfully the stone wall had an opening on the far side and, even at a sprint, we just barely passed the herd.

Not long after, at about kilometer 35, I was surprised when another woman came up behind me, an Austrian who'd I'd met in Base Camp. *Scheiße*!

I wondered how she caught me. It must have been the yaks! She must have found her way around them or they'd moved off the trail and into a farm shortly after she got to them. You never know if the yaks are traveling just across a village or miles on end.

She was about my age and was on the trip with her father, albeit in another group. When we met in the dining tent, she spoke decent English but her father did not, so we switched to German. She told me that she lives in Salzburg, but grew up where her father lives, in Lofer in the Austrian Alps, which is just about 20 minutes from our vacation home in Zell am See. Therefore when she came up behind me during the race, I knew that she would have the technical running skills to beat me since she grew up in the Alps. I thought, *Okay, if she really covered that much ground despite me giving all I can, then she deserves to take over the lead.*

That was my initial thought.

Then I changed my mind.

I wanted to win this race and I wasn't going to give it up after 35 kilometers without a fight! In any case, the race was on!

Even though I grew up on the ocean, miles away from any mountains and years away from trail running, over the past several years I had tucked a lot of hours of mountain running under my belt and finished several long-distance mountain races where I learned a lot and honed my technique. One of those races, which taught me just about everything I needed to know about trail running, was simultaneously the most physically challenging day of my life.

*(We are going to briefly leave the Himalayas and take a side trip to the Austrian Alps for some background on my trail-running indoctrination.)*

It was the Hochkönigman Endurance Trail starting in the idyllic village of Maria Alm, not too far from Salzburg. The race began at midnight but already by 11:00 PM, during the mandatory race briefing, my eyelids started getting heavy and the uncontrollable yawning started. Next to me sat my son who had laid his head on the table and fallen asleep. At the time, I can remember wishing I was at home in my bed. There were 135 runners and their families gathered to listen to the race director run down the details. The race would begin in an hour and cover 85 kilometers of trails with about 5,000 meters of positive elevation. I was hoping to finish in about 14 hours, but I'd later find out that was hopelessly optimistic.

My husband and our two youngest children were there with me, and they were planning to meet me along the route, at the refreshment stations or anywhere else that access was possible, but since the trail was very remote there would not be too many opportunities to see each other. That didn't bother them, they love following me at these races; it's just as much an adventure for them as it is for me. They fold down the back seats of our SUV and lay out camping mattresses and sleeping bags to get some occasional shut-eye. Well, the kids sleep, while my husband navigates.

So, shortly after 11:30 PM, once the briefing ended, we hesitantly headed out to the starting area where we had a quick gear check of mandatory equipment. A list had been provided on the Internet and my small backpack was stuffed full: long pants, rain pants, a long-sleeved shirt, a rain jacket, first-aid kit, 1.5 L of water, a cell phone, headlamp, spare batteries, a foil rescue sheet, food (for between the aid stations), a drinking cup, hat, gloves, and a map of the course. The weather report said there was 0% chance of rain and mild temperatures, but you still can't skimp on the warm, dry clothes when in the mountains, because if you happen to get hurt at 2,000 meters above sea level and can't run, then your body temperature decreases rapidly as soon as you stop running, and waiting several hours for help in sweaty running shorts and a short-sleeved shirt could be life threatening.

A billion kisses from my kids during the last few nervous minutes of waiting, then the countdown began, and we were rather unceremoniously sent out into the night.

The course started out of the city and immediately uphill. All headlamps were on. After only about 500 meters the incline was so steep that everyone halted to a walk. *What? So soon?* It was going to be a long day.

Any time the ascent wasn't so steep, I tried to run, but running wasn't much faster than my mountain-hiker's gait of pushing off from the quads with each step. As I looked at the other runners, I noticed that almost all of them had trekking poles. I always thought the poles looked like such a clumsy burden, but as I watched them pick delicately over the terrain and support their steps, I was beginning to change my mind. (*Yes, this was the race I'd previously mentioned which inspired me to get myself some trekking poles.*)

From the starting line, my family had jumped in the car, found a forestry road, and were waiting at kilometer 5, at a chalet on the top of the first ascent. I saw my son in the distance and called out to him, as it would be nearly impossible for him to recognize me in the dark amongst all the runners shining headlamps in his direction. He gave me a high five as I ran by, telling me I was fast, then I soon saw my daughter (on the playground) and my husband who informed me I was the fourth woman. That wouldn't last for very long as just before the next ascent another woman passed me. But I stayed right behind her. There were several of us in a group and she did a great job of leading us up a brutal ascent. I followed her almost to the Messingssattel, a ridge on top, then she slowed down and I passed her, but she'd overtake me again a couple hours later and I'd never see her again.

The first official checkpoint and aid station was at kilometer 13 in the village of Hinterthal. I saw our car parked in the distance so I knew my family was there. I topped up the bladder in my backpack with water and ate a piece of banana and a couple of slices of watermelon before quickly getting on my way again.

On the next incline I slowed to a walk and made some small talk with a woman who had passed me at the aid station. She had a local dialect and confirmed she was from *those hills*. Of course, she had trekking poles, too.

Once out of the forest and up to the Pichlalm, the clouds had cleared and an amazing star-filled sky had appeared. I alternated watching my step and taking in the beauty of the heavens which was exceptionally bright since we were far removed from the artificial lights of cities and towns.

Past the Erichütte and the trail wove in a ring along the Hochkönig mountain ridge where I could see the dotted runner's headlamps for miles. Some looked so far away. *Do I really have to run that far?* But in terms of distance, we were still not even a quarter of the way through the race.

In the dark and silence of the night, your senses are heightened, and you can hear flowing water quite clearly even at a distance, so despite the blackness I knew that a large river was nearby. When the trail opened up to river-washed stones I could see the headlamps of other runners making a sharp turn ahead and it appeared as though they were coming back in my direction for a short distance. As I got closer, I noticed a runner on all-fours. *What is going on?* Then as I climbed through some large rocks, I noticed it: a fallen tree spanning a raging river. And I had to cross it. *Oh, great.* And of course due to the recent rains and the spray from the river, the tree was wet and slippery. I was not going to risk a balanced walk across, so I straddled it and shimmied forward.

The trail was marked with reflective paint that you could see from several hundred meters away, so it was really easy to follow. Also, it was relatively flat along the next section and running was often possible, when we weren't jumping over streams or passing through cattle gates built to keep the free-roaming cows in the pastures.

Speaking of cows. It was spring and they were out with their young calves, and for that reason, on high alert. As I came across a herd of them near a farmhouse, some became very active and ran up onto the trail next to me. Okay, they are cows, and from a distance very idyllic, but up close these animals are HUGE.

And I had a very keen sense of not being welcome. I tried to run faster but that seemed to get them more agitated. I had to stop a couple of times to try to out-maneuver them. I called out hoping that someone in the farmhouse might hear me and come out to help, but it wasn't even 5:00 AM and just barely getting any early dawn light. Then I realized that I still had my headlamp on. I turned it off and this immediately seemed to calm them down. Then I scurried up an embankment and ran as fast as I could past the herd.

A few minutes later I saw my daughter in the distance and knew I had reached the second aid station at kilometer 30. Time for a sunrise breakfast. My son was apparently sleeping in the car. Once again I filled the 1.5-liter bladder in my backpack which was completely empty, ate some more banana and watermelon, and relayed my adventure with the cows. I also drank some hot isotonic drink, but after just a couple of minutes I began to cool down and knew I needed to keep moving, so I said goodbye and headed out once again into the woods.

In addition to fruit, the aid stations also offered pretzels and some other baked goods, but being a vegan I always carry what I know I can rely on. I had my own gels, roasted nuts, and granola bars with me and ate them between the stations. You can never take in as many calories as you are using in a race like that and I knew that over the course of the next week I'd be enjoying some extra meals. In a race of this duration and intensity, it's not just energy in the muscles that are getting used and calories that are burned, but the body grabs whatever nutrients it needs from wherever it can find it. The days following the race I had a massive mineral deficit which was evident because my teeth were so ultra-sensitive that even breathing over them was painful and I lost quite a bit of hair. But after a few days of vitamin and mineral supplements, rest, and lots of healthy meals I was back in good shape pretty quickly. (*Note: This is from my own personal experience. I've read no medical studies to back up my theory on this.*)

After leaving that aid station the trail made a gradual ascent and soon we were up above the tree line. At the next peak we were offered a spectacular view of the sunrise and a valley below which was filled to the rim with a bath of clouds. It was so stunning that I had to stop to take photos.

Up next was an elevation descent of almost 900 meters, but unfortunately we weren't on forest roads, tractor paths, or even well-treaded trails; no, the descent was steep and again very technical. I was reduced to walking and picking my way down at a depressingly slow pace since my quads were aching from the climbs.

It was hard to decide which was more strenuous: running uphill or downhill. During the strenuous ascents, I'd wish for descents; during the agonizing drops I wished for the pain-free work of the climb.

I soon found that I'd been keeping pace with another runner for a while, so we chatted about the trail which was really hard to follow in the early morning light now that there was no longer visible reflective paint; we had to rely on the pink markings and an occasional sign or ribbon, so it was nice to have a second set of eyes to rely on. Back out onto a pasture and ahead was another herd of cows. *Uh-oh.* We had to cross through them to a gate on the other side. I looked over at the other runner, gestured him forward, and said "After you..." with a smile. He then began to move through the herd and the last few meters before the gate a large animal came running behind him. He opened the gate, slammed it behind him and began talking softly to the cow, which then slowly moved away. The runner then opened the gate for me and told me to run! I made a mental note to suggest to the race director that adding the skill of dodging aggressive cattle should be included in the race description.

At the next aid station I had to sit for a few minutes to rest my quads. My husband was there and told me how other runners also had the same complaint. After a few minutes, I left there in a small group of seven runners. The next several kilometers were to be the most difficult ascent of the day. Nearly 1,000 meters of elevation gain over a distance of just over three kilometers. *Do the math.* The trail was narrow and one of the men took the lead to start, but he soon relinquished his role to me and I led the group up the mountain. We reached the top after an hour and 15 minutes. Running the entire way. I was completely wrecked. At the top there was a minor aid station with water containers and my family was there to meet me. A giant hand-carved Hochkönig chair was there and I collapsed into it. I placed my face in my hands and burst out crying. I couldn't control it and my poor son said, "Don't be sad, mom, you're doing great!" I told him that I wasn't sad, I was just exhausted. I needed a few minutes there and my daughter gave me a leg massage and repeatedly filled my cup with water. My family is such a huge motivation for me during these long races; I can mentally break up the day by looking forward to seeing them and getting their positive reinforcement. They also have stories to tell, which motivates me even more to see them and hear about their adventures. But this time it was different. That was the first time during a race that I was not sure if my body could support me to the finish line. I was only about half way through. Mentally I was ready and willing, but my quads were so shattered that I wasn't sure if they would give me the balance required to traverse the narrow mountain ridge that I knew was still in front of me. But I knew I had to continue. Giving up would be more painful.

The group that I'd run with up the mountain was gone. But I couldn't stop for long or I'd never get going again, so as the next runner was leaving the water station I tagged along behind him. Up, up, and up some more until we crossed over a large snow drift and reached the next summit. Then another steep descent of 800 meters elevation. This was getting a little frustrating...massive climbs, then major descents. All that work for nothing.

The trail was poorly marked in the next section. Either that or I was losing my concentration and didn't see all the markers. In any case, after running down the middle of an overgrown, grassy ski slope, I found myself on a well-groomed forestry road and was enjoying being able to run without watching every step. Then reality hit. I must have missed a turn off because this was too easy. I didn't know if I should turn back, so I stopped to take a look at my map. I dug it out of my pocket and found it to be a soggy mess that fell apart in my hands. It must have gotten wet at the last aid station when I doused myself with water. And I was getting no GPS signal on my cell phone to check out the Google map. Super. *Now what?* Then ahead I saw another runner sitting on a bench. I ran up, sat down next to him and asked him if this was the right way. He was also pretty sure we'd missed a turn-off, but he didn't really care because he said he was done, out of the race. I called my husband but he couldn't locate my iPhone. Just then two more runners were coming down the road and they also said they were sure they missed a turn off, though how far back they didn't know, but they thought the forestry road would lead down into the village of Dienten where our next aid station and bag-drop with a change of clothes was. So, without too many other options, I tagged along with them and half an hour later we showed up in Dienten, having added a little over 2 kilometers to an already incredibly long day.

During the next ascent I had a magnificent panoramic view over the entire region and despite the increasing fatigue, I could still enjoy it. Off in the very far distance I could see a chalet on

the top of one of the highest peaks. It was amazingly beautiful…
*but…that couldn't be the Statzerhaus, could it? Where the next
aid station was? No, it can't be, that looks so incredibly far away.
And so high. But there are no other mountain-top chalets in sight.
That cannot be right. It's not humanly possible to go that far…
and the race director couldn't be crazy enough to torture us to
that extreme, could he?* I ran on in denial, hoping that the trail
would turn off in another direction, but it kept on towards that
towering peak. Then eventually I saw tiny figures in the form of
runners making their way up there. The tears came, through which
I was cursing the race director, and praying that my legs would
hold out.

The only saving grace that kept me in motion was that the
Statzerhaus was supposed to be the highest point of the course
(*which it was*) and that it was all downhill from there (*which it
wasn't*). From a few kilometers away I could see my husband's
car perched on the side of the mountain just downhill from the
Haus, so at least that was something to look forward to, but it
still looked sooooo far away. And there were more snow fields to
cross, and pathless fields to navigate, and one of the ascents was
so steep I had to sit down about every hundred meters just to catch
my breath and rest my quads. *This is nuts!*

Then I caught up with another runner, who commented that I
had recovered well since he last saw me. It took me a second to
realize he'd witnessed my complete breakdown a while back. We
talked a bit and he said he ran the race last year, which is why
he knew what was still to come. Something about his comment
was foreboding and I told him that I didn't want to know. But he
proceeded to tell me anyway and said that after the Statzerhaus
we have the Schwalbenwand (Swallow's Wall), and he pointed to
a ridge of three peaks (*yes, three*) that we still had to traverse. I
laughed because I thought he was joking.

"Isn't it all downhill after the next aid station?" I hopefully asked.

"Um, no," was his response. While laughing.

We then came up over a snow bank and finally out onto the forestry road leading up to the aid station, which is where we came across a group of mountain bikers who had heard about the race and asked with astonishment if we had really been running since midnight (it was presently 2 PM). Yes, 14 hours so far, and still a way to go. They were in awe. I briefly felt heroic.

Suddenly my family was upon us and they accompanied me to the aid station. They were struggling slightly to keep up with my hiking pace and my husband remarked, "I can barely keep your tempo and you've got 70 km in your legs!" Hit repeat on the hero comment. But of course he was exhausted too after having driven through the night.

There was a large group of men playing Wiesenshießen, a sport similar to curling but on grass, in a field high up on a ridge adjacent to the Statzerhaus. It was there that I had my last chance to tank up on some fresh fruit and water. Then on to the Schwalbenwand. It was intense. Those last 15 kilometers took me almost four hours. At kilometer 80 there was even a climb on a stone cliff with ropes. It was beyond ridiculous.

But then finally in the distance I could see the village of Maria Alm. And when I was about two kilometers away I called my husband and told the kids to be ready if they wanted to join me running the last few hundred meters. I ran into the village, down the main street and passed the cafés filled with diners, all of whom stopped talking and eating when they saw me (and every other straggling runner) and all began to cheer. Then suddenly I heard my name called out, a man emerged from a café and began running alongside me. It was one of my teammates from the

Armin Wolf Running Team at home who had run one of the other race distances that morning.

Then I saw my kids, now there were three of them, since my girlfriend Stephanie (yes, Stephanie from Caged Naked in *Ultramarathon Mom*) had arrived to see me finish and she had brought another one of my kids along with hers in tow. They were ecstatic to finally see me. The feeling was mutual. They took their places beside me, my girls grabbed my hands as we ran. Then I saw Steph and then my husband. And with arms raised over my head, I heard a blur of announcements, a cheer from the crowd and I crossed the finish line, 18 hours and 21 minutes after I'd started.

Was I jubilant? Ugh, not really.

Relieved? No.

What was I feeling? Just pretty numb.

There were baby pools set up in the finish area for us to cool down in. They were filled with cold water and alcohol-free beer, and they were surrounded by beach chairs into one of which I sank. With the help of my family, my shoes and compression socks were off in no time and my feet went into that icy water as I cracked open a beer.

Now I was jubilant and relieved, but still numb.

The ride home was 30 minutes and I was fighting to keep my eyes open the whole time. I lost the battle about a minute from the house. But in the driveway my oldest daughter, who had not been at the race, helped me out of the car and into the house. She guided me into the shower and brought me a comfortable change of clothes. Then out onto the terrace where Stephanie served me a huge plate of food and ordered me to eat. I got about a quarter of the way through and almost did a face plant in the tofu with ginger and peanut sauce before I said I needed to sleep. My daughter helped me to bed where I slept deeply for the next 12 hours.

Fast forward a year and to the other side of the planet. There I am in the Himalayas, having just freed myself from a herd of yaks, struggling with oxygen deficiency and being chased by an Austrian. And I begin planning my strategy. Initially after being caught, there was a steady, jagged descent where she stayed right behind me. This did not surprise me. Despite being a pretty good downhill runner, all the experience I'd gained in those techniques were learned in her backyard in the mountains near Salzburg! I figured that she'd be just as good on the ascents too, but during the next major climb I slowly began increasing my lead. It was there that I passed Pedro, wrapped in his fluttering cape of the green, white, and red flag of Mexico, who had stopped to catch his breath. He simply stared at me pass by, shaking his head, telling me that I was a tough one. I never stopped. I had learned over the past several hours that I wouldn't get much recovery by taking a break, and with only about six kilometers left, I would just have to endure if I wanted to stay in front. There was another descent where I was worried about my chaser catching me again but I never dared turn around for fear of losing my balance or tripping on the rocky terrain. *But where is that village with the tea house signaling the last five kilometers?* I was now in thick tree cover and couldn't see far ahead except to discern another massive ascent along the mountain ridge. This was the one section of the course that we had not seen the week before, so I was surprised when I encountered a long, steep, excruciating, stone-stepped climb leading up to the back side of that small village. When I finally made it to that tea house where we had been prior to our first run back into Namche more than a week before, I knew that the trail would soon open up and for the most part be a gentle downhill into the finish. There were two more quick checkpoints, but I refused the water at those stations. I still had something in my Camelback and that would have to be enough. I was not willing to stop.

I also knew that I couldn't slow down. I'd have to really run it to be safe. And I did. I ran with all I had, still circumventing the stupas and monuments clockwise, despite the few extra steps that entailed, but bad karma would not be worth the seconds saved. I tried to concentrate on form—smooth strides, open up the chest, breathe— because I knew I was not all that fast…considering the fatigue that had seeped in after more than 7 hours on the run, but regardless of not being super fast, giving all I could was good enough. And with every last amount of energy I had, I fought it to the finish and after an official 7 hours 39 minutes, I ended up there as the first international woman, six minutes before the next international competitor.

I was overwhelmed with emotions, fighting back tears, and completely exhausted. Ricky walked up to me with a huge smile on his face. Despite being more than ten years younger, he looked at me like a proud father. I was weak and shaky. He wrapped an arm around me and helped me to a chair then brought me a bottle of water and said I was not only the first international female, but the first of Lodge Group A to reach the finish. I knew this, but Ricky seemed impressed with that fact, more so than being the first foreign woman. Henni would have certainly steam-rolled me had he not decided to take it easy and run the entire course with his wife, Cindy.

Trijan was also there and asked what he could do. He then helped me get my shoes off so that I could get the track suit on that had just been brought to me. I was cooling down fast. The track suits were really like you think of when you hear that phrase, something out of the 1970s, baggy nylon pants with the marathon logo and a matching jacket which had no form-fitting contours whatsoever. But regardless of how I probably looked, I was so proud to have it on, and it made me feel on top of the world. I was also given a certificate with my finishing time and a description of the amazing race that I'd just completed.

A woman came over to where I was sitting on that plastic chair, knelt down next to me, and congratulated me. I recognized her from the day before; she was the woman from the Island Peak group that had been in bad shape. She introduced herself as Maggy and had a German accent. Then it clicked; I also knew her from Instagram, she had posted some things prior to the trip and tagged the Everest Marathon, as I had been doing with my posts, so before the trip I had begun to follow her and her girlfriend Anja (together on Instagram they are *youareanadventurestory*). We chatted for a long time. She lives in Munich but speaks excellent English so our conversation stayed mostly in English with brief interludes in German. She and her friend Anja had done the Island Peak tour—essentially the same as ours, but with an additional hike up Imja Tse, which is a 6,000+ meter summit south of Lhotse. The mountain is nicknamed Island Peak since it appears to stand alone from the other peaks and ridges, jutting out of a sea of ice like an island. Their group had summited the peak, a strenuous climb in its own right, but when doing it just days before running a marathon, it is absolutely valiant. However, it was unfortunately too much for Maggy's body to take and on the descent of Island Peak, heading to Base Camp, she came down with a terrible flu. She couldn't even manage the walk back to Namche let alone run a marathon, so she was flown via helicopter on marathon morning.

There was a tent serving food to the finishers so I staggered over and got a heaping plate of fried rice and veggies, but I could only pick at it. My appetite hadn't returned yet and despite their best effort at keeping the food warm, within a few minutes it was ice cold and unpalatable. Maggy, clearly suffering with a deep, harsh cough that was painful to watch, was waiting for Anja to finish. She should have been in bed or, even better, in the hospital, but she was adamant about being there when her friend finished the race. She kept checking the Internet updates, but wasn't sure what the distances were between checkpoints. I wasn't really sure either since there were no markers along the course. I could only help her by telling her about how long it took me to run between the checkpoints, as well as I could remember, so that she could figure out when Anja would reach the finish. Our best guess was that it would be a couple more hours, so Maggy decided to walk down to the lodge and get some warm clothes for her friend. I left with her for the ten-minute walk, as I was in dire need of a hot shower and warm clothes myself.

Back at the lodge, I sent a few brief messages home to tell everyone the news. But my family had been tracking me, and my husband had sent me a screenshot of the finisher list with my name as the fourth woman overall, with three Nepalese superwomen in front of me. Right there in black and white! My family was so happy for me and the kids were relieved to hear that I was fine. Once showered, I dressed in every piece of warm clothing I could find in the bag that had come down from Gorakshep, but unfortunately my down winter jacket and warm hat were in the trekking bag that hadn't arrived yet from Base Camp.

Then I hurried back up to see the others finish. As I arrived, the organizers were just finishing up an awards ceremony. I stood nearby, wondering why I had not been approached. It was clear who the Nepalese winners were, with their certificates and prizes in hand, but there were also several international men walking around with brand new Solomon shoe boxes. What about the international women? The second-place foreign woman, the Austrian, was also sitting on the sidelines looking baffled.

\*\*\*

We'd later find out that the first three male finishers (all Nepali) and first three female finishers (also all Nepali) all got prizes (I was fourth). But, in addition, the first five international male finishers were awarded cash and prizes, even though the first international male finished in 18th place overall, with 17 Nepalese men before him. On the female side, there were no prizes awarded to any of the international finishers. As the first international female finishing just behind the fifth-placed international male, I got nothing whereas he received cash and a new pair of Salomons. How does this happen at an international event?!? Unfortunately that was not the end of it, as the rankings were modified several times. A 19-year-old Nepali woman, who Kyaron had told me about at Base Camp as being one of Nepal's promising young runners, was with me for short times during the race. She alternated quite a bit between walking and running. I had been at the finish when she came across the line 20 minutes after me. I was cheering and so happy to see her finally make it. I even told Maggy about her and how young she was. But later that night the rankings had been changed so that the young woman was listed as having finished before me! This was ridiculous and I pointed it out to Ricky who was sympathetic and said he would raise the issue to the organization. Once back in Kathmandu I also approached the organization and they said that they were looking into it. By the time I left Nepal the ranking still had not been changed and I began writing emails to remind them that there was still an error. Finally, after a week at home, the rankings had been changed. The young woman was removed from fourth place, where my name was on the original rankings and should have been again, but this time there was another name there instead! After looking into it, I found out that it was the name of a male competitor though they had him listed as female! Again, I began an email campaign to get the situation corrected and a few days later his name was removed, but yet again replaced with another Nepalese name, this time a female. Shocked and astonished, I wondered why it meant that much to them to have the first four places of the women's race occupied by Nepalese names, but at that point, despite right or wrong, I gave up what seemed to be a losing battle.

*\*\**

Niki had already reached the finish during the time I'd been gone, but Harry and Shaun came in right as I got back. *Nailed it!* And 20 minutes later Beatrice crossed the line with tears in her eyes but a huge smile on her face. We all huddled together congratulating each other and relating highlights, exhausted but high on adrenalin. Carolyn was still out there and Niki expected her to need a couple more hours. But Niki was freezing; she couldn't wait that long in her race clothes, so I told her to go ahead and get a shower and warm clothes and that I would wait there in case Carolyn arrived in the meantime. Shaun, Bea, and Harry left too, also in need of a warm, dry change of clothes. At just above freezing, it was too cold to stand around in sweaty stuff, so I was essentially alone, and cheering for everyone who came into the finish, whether I knew them or not. By the time Niki returned about 45 minutes later I was again numb to the bone. Even though I would have loved to have stayed and cheered on all the other finishers, I knew that my immune system defenses were weak, and I needed to get warm.

The walk to the lodge was all downhill along stone steps and packed earth. My quads were hurting this time down since the muscles had cooled, but I tried to move as fast as possible, spurred on by the prospect of a warm fire in the dining hall. Everyone who'd finished was in there, and a waiting list had formed for those wanting to use the only shower on the premises. I was glad to have that already behind me. I was happy to see that the stove was lit, although apparently just very recently, since the room was not all that warm, and even after standing for at least an hour directly next to the fire, I still felt cold.

Then finally, when we were served dinner, I began to warm up, from the inside out. The guides all seemed overly concerned about us and were waiting on us hand and foot. When I asked one of them for hot water, in my very tired and possibly not-so-comprehendible post-race slur, he did not understand what I was asking for, so he got another sherpa to come over and find out what I wanted. Once they understood and took off to start boiling water, Shaun said to me, "He's deaf, you know." *What? How could that be possible?* We'd just spent nearly two weeks with him, and although he'd never communicated much, I figured that his English was just poor, because this was the first and only time he did not understand me. How amazing is that? A deaf Nepalese guide working with tourists from around the world. Remarkable.

Suffice it to say, instead of the rowdy party that we were all expecting that night, the room was filled with a bunch of exhausted runners. But I still felt the need to celebrate in some form so, exactly 65 years after the first ascent of the highest mountain on earth, I toasted a beer with Harry and we chatted about the race, the celebrations in Namche, and where our paths would lead.

The last thing on my agenda that night was filling my bottles with hot water, rushing through the cold hallway to get upstairs, and putting those flasks and me as quickly as possible into the warmth of my sleeping bag, topped off by a reunion with my old friend, that cozy dirty blanket.

# CHAPTER 16

> *"I always take the same perspective with each new adventure. I put myself in the position of being at the end of my life looking back. Then I ask myself if what I am doing is important to me."*

–Reinhold Messner

## Day 17: Rest Day Namche Bazaar

On this day we should have begun the two-day trek down the mountain over Monjo and back to Lukla where we were scheduled to fly by small plane back to Kathmandu, but 22 of 25 in our group mutinied and said we wanted to get evacuated by helicopter from Namche straight to Kathmandu, which Ricky had told us was an option. It would cost us extra, but we were willing to pay. Several of us were ill or had injured ankles and the rest were just ready to get out of the cold, drab mountains and back to some semblance of civilization with warm sunny weather where we could recuperate. The conditions had been mostly overcast in the mountains, which meant that fixed-wing flights out of Lukla were a guessing game, and we'd heard that the previous week there had been hundreds of people stranded at the airport waiting for clear weather. That would risk missing our international flights home. A swift return by helicopter would eliminate that problem.

All in all, I felt fine. My legs were not sore at all. I still haven't quite figured out why they are sore after some races and not after others. It used to be that the short distance sprints (5 km, 10 km) gave me the worst muscle aches the following day, but not anymore. Maybe I am not giving it my all. Who knows? The day after my very first marathon—the Berlin marathon—I had to walk down the stairs backwards; I was in agony! After a 100-kilometer race in Switzerland, I was reduced to crawling up and down stairs for the first 24 hours afterwards, but I was happy to be moving at all after running that distance.

Surprisingly, the worst muscle soreness I'd ever experienced was after the Großglockner Wiessee Trail in Kaprun, Austria. I could barely walk for a week. Why? It wasn't particularly long—only 31 km—but it was almost all steep downhill and that is something that, at the time, I didn't train very often and my legs let me know it. That race was only about six weeks after the Hochkönigman Endurance (which I just described in detail), so after those two races, I began religiously training downhill, especially in preparation for the Everest Marathon, to avoid a repeat.

That said, normally after long-distance trail runs, the aches and pains are minimal; I am simply tired for a few days and need to catch up on some rest. And eat, of course. Which also seemed to be the case after Everest. I had woken up starving!

But not everyone in the group was doing well. Raemonde came into the dining hall late that morning looking like she'd been in a fight in a back alley. A black eye and completely exhausted. She'd finished the race sometime after midnight. She had been the only one in our group brave enough to attempt the 60-kilometer ultramarathon and was showing the consequences of the effort. Thankfully, the ultra runners are given a local guide to run with for the last 18 kilometers, after the marathon mark, so she wasn't alone in the night, but still, it had not been easy. Apparently she had fallen, just before I saw her on the course, the day before, which is why she had a cut on her nose and a black eye. She endured the darkness, cold, and rain, and needed nearly 20 hours to finish shortly before 1:00 AM. And who was there to congratulate her when she crossed the finish line? Ricky, of course. But despite being injured and completely spent that morning, she was still glowing with happiness.

After breakfast, the entire group went outside to take a photo: runners, sherpas, porters, yaks, and all. Okay, no yaks.

Then Beatrice and I took off to buy some souvenirs. *What to get for three teenage girls?* We entered a small shop that had local handicrafts where we were graciously welcomed by a robust local woman. I told her about my girls and she embarked upon a mission to show me everything. She had jewelry, handbags, wooden carvings, and yak bells, as well as hand-knitted sweaters, hats, and gloves of every color combination imaginable. The gloves caught my attention and the woman told me that she knitted them herself out of yak's wool. Perfect. I selected my daughters' favorite colors, and added a magenta yak-wool headband to the pile. But I wasn't through yet because there was just so much to look at. Before leaving for Nepal I had asked my girlfriend Steffi, who is also my Kundalini yoga teacher, if she had any requests from Nepal. She had nearly too many to list, having always wanted to visit but not having made it yet. Yak-wool attire was not on her wish list, so when I saw a set of chimes—actually two small cymbals attached by a leather strap—I knew that they were made for her. Then on to the next shop where I bought T-shirts for my husband and son, a color poster of the mountains of the Khumbu valley, and some prayer flags. But one thing I was looking for that I could not find was a bell, for the singing tree in Steffi's garden. The tree already had several bells and chimes hanging from it and made beautiful music when the breeze blew through. But it had to be delicate and just right, and nothing caught my eye, certainly not a yak bell though there were plenty to be had, so I was hoping to have better luck when back in Kathmandu.

Shopping completed, time for some more fun. My local newspaper had asked if I could film a short video for them of my reflections from the trek and the race. This was heaven to Beatrice's ears and she went into director mode. I walked up and down the same section of a shop-laden street several times, each time repeating my script, before the footage was to Bea's satisfaction, and then we set off to find a good cup of coffee, free WiFi, and battery charging.

The café we'd been in the week before was now closed for the season, but we ran into Niki who led us to another that she'd been to which had WiFi and was still open. The mouth-watering aroma of coffee filled the air as we entered the Café de 8848, but the cake vitrine was down to slim pickings. We were happily surprised to find Shaun and Ash there, both relaxing with coffee and several plates in front of them that were empty except for a few measly crumbs. Evidence of what happened to the cake selection. Once settled in with our steaming mugs, I checked out the videos that Bea had filmed and I found Ash right behind me in one of them. "Yeah, I saw you guys there," he confirmed, "you looked very engrossed in your work. I didn't want to disturb you," he laughed. *How did we miss him?*

We returned to the lodge for lunch where we found most everyone to be operating in low gear. The weather was still overcast and dreary, which kept the mood rather subdued. Beatrice wanted to take a nap after lunch, and Carolyn wasn't feeling well at all, so Niki and I went back to Café de 8848 to watch a film that they showed every day at 3:00 PM about the life of the Sherpa mountain guides on Everest. We ordered ginger-lemon tea, plugged in our cell phones for charging, and found a spot on the hard, wooden benches which were scattered with colorful pillows that looked inviting but were not in the least bit comfortable. The film was fascinating. Personal profiles of the men and women in the region who left their homes and families for months at a time to undertake some of the most dangerous work in the world. They would prepare the climbing routes, set the ropes and ladders, and carry the heavy gear up the highest mountain on the planet. Those specifically working to prepare the routes were called icefall doctors. Their job was to secure a route through the maze of deep crevasses, ice cliffs, and towering seracs that are formed as the Khumbu glacier moves down from the high peaks to the valley below. Traditional farewell ceremonies are conducted before departure of each Sherpa from his or her home village. Some never make it home. To date, one third of Everest deaths have been Sherpa climbers. Needless to say, we left the café in a somber, reflective mood.

Shortly after arriving back at the lodge it was time for dinner. It would be our last as a group in the Himalayan mountains. An American doctor was also there that night. He had been working at the clinic in Pheriche for the past several months and had heard that we were a large group taking helicopter flights out the next day, so he had coordinated with Ricky to join us.

Ricky Time was held to discuss exactly how we would be getting back to Kathmandu. The plan was to take two helicopter flights, a short one from Namche to Lukla and then a second flight from Lukla to Kathmandu. We would leave the lodge in three separate groups the next morning. The first group would depart very early to hike up to the helicopter pad above the city, and wait for the first helicopters to arrive. There was no definite schedule, so our guides would be in touch with each other by cell phone to let the other groups know when to leave. There was no point in all of us sitting up on the cold and windswept platform for hours. We all volunteered for the different groups and everything seemed well-planned and peaceful as we finished dinner. Unfortunately, that would not be the case the next morning.

Several of us planned to meet that night at the café and bar where we sang with Ricky on our first trip through Namche. We'd finally celebrate together, since the night before we were all too exhausted. We trekked down into the village after dinner and this time, instead of climbing the stairs to the deck and entering the café, we went straight into the bar on the lower floor to order drinks. As I walked in and approached the bar, a very drunk man started talking to me and said, "Hey, I know you...you probably don't recognize me though since I was clean shaven back then." He was Nepalese but I had no idea who he was. He kept talking about being at the start of the race and I nodded as if I knew who he was but was imagining him standing somewhere on that pile of rock and ice at the start, calling out some instructions. But he was slurring his words and it was hard to understand anything. Seated next to him was a blond British woman, a trekker keeping him company who was highly amused at the fact that I was trying my best to be polite and comprehend what he was saying despite being at a complete loss.

A beer was handed to me and I was herded upstairs with the rest of the crew to our over-sized three-sided booth. We all squeezed in and the American doctor who had been at our lodge for dinner was also there, but he sat in a chair at the head of the table, and almost immediately he began his sermon. He told us that he was some kind of super genius from New York City but had been on sabbatical at the hospital in Pheriche. It turned into a very bizarre and unpleasant situation. He went on and on about his knowledge and experience with high-altitude sickness. I felt like we were students in a lecture. We all just wanted to chill, chat, and celebrate. I tried several times to open up the discussion amongst us, but he kept dragging it back to himself, practically scolding me for interrupting. Everyone was being polite and acting like he was so interesting, and even though everyone sitting around that table had awesome stories to tell, the hot-shot doc wasn't interested in hearing anything about us, he wanted to talk about himself. Maybe there had been a major lack of social contact during his stay in Pheriche and he needed to talk, but I was almost ready to leave because it was just about unbearable; I'd rather be with the drunk guy downstairs. But then Ricky showed up with Kiki and the conversation lightened up. Nobody can steal the show from Ricky and Kiki, which the doc apparently realized, and since he was no longer in the limelight, he left.

And that's when the party began. We could finally enjoy the company and closeness of our fellow trekkers, who'd we just spent two and a half weeks with, without the stress and worry of the trek and marathon. We could relax and be ourselves.

The drunk guy, who I'd since found out was one of the race organizers, also soon joined us. And he was in fact hilarious. He looked just like the actor Jimmy Smits but younger, like Jimmy Smits from *The Cisco Kid*. He was slurring his words so badly that we couldn't understand anything but we laughed so hard anytime he opened his mouth that he believed he was the life of the party. And he actually was!

After not having had alcohol for a couple of weeks, it went straight to my head. That was probably the case for everyone there, except Beatrice who doesn't drink at all, but she's naturally giddy anyway. We sang and laughed and were brought beer after beer until someone smart decided it was time to call it a night.

Back in the lodge, Beatrice and I continued to chat and laugh. I knew the walls were paper thin and that Harry and Ray next door were probably being kept awake by us, but as much as we tried, we couldn't keep it down, so I wrote a text in apology to Harry (though I could have probably whispered and he'd have heard me). I wrote, "Sorry 4 noise, Harry," then I added, "But we r actually not sorry."

"No problem," he replied, "that low-oxygen-and-beer cocktail does it every time."

# CHAPTER 17

*"We do not live to eat and make money, we eat and make money to be able to enjoy life."*

–George Leigh Mallory

## Day 18: Crazed Helicopter Flights From Namche to Lukla, and Lukla to Kathmandu

The next morning was dreary and cold. We were more than ready to get back to Kathmandu where summer weather was waiting for us, so after breakfast we packed up our bags and then gathered in the dining room to wait for our flight. Two groups had already headed out for the 15-minute walk to the helicopter pad. Bea and I were supposed to be in the second group, but a few people, including the American doc, busted up there at the crack of dawn hoping to get out earlier and there was a backlog. Ricky was still at the lodge with us and was in contact with Pemba who was with the others up on the mountain. Pemba had relayed the information that no helicopters had arrived yet, so we were told to relax.

Bea, Niki, Carolyn, and I sat together at a corner table and bought a can of Pringles potato chips from the reception. Almost all the chips were broken. We were all bitching about it, and since we didn't have much else to do, I turned on my voice memo app and we went live:

## Four Girls JAM SESSION

**H:** Let's talk about race day, starting in the morning when we woke up...

**N:** Nobody could feel their toes...fingers and toes. It took me until about Gorakshep until I could feel my feet. You (Holly) were probably a bit sooner than me.

**H:** Yeah, just after starting I was okay. But before that I felt like I had rocks tucked into the front of my shoes.

**C:** I was so nervous, and I was getting silent and you (Niki) were like, "What's wrong?" And I'm like, "Can't you leave me alone? I'm nervous."

**N:** I didn't know you were so nervous until I saw your face and was like, "What's wrong with you?" I've never seen you like that.

**C:** I just felt nervous because I knew it was going to be a fucking long day.

**B:** I was nervous about not being a daylight finisher. I was afraid of being stuck in the cold and if it started raining... I knew I could find a lodge, but.... My main goal was 12 hours and be a daylight finisher. I was scared about wet and cold.

**C:** That's exactly what happened when the sun went down and it felt wet and cold.

**B:** And that's dangerous. And it's no fun anymore.

**H:** I was surprised at it actually being runnable in the beginning.

**C:** It was more runnable than I remembered it being during the trek up.

**H:** I was thinking there was no way we would be able to run the first couple of kilometers. I thought it would be so frustrating at the start. But it opened up. No problem, there were a couple of people that wanted to pass but it wasn't like people couldn't get by.

**C:** Yeah, no problem. I let people past me. (Carolyn coughing.) Shit.

**H:** Then there was a long stretch that was runnable. And there were so many trekkers that were so supportive!

**N:** Yeah!

**B:** Yeah, that was nice.

**C:** That was amazing.

**H:** They were all cheering for us like we were superheroes! There was one group of trekkers that yelled to me, "Where are you from?" And I just answered, "It's a long story." (Laughter from the girls; sneezing from Carolyn.)

C: Well, some of them saw my start number and saw the flag, since I was at a slightly slower pace than you, Holly, they actually had a chance to see my start number (laughter from the girls), and they were like "Yay! Canada!" Yeah, that's right, fuckin' Canada!

N: So, the wind didn't bother you guys all day? I mean, the wind got to me after a while.

H: Nope, didn't bother me. I felt it; it was a bit annoying, but it wasn't a factor.

N: And the cold.

(Picking through tiny pieces of Pringles chips cupped in our hands.)

C: That's funny because when I came into the finish people were talking about the wind and I was like, "What wind?" And then I thought about it and thought, yeah, it was kinda windy.

N: Yeah, very windy!

C: That wind was actually a blessing for me because it kept me cool. We were just sweating. (Sounds of Carolyn chomping on chips then brushing crumbs off her lap and onto the floor.)

H: Did you guys take off any layers?

C: I ran in exactly three layers the entire time. The only thing that came on and off were my gloves. On and off. The whole fucking day!

**B:** Yeah, me, too.

**C:** Otherwise I didn't change anything.

**N:** I put my jacket on when I got caught behind that yak train.

**B:** Yes, let's talk about the yaks.

**H:** There were no yaks in the beginning. Didn't they shut down the trail for yaks between 7 and 9, something like that?

**N:** Yep, something like that, but then when they finally were allowed on the trail, they wouldn't let us pass. I got caught behind them right when you came down to one of the hanging bridges, we were on the bridge and there were like 45 yaks on the bridge.

**H:** And you can't pass a yak on a hanging bridge!

**N:** No! And it was probably like 30 minutes, like at least 6 people caught up to me, it was so frustrating, and he wouldn't let us pass because the yak at the back was aggressive.

**H:** Never met a yak that wasn't.

**N:** And there were too many, the train was just too long.

**B:** (to me) Did you run on the suspended bridges?

**H:** Yeah, that was strange, bouncing all over the place.

**B:** You really did run across?!?

**H:** Hell, yeah, it's a race!

**B:** Wow, that is fantastic because the first day she is crying and then when there is competition she runs. Pazza!

**H:** I would have run them on the first day too if there hadn't been people in front of me 'cause I just wanted to get off them fast.

**N:** Yeah, yep. That's funny. I didn't want to run them, but didn't have much choice.

(Door squeaking as Ricky enters the dining hall.)

**H:** So what was the most difficult part?

**C:** Well, it would have had to have been that last 32 to 37 kilometers. I just couldn't handle it, that last climb was so friggin long!

**H:** We didn't know, we hadn't seen that climb during the trek since we took another route up.

**C:** We knew about it, we knew it was there, that was all, but we hadn't trekked there. (Coughing fit.)

**N:** I think for me it was my footing and all the rocks, 'cause I was so conscious of not rolling an ankle. And I was constantly looking at the ground. So instead of looking up and around at all the different places that I'd been, it was just constant mental focus on where I was placing my feet. The whole time. I didn't fall, so that was my goal. I almost had a couple, my left leg started to drag towards the end so I kept catching it. And then, um...so I think the footing was the big thing. It wasn't the descent, it wasn't the drop, it wasn't any of that.

**B:** And for you?

**H:** Yeah, the climb before the monastery at Tengboche. That was like never-ending.

**N:** I know, I'd even forgotten about it and then it was like, wow, it just came out of nowhere.

**B:** And how about at the end, the part that we had run back at the beginning, when we were in Namche? We thought it was so easy then.

**N:** Yeah, everyone was like, it's flat, but it's not flat.

**C:** I wasn't running, and I was like, "Shouldn't I be running this?"

**H:** What about your interaction with other runners?

**N:** Mine was positive. I had a good experience. I said hi to everybody, hi to all the porters. And for the most part they all said hi, but there were 2 or 3 that were so focused, but where I was in the race, they didn't need to be focused (laughs).

(Lots of commotion... Ricky's voice, asking if we want tea or something else to drink.)

**N:** Oh, I'll have a coffee.

**R:** Black?

**N:** Black.

**H and B synchronized like twins:** I'll have whatever. Something. Hot.

**C:** Black tea, please. Black tea.

**C:** Well, I mended fences with Pork-belly Pub (a nickname we gave a woman from another group). I ran like three-quarters of the race with her.

**N:** Yeah, that's right. That's nice.

**C:** And the only person who gave me zero love, who I gave a lot of love to was the English woman who Shaun knew, the woman that walked, like, the non-runner, although she was kicking my ass.

**H:** She was walking?

**C:** She was walking. Like I would pass her and I'd be like, "Excellent. Great job." And like she never said one word to me the whole entire time. And like I would stop then and stretch so she and her husband, who I am assuming was her husband, would catch up to me, and he was really nice to me and was like, "Is there anything I can do?" And I'm like, "No, no, I just need to stretch my back." And I was like, "Don't worry about me, I'm fine."

**H:** Were they running together?

**C:** Yeah, they were together. Like he would sit and wait for her. Then I would catch them. I was like super positive to her, but I think she was just dead exhausted.

**N:** I felt that male runners were much more friendly than the females. I think it was because I was back in that 3, 4, 5 pocket so...

**H:** There weren't many women around.

**N:** No, just that English girl that I was trying to catch, and then, I don't know who was behind me, but it was all male runners and they were nice.

**H:** I felt like the guys around me kind of needed support. I felt like I needed to encourage them. They seemed to be mentally discouraged and were having a tough time with the terrain and breathing and I felt like I was just trying to pep them up. Telling them that we were still over 4,000 meters so it was only normal to feel exhausted... stuff like that.

**N:** Yeah! I felt the same thing! The guys were kind of struggling.

**H:** It was weird.

**N:** Yeah.

**B:** I had one of those situations where you would think that I was making up a story, but I got hurt and there were four nice men that helped me.

**H:** With your foot, right? Because men are all over you whether you are hurt or not, you know that, right?

**B:** (Ignoring my comment) Yes, well, I fell in a village. It was very theatrical, and I was like, "Oh, shit!" but it did really hurt and so these guys came running, but I think they were trekking men from India, they were not from the village, so one started to massage and I yelled, "Ahhh!" You know, it really hurt. And then people started to laugh 'cause I was like, "Don't even touch me!" And then more people arrived from the village. "Where are you from?" Italy. "Yay!!!! Italiano! How old are you?" 52! Craziness! So, they had a bag with first aid and they gave me a pain killer. Then I started really limping about, maybe a total of half an hour later, the golden painkiller started to work, thank you! And I just got going.

**H:** What was the magic pill they gave you?

**B:** I have no idea! But it really was like magic. Because I thought, I really thought, this race is finished for me. I'm out.

**H:** Looks like some of that good karma found its way back to you once again.

**N:** Yeah, amazing, you were lucky. Those hills were tough, especially the one at the end there, I did like 50 steps and then I stopped for like 20 seconds.

**H:** I found stopping is worse because you never catch your breath.

**B:** (Doubting sounds.)

**N:** Yup, yup (in agreement).

**H:** Yup, just keep pushing through.

**N:** So, halfway up the damn hill I'd be like, just put one foot in front of the other.

**B:** Yea.

**N:** It doesn't matter that you are walking. Just keep moving.

(Squeaky door opening; coughing; lots of overlapping talking and noises.)

**H:** What did you think of the water stations and the checkpoints?

**N:** Yeah, um the water stations, I thought they were supposed to be every 5K, but I think some of them were longer.

**H:** And then at the end they came one right after another. At the last one, it was right before the finish, I was like, "No, thank you, I'm all set... Duh."

**B, N, C:** Yeah. (Laughter.)

**B:** And at the finish it was really nice, people were really teary.

(Hot drinks being delivered to our table.)

**B, H, N, C:** Oh, yay!

**B:** Amore mio.

**N:** Yep, right here, thank you so much, appreciate it.

(We just got ginger-lemon-honey paradise. Ricky is saying something indiscernible.)

**C:** I only had the juice...where was that? In Dingboche? I only had the juice.

**H:** They had that soup and they said, "You need to eat," and I looked at it and felt my stomach turn, and was like, "No, thanks."

**C:** Yeah, maybe not...it looked yucky.

**H:** I was already empty on water.

**B:** We stopped and had the soup.

**H:** Did you guys refill your Camelbak at all?

**N:** No, no. I didn't eat enough or drink enough, but as soon as I crossed the finish line, I forced some vegetables and rice down, which was important.

**B:** I also did not feel thirsty. I drank very little during the race.

**H:** But I tried to drink at least a full cup at each water station, at least at the beginning.

**N:** Oh, yeah, I drank a full cup at each water station.

**H:** Drinking is so important.

**N:** Yeah, I had several cups of water and some juice.

(Ricky incoherent talking on the phone, but his tone sounds serious.)

**B:** I have this rule that I can only skip the last station, even if I'm not thirsty. If I don't drink enough, I get side-stitches.

**Ricky:** They are having a fight.

**N:** What? Who's having a fight? Our people?

**R:** Yeah, who's going first (on the helicopter).

**N:** Are you serious?

**Ricky:** Pemba is calling me, "Who is going first flight? They are all wanting to go first." (Ricky laughing.)

**N:** Whether you wait here...or there...I'd rather wait here.

**H:** It's probably cold up there.

**N:** That's probably why they are fighting.

**H:** Yeah, didn't we take care of that last night, who goes in which group? Isn't that why we are sitting here now because it was already planned?

**Ricky:** It's because I am not there, that's why.

**C:** Yeah? And they think they can take advantage of Pemba.

**R:** Yeah...What am I doing? (Imitating Pemba) They are all asking who is first, but they should know.

**C:** They are playing stupid if they say they don't know.

Ricky and Ray begin discussing about how the group was reacting. Then Ricky started talking about hiring the sherpas and how they are not given lodging as part of their pay (same as the porters who find porter houses for sleeping). But the sherpas are in the lodges with us till late at night serving our dinner, heating the water, cleaning up, and they are essentially expected to be there for us and that means spending the night in our lodges. (I think many nights they slept on the benches in the dining halls, which is actually pretty smart considering it's the warmest place around.) Although being a sherpa is a relatively good job for a Nepali, it is still a tough life, and having to play babysitter to wealthy foreigners shouldn't necessarily be in the job description, which is now what Pemba was facing.

Finally we got the nod to head up to the helipad. It was a trek through the village and out the other side, up steep rocky steps to a reinforced outcropping high above the city with an amazing view. We were accompanied by porters carrying our trekking bags for one last time. I tucked some small bills into my pocket which I handed to my porter, Milan, along with a humble thanks for all his efforts over the past ten days.

As we arrived, a helicopter was positioned there with rotors turning, while bags, supplies, and passengers were being loaded on. We were standing less than ten meters away as there was really nowhere else to go, so when the engine starting gearing up, and the blades were turning faster, creating a massive downdraft of air, we had to back into the stone wall behind us to avoid being blown away.

As I mentioned before, there are no scheduled landings or departures at the Namche Bazaar helipad. All flights are chartered and are largely dependent on availability and, of course, the weather, so we had no idea what we were in store for, but after a wait of about 15 minutes we saw another helicopter in the distance and things got buzzing. The next five people were ushered up to the front, Beatrice and I among them, and our bags were separated from the others and brought forward. The machine steered towards us, seemed to almost dip down below the overhanging cliff, then, like a falcon, quickly swooped up over us and landed. We all hurried in and our laps were piled high with our trekking bags. I searched for a seat belt. There were some random nylon belts which seemed to have been stretched to their limits, twisted and tangled, but none of them appeared to attach to anything, so none of us were buckled in and I just held on tight to the bag on my lap, said a short prayer, and in an instant we were off. We shot briefly up over the helipad, then suddenly dipped down into the valley. I felt like I was on a rollercoaster and my stomach had found a new home in my throat. Beatrice was whooping with delight. Dave was filming us. I was in hell.

It was another minute before I think I started breathing again. Then I realized that my right arm was reaching across my body and grasping the bicep of Pierre who was sitting on my left. My fingernails were deep into his jacket—thankfully it was thick, otherwise he'd have needed stitches. I apologized but did not let go, though I loosened up a bit.

The ride was less than ten minutes to Lukla where we would then wait for another helicopter transfer to Kathmandu. Beatrice was in the front filming and chit-chatting with the pilot who had revealed that he was Italian. At that point, I saw the fire in her eyes and could almost feel the heat of her heart melting as they switched to their native tongue.

Landing a helicopter at the airport in Lukla is a heck of a lot easier than landing a plane, and once we were safely down I was almost disappointed that it was over. Almost. But we'd have another trip that day and whether the wait would be 30 minutes or 8 hours, none of us had any idea.

There was a small lodge with a restaurant adjacent to the helicopter landing field and the five of us filed one behind the other inside to find a comfortable seat to wait. Unfortunately, we were not the only ones with this brilliant idea as the single-room restaurant was packed with trekkers and their gear, also waiting for a lift out. Most of our marathon group had already arrived and within the hour the rest were there with us too, so we went back outside and sat on a stone wall that overlooked the landing field. We dangled our feet over the wall which dropped down several meters to a littered stream, where just on the other side a worn dirt path connected the village to the airfield. There was so much action going on around us I wasn't sure where to focus. It was like being in a movie theater but better. Trekkers were coming and going from the lodge. One lone security man was yelling at tourists to stand behind a fence. There was a constant stream of people entering in and out of the tiny squat toilet in front of us. An airplane occasionally landed on the airstrip 100 meters away and helicopters set down randomly where they could find space. At one point there were six helicopters there, whereas in the Western world there may have been space for two. There were no large circles painted in white with a giant H in the middle directing them where to land. It was rogue. But it seemed to work.

The first five from our group were then told that they could go down to the airfield, find their trekking bag in the pile of dozens sitting next to crates of perishable food, and then wait for the next helicopter. But why was the hot-shot American doctor in the first group with our trekkers, we wondered? How had he finagled that? We were all more than ready to go.

Asking around we were told that apparently Mr. Hot-Shot had convinced everyone that he had an international flight to catch and for that reason he needed to be in the first group. Later we would find out that his flight was very late at night, long after we all were back in the city.

First impressions are sometimes right on the button.

Then we saw a woman being aided, practically carried, by two companions down to the airfield. She was first led into the toilet cubby hole where she stayed for several minutes, then she was helped down to the side of the field where she subsequently collapsed. Several of us witnessed this and tried to signal to our group's doctor, Prajwal, and Mr. Hot-Shot who were standing on the other edge of the field waiting for their flight. Carolyn's shrill voice finally was loud enough to catch their attention and we all pointed to the woman lying on the ground. The doctors hurried over and knelt at her side. Shortly thereafter a helicopter arrived and she was given priority (Mr. Hot-Shot got bumped!), but she could not stand on her own so they tried to lift her and carry her to the aircraft. She appeared to be simply dead weight and the look on her face revealed that she was in agony. They loaded her on board like a pallet of goods and took off, speeding down to a lower elevation, where she would hopefully recover.

Prajwal came up to where we were waiting and watching, informing us that the woman had cerebral edema, and the prognosis wasn't good. Apparently she had already trekked up to Dingboche, then had trouble with the altitude and had to go down, after a day of rest she tried it again but was now in a life-threatening condition.

We had no idea how long we would have to wait for our flights so I went with Harry and Henni to pseudo-Starbucks where Henni told us stories of dangerous road biking in South Africa and an attempted hijacking that he narrowly survived. Apparently, on a weekend ride with a friend, he was accelerating down a long sloping hill, when suddenly at the bottom, a man jumped out in front of them, blocking their way, and had a gun pointed right at them. His buddy swerved past him but Henni didn't have the same speed, so for some reason he stopped and turned around. But in the high gear that he was in, he couldn't accelerate, and the guy with the gun was running right behind him threatening to shoot him and take his bike. But he kept pushing himself, pedaling as hard as he could, and somehow got away.

Henni had ordered burgers-to-go for himself and Cindy and when the food was ready he left, while Harry and I finished our coffee and tea. Then 15 minutes later Henni was back and out of breath, winded from running to tell us that the departure was on the roll! After a quick trip to the bathroom (you never know when you'll find another one that is cleaned daily), we booked it back to the airport as fast as we could.

But, once we got there, we realized, of course, there was no real hurry.

Groups of five were formed for departure. Harry and Shaun were sent out onto the field with their group, while Bea and I went into the adjacent lodge and observed the chaotic scene from the large windows. Raemonde had ordered a sizeable dish of pasta and begun eating when we were suddenly summoned out as the next group of five. She was supposed to have been in the last group, but with the passenger-bumping and occasional seven-seater helicopter, things were not running according to plan and Raemonde was forced to leave her nearly full plate on the table.

Again, that rush was unnecessary.

Down on the field we picked out our trekking bags from the dwindling pile and placed them forward so that they would be loaded onto the next flight. We weren't really sure where to stand though. There were no markings and no one apparently in charge of organization and departure safety. We just tried to stay out of the way and huddled in a corner wedged between the two levels of helicopter landing fields and the fixed-wing airstrip.

Then suddenly from somewhere down in the valley a helicopter swooped up over the ridge and came right at us, landing about 30 feet in front of us. The wind from the rotor blades was ferocious and it was an effort to just remain standing. Unexpectedly a second copter was right behind the first! It flew just meters above our heads and landed on a narrow ledge not 20 meters behind us. Now the turbulence was too much for feather-light Beatrice and it would have thrown her to the ground had I not grabbed onto her in the last second. We tensed every muscle in our bodies just to hold our position for the few seconds before both machines turned off their engines.

"Your hair is a mess, Beatrice," I snickered as we were ushered over to board our flight to KTM. "Thanks, dear," she replied, "but tonight we will have a lovely shower and I can use my flat iron!"

The simple pleasures in life are what make it worth living.

# CHAPTER 18

*"Let it all go. See what stays."*

–Anonymous

## Day 18 Continued: Back in Town

After about 30 minutes, the Nepali capital came into view. The air was thick with pollution, gray cloud-like masses hovering low over the city. Directly below us we could see miles of small apartment buildings, mostly under ten stories high, but almost all of which appeared to be unfinished, in various stages of building, renovation, or repair. Prayer flags could be seen on some rooftops and the peaceful, serpentine curves of the Bagmati River tried to fool us into believing that its waters were clean and pure.

After landing somewhere at the outer reaches of Tribhuvan International Airport, we were brought by minivan to the domestic terminal and exited to the chaos of a big city. Following two weeks of near solitude in the quiet of the mountains, it was almost too much to bear. The people, the noise, the stress of making decisions. *Where to now?* I followed Beatrice who was just about to walk inside the terminal when I spotted Shaun around the front of the building. I called out to Beatrice and motioned that she should follow me. The rest of the group were right behind. Once within earshot, I also yelled out to Shaun who then waved us in his direction and we dodged the crowds to catch up with him.

"We've got a mini-bus lined up to take us to the hotel," he said. Awesome!

But as we got to the bus we realized we were too many people to all fit. A few people would have to stay behind. I told Beatrice she could sit on my lap for all I cared, but I definitely didn't want to have to hang around at that airport for another hour hoping that the bus would come back.

Then I noticed who was at the front of the line to get on the bus: Mr. Hot-Shot! He piled in as soon as the door was opened and I was suddenly struck with the reality that Beatrice and I, standing in the back, would not get a seat. I was fuming!

But then the driver, who had opened up the back of the bus to load in our gear, had gone around to the front for a minute but left the back cargo door ajar. I grabbed Beatrice by the arm and pulled her along behind me, jumping into the back and clambering over the pile of trekking bags then hurling myself into the backseat. Bea was right behind me. We were in! But even squeezed in with Bea on my lap, several from our group were still standing outside wondering what to do.

After a few minutes of confusion, the rest of the group decided to take a taxi, paid out of their own pocket since they preferred that instead of waiting for the bus to return. I was wondering why Mr. Hot Shot hadn't volunteered to get a taxi instead of taking the place of one of our group members who was essentially covering the cost of his transfer via our pre-paid travel package. Beatrice tried to calm me down. "There are people like that in this world.

You can't change them. Don't let it get you upset," she consoled in her Italian-British-Swiss accent.

She was right, so I focused instead on the fun days ahead of us back in civilization.

First stop: Hotel Shanker. Since we had taken a helicopter from Namche instead of trekking back to Lukla and then taking a flight as planned, we were back in Kathmandu a day early, and Hotel Shanker did not have vacancy for all of us. So after paying for the heli ride with our credit cards, we picked up our suitcases and were then transported to another hotel. Hotel Pilgrims in Thamel. It was by no means up to the same standard as Shanker, and Bea even thought the lodges in the mountains were better, because up there at least we had no expectations, compared to this one that was very basic and not as clean as normal Western standards. But we had an *en suite* bathroom with a hot shower, and that was all I needed. Pure luxury.

Our room was at the end of the hall and just outside our door was a balcony overlooking the side street running in front of our hotel. I went out to look and found the entire length of the street was strung with prayer flags in both directions as far as the eye could see. Such a peaceful, beautifully romantic spot. After I finished showering, I took a chair out there and spent some time just daydreaming, wrapped in the arms of my entrancing surroundings.

After Beatrice showered, she announced that she still absolutely needed two hours of beauty time. No less. But I wanted to explore, so I took a walk with Harry through Thamel. I had been to Kathmandu before, in 2015, and left ten days before the earthquake struck. Harry had been in Kathmandu at the time of the earthquake. Yes, *during* the earthquake. And he relayed stories about that day and what had changed since. He knew the city inside and out. Or so he told me. I had my doubts, but considering that we didn't get lost, either he was telling the truth or was secretly consulting google maps as I was admiring the merchandise in the shops.

Thamel is the tourist center of the city, with many souvenir shops and outdoor outfitters as well as lots of hotels, cafés, and restaurants. But navigating the streets requires concentration, since the roads are not well paved and are stricken with gaping holes, where bikes, cars, animals, and motorcycles are all contending with the pedestrians for space. Drugs are also available in plenty, a relic of the hippie days when artists from around the globe gathered there to stay for weeks or months on end.

Two hours later, after buying a scarf for me and finally finding just the right bell for Steffi at home to hang in her singing tree in her garden, we wove our way back to the hotel where we met up with Bea, Shaun, Niki, Carolyn, and Pierre and made the short walk from there to the New Orleans Pub for dinner. They had Western standards with Nepalese and international fare in a courtyard setting filled with plants, warm lighting, and the cozy feeling of home.

Shaun took photos and then posted a boomerang in his Insta story, tagging the restaurant we were in. Not half an hour later a fan of his came by to meet him. A local body builder who apparently owns a gym in Kathmandu, he talked with Shaun for a few minutes then asked if it would be okay if he called his sister to come over and also meet him. Of course Shaun was cool with that and the fan politely waited in the entryway for his sister while we got our drinks and appetizers. Either the apps were really filling or our stomachs had shrunk over the past two weeks but all of us had trouble finishing the delicious food we were served. Another round of drinks and the mood was laidback, mostly just telling jokes, until the fan's sister arrived and we turned our attention to taking photos of the three of them together.

Back out on the streets, the atmosphere in the narrow alleyways was different at night, a younger more energetic crowd, but the air felt almost stifling compared to the cool mountain freshness that we'd gotten used to. The shops were still open though they were mostly empty as interest had moved into the cafes and restaurants rather than shopping, but we were all tired after another long day and getting into bed was the priority.

Back in the sanctuary of Hotel Pilgrims, after some rearranging of the furniture and trying to adjust an air conditioner that wasn't working right, we spent a long hot night tossing and turning in the bowels of paradise.

# CHAPTER 19

........................................................................

*"You can check out any time you like, but you can never leave."*

–The Eagles

........................................................................

## Day 19: A Prisoner in Paradise

The breakfast served at Hotel Pilgrims was the worst we'd had the whole trip. The coffee was undrinkable, the juice was artificially flavored water, there was no fresh fruit, and the only thing I could force down was a piece of toast with margarine. That wouldn't hold me for long. Thankfully, Harry, now our official tour guide of the Nepalese capital, offered to take me and Beatrice to a great coffee house. So with Jesper also in tow, the four of us started out into the streets of Thamel once again.

Beatrice and I were courted by the shopkeepers into almost every little place along the way. I politely looked at their wares, while Beatrice politely flirted. After a few minutes in each spot, we were back on the street where our chaperones were civilly waiting. When we arrived at Himalayan Java on the edge of

Thamel near The North Face store, I thought we must be back in Europe. A modern bohemian-style café with over-stuffed couches in earth tones, grand library tables where one could open up a laptop and, with their high-speed Internet, have a business meeting, as well as bookshelves lining the back wall with a selection offering something interesting to everyone while sipping their cup of joe. We ordered coffee and oversized pastries.

I could have stayed curled up on that couch all day, but we were supposed to be back at Hotel Pilgrims at noon in order to check out and transfer back to Hotel Shanker for our last two nights before heading home.

The weather was mostly sunny that afternoon so once back at Hotel Shanker we changed into our bathing suits and headed out to the pool. Maggy and Anja were also there and I finally got to chat with Anja and get her perspective on the race, the hike to Island Peak, and Maggy's illness (yes, she was still coughing, but much better than she had been when I met her at the finish line on race day).

As soon as Niki and Carolyn got to the pool, they started in on the cocktails. The rest of us joined them with beer and mojitos once we got a pool-side table and ordered lunch.

At that point, everyone was a little anxious to pack up and go home. It was only Friday and most of us were scheduled to leave on Sunday; Harry not until Monday. We'd been away for three weeks and all had long flights ahead of us, but there wasn't much we could do aside from trying to rebook a flight a day earlier and pay an exorbitant sum in doing so.

Everything that we required was there for us: a beautiful hotel, great food, a pool. But I felt like we were prisoners in utopia. The song Hotel California kept popping into my head... *You can check out any time you like, but you can never leave...*

The trip organizers did a great job of keeping us entertained though, and planned dinner for us in a chic restaurant called Trisara which was on King's Highway, near the Palace, and within walking distance of our hotel. It was in an old, renovated warehouse with a huge open space below and a large balcony up above where our tables were located. About 15 of us were there and we all chilled on couches around low tables. Carolyn was having stomach problems again. She didn't eat much, drank no alcohol, and appeared to fall asleep at the table after she was through picking over her meal.

After we finished eating, a hookah was passed around and a band started playing. But Ricky's plans for us that night weren't over. His band was performing at the Senate Nightclub and he invited us all over there. We staggered out of the restaurant in a mish-mosh and somehow all got split up in the crowds on the street. The last I saw of Beatrice was her being whisked across a frenzied intersection through a red light holding onto the arm of Pedro, while Niki, Carolyn, and some of the others headed back to the hotel. Ricky was nowhere in sight and though surrounded by throngs of people, I suddenly realized that I recognized no one. *Shit.* Then I saw a familiar face coming back towards me. *Who could it be?* Of course it was Harry. He said not to worry, he knew where he was going, so I followed blindly, but I soon realized he had only a *vague* idea of where he was going. The coffee shops of Thamel were his *revier*, but he was certainly no expert on the club circuit. First we ended up in the Reggae Bar, touring all three floors top to bottom asking for Ricky. Everyone seemed to know Ricky and said he was there, but we were clearly talking about a legion of Rickys. Finally, realizing we were in the wrong place, and that the Senate was just around the corner, we exited, ended up in a back alley, soon found the golden lion of the Senate club, made our way through the steel gates, past the bouncers, and there was Beatrice happy as a clam to see us! We got there shortly after 11 which was apparently way too early and the place was nearly empty, but people kept streaming in and within an hour the dance floor was full. We appeared to be about the only foreigners there that night, but in Ricky's company we were accepted by everyone. Someone ordered a giant beer tank with a spigot so we drank unabashedly, thirsty from dancing and singing to the classic rock songs. Ricky sang "Smoke on the Water" and rocked the club with his strong, raw voice. The place stayed open until 6 AM, but by 2:00 we'd had our fill. As we left the club there was a huge crowd of young Nepali men, all wearing their best white, pressed shirts, waiting to get inside. Stumbling through the night we somehow made it back to our hotel and tumbled into bed where we slept till the sun creeped in from behind the drapes and the smell of coffee percolated through the air vents into our room.

# CHAPTER 20

*"All the earth is seamed with roads, and all the sea is furrowed with the tracks of ships, and over all the roads and all the waters a continuous stream of people passes up and down—traveling, as they say, for their pleasure.*
*What is it, I wonder, that they go out to see?"*

–Margaret Bell (1868-1926), English writer, traveler, political officer, administrator, and archaeologist

## Day 20: Durbar Square and Marathon Party

That morning we said goodbye to Niki and Carolyn who were the first two to leave from our group. They had an early flight and would miss the big marathon celebration party that would be held that night in the banquet rooms of the hotel. But they were both more than ready to head home and didn't mind skipping the party.

Until dinner we had nothing planned on the agenda and, being overcast and cooler, it was not pool weather. Just as well, since

I wanted to go to Durbar Square. I wanted to see what it looked like after the devastating earthquake and was hoping to confirm it to be on the road to recovery. But Beatrice mutinied on me and opted for a massage while Shaun retreated to his room to work.

So, while contemplating the maps in the lobby and trying to figure out if I should walk or take a taxi, Harry wandered up and, looking over my shoulder, asked what I was doing.

Harry. My savior. Again.

Of course he was game and led me on another tour through the narrow jumbled streets, on which I'd been many times in the past couple of days though I was still at a loss for direction. So much for my keen orienteering skills.

Durbar Square in Kathmandu dates back nearly one thousand years and is at the site of the Hanuman Dhoku palace, which was the home of the royal Nepalese family until the 18th century. The palace now houses a museum while the square has many temples preserved as national heritage sites, some open only to those of the Hindu or Buddhist religions. There is also a large marketplace, Basantapur square, with vendors selling souvenirs such as singing bowls, wooden carvings, daggers, masks, and pottery.

I had seen images on television and the Internet of the city in the aftermath of the earthquake, but I had no idea what to expect now that three years had gone by. The destruction was shocking. The place was absolutely unrecognizable. Visions of the exquisite temples were imprinted on my mind from my trip just a few years earlier. I even remembered some of the faces my family and I encountered while there, including the young men selling water at the top of the Maju Dewal temple, and a very young girl in a yellow dress who coveted a small piece of paper in her hand at the Shiva-Parvati temple. I could not make sense of the piles of rubble. It was a giant construction zone but with no (seeming) order and absolutely no modern building equipment. Bamboo stilts and metal scaffolding, men chipping away at dusty piles of stones behind chained-link fences, wooden bracing at 45-degree angles propping up walls to avoid collapse. Everything looked to be in the process of rebuilding, but moving unbelievably slowly. At that rate it would take a century before it would be complete.

It was a rather disheartening walk back to the hotel, past various candle-lighting and flower ceremonies, the peddlers, rickshaw drivers, lovers kissing on the Le Bistro balcony, the New Orleans Café where we'd eaten our first Western meal after two weeks on rations, the shops where I'd bought the bell and my scarf, and past the prayer flags of Z-Street.

But that night, our last night in Nepal, was to be in celebration with the entire marathon crew, organizers, and runners, both international and Nepali. Everyone showed up in their best attire. Drinks were served in the entry hall, then we were ushered into the dance salon where white linen-covered tables were under the arches on the perimeter while rows of cushioned chairs lined the dance floor. At the head of the room was a stage with a podium and large screen where the now clean-shaven and sober Jimmy Smits from the Namche pub was making announcements. Wait staff were soon upon us like flies, offering trays of spicy meatballs, dumplings, nuts, deep-fried vegetables, and drinks for every taste. Most were drinking beer or wine, but D3vil, with his long, dark wavy hair hanging loose, went hardcore and was drinking whiskey at an impressive pace.

A short recap photo stream of the race was shown, as well as a speech giving accolades to the organization. I was hoping for some type of awards ceremony for the winners, but apparently that had been completed in full at the race finish since nothing further was mentioned. Naturally, I was disappointed.

On into the grand dining hall for a magnificent buffet dinner. I loaded up on salads and piled that high with papadums. I love those spicy, crispy chips and just can't get enough. So, after polishing off the ones on my plate, I mentioned how great it would be to have the whole giant basket of papadums from the buffet right here in front of me on the table. As if on command, Shaun stood up, walked over to the serving table, swept up the basket as though it were the most normal action in the world, and gallantly presented them to me. I loaded up, as did everyone else at the table, and then Shaun politely returned the meager rest to the buffet table.

There was music, dancing, and a laser-light show back in the salon after dinner. Beatrice was working the dance floor and keeping every male in the room out there with her. She looked great in her skin-tight red dress under which even her tiniest string thong wouldn't have fit.

I wasn't up for dancing a second night in a row, and the loud music combined with the large crowd were suddenly too much for me, especially after spending two weeks in near silence, so I walked outside into the gardens, found a lounge chair, and enjoyed the cool night air. Shortly afterwards Shaun had also had enough of the night and needed to finish packing his bags for a morning flight to London. On his way back to the main building he spotted me in my idyll.

"Whatcha doin' Zimmermann?" he asked.

"Just enjoying my sanctuary," I replied while gazing up at the stars. He laughed, gave me a peck on the cheek, and said goodnight for the last time on our magical adventure.

# CHAPTER 21

*"Nailed it."*

–Shaun Stafford

## Day 21: Kathmandu and Late Afternoon Flight to Abu Dhabi

We made our sad goodbyes to Shaun at breakfast. He was the next to be released from our hotel penitentiary. But I was fairly sure I would see him again since we both ski at the same mountains in the Alps, so there were no tears shed from me, though I can't say the same for Beatrice.

And since today was our last day, I wasn't about to let Beatrice disappear into the viscera of the hotel for another massage. I planned to take her to do some sightseeing and combine that with some photography. (I can always sell her on photos.) I knew a perfect place to do both, Swayambhunath, and after running into D3vil at breakfast and telling him about our plans, he decided to join us. He was full of energy with apparently no residual effects from his whiskey binge.

Swayambhunath is an ancient temple complex on a hill in the western part of the city, a sacred pilgrimage site for Buddhists and followers of Tibetan Buddhism. A large stupa with Buddha eyes dominates the site, which is surrounded by temples and shrines. The entire hillside encompassing the complex is a forest with many varieties of trees where thousands of monkeys make their home, inspiring the local name, the Monkey Temple.

We took a taxi to the south-west entrance and paid our fee to get in. D3vil was free. He immediately pulled out his camera at the fountain as we entered and Beatrice began posing. The stairway and walls lining the path up to the complex were riddled with monkeys, but thankfully they were used to being around people, were fairly reclusive, and seemed to be busy with grooming each other, except for the small ones who were crazily chasing each other and swinging on the railings.

I was relieved to see that the place looked pretty much the same as it had three years before. D3vil said that there had been some damage from the earthquake, but much of it had already been restored. Burnt offerings emanated from each of the dozens of small temples on top of the hillside, filling the air with smoke and exotic aromas. Artisan's crafts, souvenirs, and prayer flags were sold in small shops. I bought two large strings of prayer flags to hang at our Austrian chalet.

Beatrice spied a beautiful bright turquoise-painted old wooden door and had to get some photos of us together there. Salt and Pepper at the end of another adventure.

After strolling around for about an hour, we took our time walking down the hill, past the vendors and preening monkeys, to find the taxi still waiting for us. Then winding our way into the city, D3vil asked to be dropped off somewhere in the heart of Kathmandu, and that was the last we saw of him.

Back at the hotel we went straight out to the pool for lunch but while waiting for our meal to arrive, storm clouds quickly swept in and we got caught in a terrible rainstorm. Not just a shower. It was coming down in buckets. Torrents. And the temperature plummeted right along with the arrival of the rain.

A sign from Mother Nature. It was time to go home.

As I looked around me at the surreal scene of waitstaff running about with umbrellas over their heads, jumping over the puddles forming in the garden to bring us our food and drinks, and the shadow of the magnificent Hotel Shanker looming above us, I thought of my family waiting eagerly for me to return. And although I longed to be with them, to enjoy the comforts of my home and family, rather than being in a cold downpour halfway across the world, I knew that at that moment I was right where I was supposed to be. Everything has its time and place; yes, everything has a reason. The adventure had given me invaluable wisdom and experience to enrich my life, to share with my children and others, and on top of that, I gave myself a priceless gift: the knowledge and contentment that I was living my life to the fullest.

I don't ever want to wake up one day and wish I had traveled somewhere or done something for which it will then be too late. Because in truth, what I fear most in life is not those hanging bridges, the world's most dangerous airport, nor even those filthy toilets, what I fear most is regret, and I have found that *adventure*, by any definition, is an effective prophylactic for that.

\*\*\*

Those first two nights back home in my own bed, I dreamed of the high mountains, the ice, and the silence. I woke to the most serenely peaceful happiness that I could ever remember experiencing. Like a newfound love. A peaceful contentment. I tried to hold onto it, but after a few hours, with the duties and expectations of everyday life, the serenity faded with my dreams.

The Himalayas had snuck in and occupied a piece of my heart. I hoped that they would stay there. At least until I could get back for a refill.

Namaste.

***

# POSTSCRIPT

*" My mission in life is not merely to survive, but to thrive; and to do so with some passion, some compassion, some humor, and some style."*

–Maya Angelou

So how did we stand up to the litmus test? Do today's adventure seekers have a genetic mutation? Or is our species becoming less risk averse?

This book recounts a story about people from a dozen different countries and cultures with widely varying backgrounds. Most work full time, have a spouse or partner, and many have children. Some participate in high-level sports, while others were running their very first marathon. One of them was even travelling abroad for the first time.

When reading the appendix of this book, leafing through the character biographies and interviews, one thing should become startlingly clear, and that is, each and every one of those human beings who hiked up to the base of the tallest mountain on earth only to run back down are none other than the boy next door, the local realtor, the teller at the bank, and the spinning instructor at the gym. A random selection of everyday people with one common thread: Adventure. That is what they seek, that is what they crave, whether they are introverts, extroverts, have OCD, AD/HD, low self-esteem, or a healthy balanced life. It doesn't matter what they do, where they come from or whether they are travelling alone or with the nudge of a friend, deep inside of them and all of us is a thirst for knowledge, not only factual wisdom, but insight into who we are and what we can achieve. And the more people that get out there and do that, travel the world, explore their boundaries, and push back the norms of expectation, then the more inspiration and confidence is parlayed onto others to make that jump... or at least take that baby step.

So, if you haven't already, then ask yourself, where are your borders? Your boundaries? If you don't know the answer, then close your eyes and think about the last time you were chilled with goosebumps when hearing an amazing story and feeling just that little bit envious that it wasn't you doing those marvelous things.

There's your answer. That's *your* adventure. Go claim it.

# APPENDIX I

## Bios

### Beatrice Lessi

Beatrice is a diamond in the rough.

Born in a sleepy town in the Tuscan hills not far from the sea, Beatrice's talent for social communication, her art of persuasion, and her elegant style were quickly discovered in the workplace as she rose to be a top bond broker in London in her mid-20s. After marrying and settling down with her Swiss husband in Zurich, she fell deeply in love three more times before turning 40—that is, in love with her three daughters. But her thirst for challenges never subsided and after being diagnosed with arthritis, she turned her back on the doctors and instead began running long-distance races including the 100-km del Passatore in Florence.

Beatrice is now a top fashion blogger with ASKTHEMONSTERS where she can be seen at red carpet events and luxury resorts, sporting the most beautiful clothes and jewelry. But the surprising thing about Beatrice is that she is completely down to earth and approachable. Anyone can go right up and talk to her and she will be genuinely delighted. She has a keen sense of fair play and believes strongly in karma: good acts and intents towards others will somehow find their way back to her and those she loves.

Holly and Beatrice met in 2016 when they shared a tent together during the 257-kilometer Marathon des Sables race through the Moroccan Sahara Desert. Since then, they have formed an inseparable bond. A better example of opposites attract cannot be found.

# Shaun Stafford

Shaun is a Londoner, though he is rarely there, since he travels all over the world for work, but his favorite place to be is at home with his wife and young son. The first thing one notices about Shaun is that he is the living embodiment of Hercules, and although his official title may be personal trainer and director of City Athletic Gym in London, his resume is long, as is his list of skills and achievements. In 2014, he was WBFF Pro Fitness Model World Champion in addition to being an international cover model and fitness writer.

Although, quite honestly, neither his physical stature nor his resume are what make Shaun who he is.

Kind, generous, funny, and humble, he was the glue that held our group together, kept us laughing and in positive spirits, with the unique gift that makes everyone around him feel like his best buddy.

Clearly no stranger to sport, in addition to being a champion bodybuilder he used to play rugby at a high level. But Shaun is not a runner, or at least he never took it seriously as a sport in and of itself, having never run more than 5 kilometers about six months prior to the Everest Marathon. Thus, he decided to prepare and train for the Everest marathon for reasons different than most.

He wanted to use his presence at the race to raise funds for The Himalayan Children's Charity (HCC), an organization that supports and educates orphaned and abandoned children in Nepal (see appendix V).

In the end, his efforts raised nearly $20,000 US for the cause.

Nailed it.

# APPENDIX II

## Interviews

The following interviews, presented chronologically, were recorded at random times and locations during the trip. Each was recorded in one sitting, with various bystanders, and later transcribed. **Bold** text are my comments and questions, which are then followed by the words of the interviewee.

### Jesper Floyd Kristiansen

Export director; Danish but lives in Poland with his wife and two kids.

**Road to Everest Marathon?**

It was quite special because in fact I had signed up for the North Pole Marathon and I was going to pay the 15,000 Euro for going in, but by coincidence the money didn't come from my Belgian employer so I didn't want to change my home currency—the Polish currency into Euro—so I said, "Ah, let's see if there are some other runs which could be as interesting as the North Pole." So I looked for adventure marathons and then I saw the Everest

Marathon and when I started to look at it I said, "Yeah, why not the highest marathon on earth?" Then I signed up straight ahead for this one.

**Previous races?**

This is marathon number 16 and I'm a member of the 7 Continents Marathon Club. So I have done the seven continents. Here and the Bagan Temple Marathon and the Antarctic are the most special that I have run so far. And I have run several in Europe as well. And the North American one was the Polar Circle marathon in Greenland.

**Do you also run road races? Or just trail races?**

No, I mainly run on asphalt. The Antarctic one, Polar and Bagan, and this one are the exceptions.

**How is your experience here so far? Is it what you expected?**

I knew it would be a tough one; somehow I expected the trail to be not as stony as it is. I'm looking forward to the race. I do expect some challenges with some parts of the race where the big stones are. Where we have the 500 meters downhill and straight out into the 500 meters uphill are the two main parameters there, I think. It looks okay I would say; challenging, but okay.

**What are the best and the worst things so far since you've been here?**

The best is very easy... it's the nature, the possibility to see the landscape around. It's the first time ever I've had the chance to walk the marathon route before I have to run it. On the other side, I don't think you would have seen much of the landscape if we would have been dropped at Base Camp for the run because our eyes would be looking in front of our feet and I think that is the best thing—that we have been surrounded by mountains, the most beautiful mountains in the world. The worst is either the temperature in the room (Gorakshep) or the toilets.

**Are you typically drawn to these extreme events? I think we already got our answer to that. And if so, why? Something in your character or has it developed?**

No, I like to challenge myself both to find out where I have my own border plus from very young I also did a triathlon in Norway doing 57 kilometers cross-country skiing in the mountains with a backpack and one month after doing the bicycle race from Trondheim to Oslo which is 540 km.

**How old were you then?**

Oh, 20, maybe 20, something like that. And then one month after that, I did the Oslo Marathon. And of these three, no doubt, the hardest was the 540 km on the bike. I had never had a bike before that race and I had only 3 weeks to train, so it was terrible but...

**Have you done a bike race since then?**

Uh, no. That was the first and only. I do have my bicycle boundaries. Why I did it also is I have my own sort of running association. In Denmark I come from a small island called Bornholm. And I moved out of Denmark in 1995. I thought that in 2012 it was time to promote my birth island and at the same time do my running, so I have established an association in Poland called Bornholm Runners where the aim of that association is to support seriously ill children in Poland, and by me running the more… how to say… challenging runs, it is easier to get sponsors. So, for instance when I ran the Antarctic marathon it was supposed to be about 17,000 Euro myself, then I gained I think it was around 7 or 8 thousand Euro for the hospice for children in the city I am in.

**So that's the second motivation.**

But if you have a sponsor who pays, for instance, per kilometer you are running, you can't stop, you just continue.

**Commentary:** Jesper looks like a traditional, conservative business manager (which he is) and talks like a news reporter (which he is not). A family man who spontaneously agreed to a 540-kilometer bike race without ever having owned a bike.

**Conclusion:** Adventurer

*Interview: Recorded pre-race in Gorakshep lodge, rest day.*

## Niki Jacques and Carolyn Caranci

My name is Niki Marie Jacques, age 44 from Vancouver, BC, Canada and I'm married with two kids, 12 and 11.

My name is Carolyn Caranci...I am in deeply love with my boyfriend of 17 years, we have a dog and two cats.

### Road to Everest?

**C:** So, it came about maybe almost 2 years ago, like 1.5 years ago and of course I have this wacky friend named Niki Marie who says that, okay, we're gonna do the Everest marathon to celebrate our 45th birthdays. And I was like yea, right, I think this is out of my scope, I'm not doing the Everest marathon, you crazy broad, and then, uh, she assured me that you know they'll be no...we'll get lots of rest before the marathon itself, we'll have 12 days of easy trekking before and we'll have free afternoons where we can be lazy and read and stretch and roll...that's how she sells me on it, right? So, of course I take a look at it. I agree. Whatever.

**N:** So, I am a total adventurer and I will try anything, anywhere. I just love to be outside doing crazy challenges and I said to her, so let's go try the Everest marathon.

**C:** I think she's always googling. She says this is on our bucket list. This is what we are doing next. Googling and then she is always sending me stuff. Always, always, my answer is no. No. And then like a half an hour later I'm like, okay, I'm in.

**N:** It takes her awhile, but there's so much to do. I have a bucket list like three miles long. And I think it's just great to have your best friend to tow around with you on all these trips. And you know, our big competitive days are behind us but now I'm just like, let's go do this, let's do that. Like I want to go to Patagonia, I want to go to South America with her. And so with the Everest thing, it was like, we get to go to Everest Base Camp and it took a little bit to sell her on it, but eventually it happened, I'm like it'll be okay, it's not really about the marathon, but the journey up there.

**So you guys are best friends? How long have you known each other?**

N: About 7 years. But when I first met her I couldn't stand her. No, not that I couldn't stand her, but I owned a fitness studio...

C: She thought I was a little obnoxious.

N: Yes. I was teaching a spinning class and I was literally on the bike. Class had just started, and I could hear her in the parking lot screaming. I'm like who's this broad?

C: Like I was trying to say hello to someone I was meeting. Like GOOD MORNING!!!

N: Yea, that's what she does when she comes in and I'm like, "Oh, God." And so I just was like, I don't know if I can handle her **(Note: This is exactly what I thought when I first met Beatrice.)** and then...

C: And then she realized that we shared a love of running. So I was spinning there and she finds out I'm a runner so she invites me away for a weekend on a relay with a bunch of people.

**N:** Which one was it?

**C:** The Whistler 50. And so from there, the rest is history.

**N:** So something between us is that we are both very authentic people, what you see is what you get. Generally, we love everybody, generally, um, there are exceptions, but we are just very authentic and very real and we just call each other out on all our bullshit, like if she's mad at me or if I'm doing something that you know, she doesn't think is appropriate then she'll be like, hey, this is not cool,....and same with her, it's just very raw.

**C:** And I think that Niki is, well, I know that Niki is somebody that doesn't listen to anything that anybody says, right? She needs to learn on her own and make her own decisions but for some reason like she would listen to me when I just slide some stuff in there. So that I think really builds our connection.

**N:** Yes, she's loyal to a bolt.

**N:** We run like 6 days a week together. We go to movies together. We travel. I have kids and Carolyn doesn't, but it's like she does 'cause she loves my kids.

**C:** You know we used to go for drinks and stuff much more often but now we've cut down and really might go to a movie together more often.

**N:** We run longer so that we can have extra layers of butter on our popcorn (at the movies).

**C:** We're spending like four hours together on Sunday; two or three hours together on Saturday. Two hours Tuesday, two on Wednesday. Like count those hours. We're spending a lot of hours so....

**N:** And then this year I was like, okay I'm gonna get a dog and then she called suit and got one right after.

**What kind of races do you run?**

**N:** Mostly marathons and some ultra marathons. We train together but we always race separately, um, and then like if we're gonna do trail races, then we train on the trails and then we find trail races to do, but we're not competitive on the trails. More road races.

**C:** Regardless of what road races we do, we always spend Sunday in the trails...long.

**N:** Always. With the dogs.

**C:** Cause our 40+ year old bodies need that.

**N:** And then if we're gonna do trail then I'd like, prefer to go away and do some crazy trail, as opposed to like an 18 or 20k, I'd prefer to do the longer stuff. Her not necessarily but ...

**C:** Yea, I'll do like 50k. She's like we're doing the 50k and I'm like oh, and there's a 25k! And she's like, yeah but we're doing the 50k.

**How is your experience here so far and is it what you expected?**

**N:** Oh, my god, it's way more than we expected. Like it's been mind blowing. It's so different. Like for me, it's been...cause I have such a high stress job at home (family business), ah...like I cried when I got up there this morning (Kala Patthar)...right when I got up there, it just started coming out. Um, it's been very emotionally releasing for me, but it's just blown away any expectations that I had.

**C:** Yeah, I think that, well, I'm naive in general in geography and what's going on in other places in the world so it's hugely eye-opening for me...the culture...just like I knew I was going to see amazing things, but it's impacting me really deeper than I imagined.

**How?**

**C:** 'Cause it's so mind blowing that I just didn't understand how wonderful it would be. And then the same with the culture like, yeah, I know we are going to be in a lodge and I'm going to be trekking to Everest but like these people are catering to us and they are feeding us and I don't know, I just can't really wrap my head around it.

**N:** My experience with the people, like you enjoy getting to meet all the different people and it's funny because you meet somebody at first and you go ah, yeah, yeah, but then when you get to know them it opens up a lot and that's big for us, like huge. So, it's been good.

**Best and the worst?**

**C:** So the best for me is yeah, that mind blowing theory. And the worst is like I can't wait to sit down on a toilet for life.

**N:** The best for me is by far being surrounded 360 degrees by the mountains and the worst for me was when Carolyn was sick at the beginning cause I've gone through this before with her...usually it's me taking care of her, like...

**C:** It always is. I'm the weakling.

**N:** I wouldn't call her a weakling, she's just different and so when she was cradled on that bathroom floor before we even left Kathmandu, I thought oh, crap, so that was the worst part. But oh, ah, as a celiac...rice, potatoes, and eggs, three meals a day, every day, that's been the worst thing...and it's not a fault of the organization, there's nothing they could do, it's just, I'm bummed out and I can't look at another potato.

**Okay, one last question, are you typically drawn to extreme events and why? Have you always been extremists, or has it developed?**

**N:** As for me, it's absolutely 150%, I'm like a full extremist and I've always been like that ever since I was oh, 22. Um, for her I would say no, but I just drag her along.

**C:** Yeah, for me no, not extreme, yeah a marathon but in my mind I want to do more but I'm not as strong in my mind (as Niki) and so not as attracted to those...but there is something in my mind, that I want to, but there is a lot of doubt. I wouldn't be here without her, that's for sure.

**N:** I like to be self-sufficient, like I like to be off the grid. I love to be with a mountain compass and just out, like peace'd out somewhere. I think society has become so dependent on the cell phone and nobody can even have a conversation with each other anymore and nobody deals with conflict anymore and when I'm out it's like a switch goes off, but I've always been like that. But definitely as I get older I'm into the more extreme...so it has developed.

**Commentary:** These two were an interesting pair to say the least. Niki is a self-proclaimed total adventurer and has always been that way, although she is clean-cut, quiet, and by far the most reserved of the two. Carolyn, on the other hand, is nuts; she is loud, obnoxious, and funny as hell. It takes a while to warm up to her, but when you get to know her, you appreciate her all-out style. But Carolyn says she would never do any of these races by herself and certainly not without the prodding and support of Niki.

**Conclusion:** Adventurers (one natural born, the other force-fed)

*Interview: Recorded pre-race in Gorakshep lodge, rest day.*

## Raemonde Bezenar

I come from Edmonton, Alberta in Canada and I live there together with Darcy [her partner/husband].

**Road to Everest Marathon? What brought you here to run this race?**

Well, the first thing is, I always wanted to see the big mountains of the world, and you know it takes a lot of effort to make a big trip instead of going to the same place all the time. And with my mum being in a home, I realized that there are only what 25, 27 years between me and my mum, so if it's gonna happen, I'm gonna have to do it now. So this is my one bucket list that I have is to see the big mountains, and a friend of mine had told me about the Everest Marathon, so I tied that into my bucket list. And I figured if I'm gonna do the marathon, I might as well do the ultramarathon. Because I'm somebody who likes to go the distance. I always like to challenge myself ...in everything I do, I always challenge myself with thoughts of the next one. And I'm really into gorilla conservation and I thought, what would be better than to run in my gorilla suit at the ultramarathon? And that was my inspiration. I like to challenge myself doing marathons and it had to be something big to not travel instead to Africa because that's usually where I go.

**What are some of your previous races? Favorite races? Or favorite distance?**

Um, I like to think that I can do big distances, but the only big distance I ever did was in Florida. I wasn't into the running part but I can walk fast. I did 80 km (a 50-miler), starting at Marathon, in Florida to, um, I think it was Key West, and the 100 miler started in Key Largo, I think. And um, it was really good, really flat, it was like 85 degrees (F) the whole day and I didn't wear my gorilla suit for that, but the only time it wasn't flat was when you were going over bridges but it was absolutely spectacular. So I basically ran 1 mile and I walked 49 miles. But I passed people that were jogging. And it took me 14 hours, 5 minutes, and 59 seconds to cross the finish line. Yeah, so that was my big one and ah, the other ones, I went to Kigali, Rwanda, and I wanted to do the International Peace Marathon in Kigali in my gorilla suit. And so I got with the organizers and asked them if it was okay that I wore my gorilla suit and they said yeah, sure, and then I asked them if I could be in the front, and it was really wild because there are all these Ethiopians and Kenyans and they are looking at me, and that's all fine, and then I was able to go right to the start line and they were all back, and then when it came time to move to the start line, I was right there in front and they were like, "Who is this person?" But anyway it was neat that they allowed me to do that. I mean, gorillas are in Rwanda, so it's both conserving the gorillas and raising awareness and stuff, so I wore my gorilla suit the whole time and that was a really good experience.

**Well, then why don't you talk a little bit about your passion for gorillas and what do you hope to do to help them in the future.**

I have done 15 gorilla treks, in Uganda and in Rwanda, and then after experiencing that, it was absolutely incredible and to see them in their natural habitat you can see yourself in them, you really can. And then you see off to the side the babies and the toddlers they are acting just like our children do and it's like oh my god, that's what I do. You know they preen and they twist and they are climbing these bamboo trees and vines and then they go on attack and start wrestling and stuff and then they stop for a second and then they'll eat something and then they are back on the attack. It's just playing. And the thing is, is that it does remind you of where you come from and reminds you that's what a family is like. It's not being on your cell phone, watching TV, or being on your computer.

**So, you run these extreme races in the gorilla suit to raise awareness that they are there and they need help.**

Yeah, yeah, they do. They are on the critically endangered list and after I had done my initial 9 gorilla treks, I came back to Canada and I started a charitable organization called the Mountain Gorilla Conservation Society of Canada and, so what we do is we provide scholarships and other forms of financial assistance to veterinary students who are pursuing a university degree in veterinary medicine in Uganda, Rwanda, and the Democratic Republic of Congo.

**So, let's get back to this race... What has been your experience here so far and has it met your expectations?**

Oh, I think it's exceeded my expectations, first of all, we've got a good group and that really is essential...it's so key. I've been on safari before in a very small group and when you've got two people that are completely out to lunch, it makes it really bad. That's why I did my gorilla safari solo and my driver was my tour guide. But I think the organization and organizers are really top notch because you know that they focus so much on getting us to Base Camp and acclimatizing us to the altitude and when they tell us "Don't drink coffee, don't do this, and don't do that, don't sleep more than five minutes if you want to have a cat nap," you follow those things because they know and I'm most impressed with the organizer and how focused they are on making sure that we are healthy and being able to do this marathon and being acclimatized properly.

**Best and worst?**

Oh, god, the best has been the organizers and the people on the trip, also the best has been the beauty, the scenery. This is just incredible, it is beyond words. This part here (Gorakshep) has totally met my expectations, probably exceeded my expectations and when you are actually looking at majestic Mt. Everest, it's hard to believe...it's very surreal that you are actually looking at Mt. Everest instead of just hearing about it, 'cause to see it is just so much different than just seeing it in the newspaper or on TV or in a book. And the worst? Oh, I try, because this is my bucket list, I try...

**This place is a fuckin' shithole.**

It is. And when I said this is a fucking shithole and I found out that it was the manager I was talking to, I told him again... this place is a fucking shithole...you can do better, you must do better. They can and should do better. Because people don't deserve this. You know, I think it should be a lot cleaner and I think if you want to have people come back, you have to give them a good experience, it's not just the mountains, it has to be everything. If people are teenagers, 18-35 party-goers, but everyone has to have adequate toilets and adequate sinks and not things that have hair all over it and is totally busted. You know, charge people a little more. I would appreciate more, so-called, luxuries, because you know what, if I have such a great experience and love this I'm gonna come back again. But when we are dealing with this...it's terrible. I mean, somebody had mentioned that one of the ladies was wiping the floor with a mop and then she took that mop and was wiping the dining room tables with it. So, I'm just saying that, and some of the outhouses that we've gone to, the worst I've ever been in, they get the blue ribbon for the worst. People do not need to live like that. No, it's like, I go to Africa and these people, some of these people, don't have anything, but what they have is clean, is very clean, but the stuff that we have seen in these lodges and these tea houses is absolutely pathetic and they don't need to live like that and if that's the way they live you know they need to step up a bit because this is a tourist place so hygiene is definitely not high on their level of thinking.

**So, one last question, are you typically drawn to such extreme events and if so, why do you think that is? Is it something that has always been in your character or has it developed?**

I think, well, I'm my own dog. I really am. I like to do things that are challenging. If things are not challenging they are boring. I don't have to scale Everest in order to do that, 'cause I wouldn't take the time to do that but I like to do the extreme stuff. It is part of my personality. You know, I like to go to the max. I've pretty much always been like that. In a group, I'm not a really big talker and I'm not a party animal and I don't become loud or anything. I'm kind of quiet and I'm actually shy, believe it or not, and in conversation I'm getting better about being able to step out of myself to portray that (effort) you know what I mean, to not be that shy person and to actually be standing in front of a whole bunch of people and talking and that's because I believe in gorillas and you know we don't just want to conserve gorillas, we want them to flourish.

But yeah, to answer your question, I'm drawn to extreme stuff, not like the bad-boy image but as far as races and stuff if it's something that I think I can do, absolutely. If it's something that is way too extreme, then no, I know my limits.

**You are a very focused person, you are kind of black and white.**

I am definitely black and white.

**Commentary:** Whoa. She is an amazing person. A true fighter that is so full of energy and ideas but lacking the finesse and know-how of what to do with it all. But she takes on her quest step-by-step, making mistakes along the way, learning and adapting from them. She says herself that she is shy, but once you get her going, she is unstoppable. She ran an ultramarathon dressed in a gorilla suit at the foot of the highest mountain on earth. Need I say more?

**Conclusion:** Adventurer

*Interview: Recorded pre-race in Gorakshep lodge, rest day.*

# Aayush Bista and Anuj Dhoj Adhikary

Two of the cameramen working for the Everest Marathon

# Anuj Dhoj Adhikary (Photographer of cover photo)

I'm 30 years old; I live in Kathmandu. My family is my mom, dad, and brother.

I've worked for this race three times. Other adventure races I've done include UTMB and UTMR, and others in Nepal.

My job was to take videos and photos of the entire trek and race. I will make a highlights video and three other videos...action, expression and landscape, and culture. I was also planning on taking before and after photos but there are too many people. I don't want to stick a camera in everybody's face.

**Do you need an extraordinary fitness level for this race?**

There are a lot of good photographers in Nepal. In order to take good photos, at this altitude, over this distance is kind of crazy. I wouldn't call myself exactly fit but I am not that bad but not that good either. I am average. If you look at the porters, they are super men.

**Best and worst?**

Everything has been the best. The worst are the smelly clogged toilets.

## Aayush (D3vil)

I'm 24 years old; I live in Kathmandu with my family of five: my father, mother, grandparents, and 3 dogs. This was my first time covering this race, but I like doing adventure races and it will not be my last.

How is the trek?

Lots of stress, have to carry a lot of equipment with not much space. And battery charging was difficult. We have power banks too but not everything is chargeable. The older cameras are not. Rationing our budgets was hard.

**Best and worst?**

Meeting a lot of new people. At times inspiring and at times fun. Nothing worst. An experience for everyone. Highs and lows.

*Interview: Recorded pre-race in Gorakshep lodge, rest day.*

# Hendrik (Henni) and Cindy Pelser

Henni, 43 in two weeks time, we are from Pretoria, but we have been living in Japan for the past 11 months, and it was a nice change of scenery to come out of Japan to this.

I'm Cindy Pelser from South Africa, and I'm 39. We have no children.

**What do you for a living?**

**H:** I work for Nissan South Africa, but then about a year and a half ago I was given the opportunity to go and work in the head office. I am in finance and I am in charge of Africa, the Middle East, and India.

**Okay, and do you work there Cindy?**

**C:** No, I used to be a beauty therapist, and I used to be a pharmaceutical rep but I left work.

**H:** She works for me (laughter). So she gave up her job to support me.

**Sounds familiar.**

**C:** Yes, sounds very familiar.

**Tell me about your road to Everest?**

**C:** We've done the Base Camp Everest trek before, that was in 2016 and we like Nepal, so we thought we'd come back again.

And then last year Henni told me about the race and there was a South African lady who couldn't finish the marathon, and there was only one, and she would have been the fifth woman (from SA), I think, and I might be the sixth one, I'll just make sure of our facts, yes. So Henni sent me the information and I said well I'm in and he's in and that's how we got here.

**H:** Of course throughout the year we run, we cycle, so it was just a matter of doing what we do and coming here (for preparation).

**So what are some of your other past really exciting races or events?**

**C:** I've done eight Comrades Marathons in South Africa. I started ten, but two I didn't finish. And also the Two Oceans Marathon which is one of the most beautiful marathons in the world.

**Yes! Commentary from Beatrice who is also there and also did that marathon.**

And then I've done some triathlons, mountain biking, road racing, adventure racing when I was younger.

**Oh, wow, what distances?**

Short ones—35 and 60s.

**Sport disciplines?**

Paddling, walking, running, climbing, kayaking.

**And how about you Henni, anything extreme?**

**H:** Well, I started out by drinking and smoking too much. Then my girlfriend dumped me in 2001, I wanted to get out of the house so I started cycling and I became a pretty good amateur cyclist for seven years.... raced for a few local teams in SA in my age group. Then I got tired of road cycling, switched to mountain biking, then came Cindy...um...she was more running than mountain biking, so if I continued just cycling and she continued just running, we wouldn't see each other on the weekend, so I started running as well and we both had a few mountain biking wins together, and then we both went to trail running as well. Last year in Japan I did a 72 km, 4500 m ascent trail run, and it was 11.5 hours of hell. It was probably 60 km just pure steps up and down.

**How did you place?**

When I finished, I think I was in the first third. I think after 11.5 hours and two-thirds were still out there in the dark.

**Did you do any special training for this race?**

No, we just showed up. I went to Dubai and Egypt on a business trip, and we went on holiday to Vietnam, so that made it difficult to do a lot of training.

**Extreme...is that part of your character?**

**C:** Because of the Comrades. I think if you've done one of the Comrades and you go back and back and back, I think it's something that's all in the mind, so I think that this, although it's going to be extreme, I think it's going to be a race that's all in the mind. 'Cause for us, we didn't prepare for this and it's quite a hectic race and for me, it's just see what the body can do but also what your mind can do 'cause if your mind is not going to be right you are not going to be able to finish it.

**H:** I grew up pretty conservatively. I grew up on a farm. I wasn't really into sports. I was bad at rugby. I only started cycling at 28. Um, but I think that kind of triggered it a bit. But still, I didn't do any traveling. I traveled for the first time in my life in 2004 for work. When I met Cindy, she basically took me and pulled me a little bit out of the comfort zone and traveled from there...we went to Egypt, the Middle East, Nepal, the Med, Europe.

**A strong woman.**

(laughs) Yup, well, she pulled me out of my comfort zone.

**How is your experience here so far? Is it what you've expected?**

**C:** The conditions are. That's because we've been here before. I'm not a person that likes group things, so for me the group thing is difficult. Um, I should have known it since I'd done group things before. But this is just a once in a lifetime experience. I'm a very black-and-white person. It's either right or wrong, there's no gray areas. And my personality is like that as well. I'm quite a perfectionist. Obsessive-compulsive. And everything needs to be 100% right, so this is difficult.

**H:** I'm happy-go-lucky. Whatever....

**So then you are a perfect match. Best thing and worst thing?**

**H:** Best thing: sunrises and the views. And the worst thing would probably be that toilet this morning (laughs) (the second day overload at Base Camp).

**C:** Best: the mountains and to see how small we actually are compared to this. Worst: I can't choose my food. I prefer to know what I'm going to eat. Just given my food, I don't know what I'm eating.

**Anything you want to add? Running for a charity or have a cause?**

**C:** Not like it's not out there, but I'm an animal fanatic.

**We noticed that, yes.**

**C:** For dogs especially. And this is an emotional trip, the second time...I don't know why I'm doing this again. 'Cause the last time I was very emotional about the yaks, the horses, the dogs who don't get looked after. So I thought to myself that when I come here this time I will make it my aim to feed the dogs at least at every place we are, to take the food that there is (leftovers) and find them and feed them. But I did have a lot of emotional...

**[She starts crying.]**

**H:** As you can see.

**What about you Henni? A cause?**

**H:** No, nothing from me. I'm just here supporting my wife. But if I can say something, I basically just showed up for this trip. I didn't do any ounce of packing. Nothing. Cindy organized the whole trip from start to finish. So I really appreciate what she did for the trip. She did everything. I didn't do anything.

**Commentary:** When Cindy admitted that it was difficult for her to be in the group, it brought tears to my eyes, because I had seen that in her, and I sympathized with that. I find it truly amazing that the desire to travel and push her body to her limits was strong enough to overcome her emotional attachment to the animals and the social environment that she found difficult to be in. Henni, the more outspoken of the two and a gifted athlete, clearly needed his reticent wife to explore his boundaries.

**Conclusion:** Adventurers (one reluctant by nature, one by proximity)

*Interview: Recorded pre-race, sitting outside their tent at EBC*

## Ricky Yonzon

I'm 34 years old and I live in Kathmandu with wife. I'm a group leader for trekking groups. No children...yet. Been married for 7 years, but she studied in the UK for 5 years and has been back for 2 years. Since she has been back, and even before she went to the UK, thinking about adopting a daughter because in Nepal and other third world countries it is hard to get by in life, and I am lucky enough that I have a job. It's a challenge. So we thought maybe somebody who has already arrived, we would provide a life to her rather than make one (a child).

**How did you become the leader of our Everest Marathon group?**

I have some history with the event manager. I've been working with him on expeditions for a long time. So he wanted me to be more a part of the marathon so I am the Base Camp manager and do some logistics and paperwork and registration for the marathon as well.

**What has been some of your past work?**

First work in life doing dishes in a restaurant when I ran away from home. My father knew where I was but didn't say anything. He probably also wanted me to know what life is. I do some mountain biking in the off season and I have a band so I do singing in pubs. I also do trekking, everything that is adventure.

**Dream job?**

Well, if I were single...this would be it, right in front of the Icefall, but when you have a family, I have to think of my wife, so in this case I want to have a job which is not too risky so that my family will not be frightened and have financial security as well. So I will probably be somewhere in Dubai.

**Why?**

I don't know, but people go to Dubai. I don't know, let's see what my wife wants.

**Best and worst?**

There are no worst. Yes, it would be if someone does not make it to Base Camp. Because I have worked in this field for a long time so I know there are people who have saved money for years to come to Base Camp, just Base Camp, the race is different, so if somebody from my side, if I have to tell them that they cannot come to Base Camp, then that would be the worst thing for me but also it's for their safety. But the good thing is that everyone is coming here to Nepal supporting the economy. That's the good thing for me; people can find jobs, lots of Nepali people, indirect jobs as well. Like the kitchen workers in Base Camp, they do not work directly for the marathon, but they are here because of it.

**Anything special about this group?**

Well, I like challenges and mixed groups are challenges. Yeah, in the dining hall you can see; there are Mexican guys in the group, and gluten free. This time around everyone is at least happy. After the marathon they write it down, that it was good. But now, this time, everyone is coming to me and saying, whatever you are doing with your group, with your guys, is fantastic so I appreciate that. For me, it's the guys (guides, porters, etc.) rather than myself. Without them I would be nothing.

**Commentary:** Ricky is a trekking guide out of choice, for which he is paid. But don't get me wrong, he can't resist the mountains, meeting new people, and experiencing something new every day.

**Conclusion:** Adventurer

*Interview: Recorded pre-race at Everest Base Camp.*

## Harry Hilberdink

I'm 54 years old; I live in Dalfsen, near Zwolle, The Netherlands, with my wife. I'm a software engineer, specifically point-of-sales systems. I went on this trip because three of my friends did it also, one of them did it twice and it planted a little seed in me, that grew, so I'm now doing it as well.

**And how was your training? Was it any different than normal?**

Yeah, I made more length in my training.

**Endurance.**

Yeah, endurance.

**In running or biking?**

Four or five hours... no, only running, no biking. Very slowly. Five minutes of running, ten minutes of walking, and I extended that to six hours, seven hours.

**Did you register a long time ago or just recently? Have any doubts?**

No, no. No doubts. I registered sometime after January, I think. 'Cause I wanted to first begin with my training and see how that turned out.

**What other kinds of races do you run? What are some of the highlights?**

I've done the New York Marathon twice. And that was also the end of my marathons on tarmac. I just love trail running far more than running on asphalt. And I love to be running in the hills of the UK and doing orienteering races twice a year; they are called Mountain Marathons. You have to run there with your mate, and you have everything with you: your sleeping bag, tent, food, etc. And you have to search for control points with map and compass. And I just love it.

**Yeah? That's your thing.**

Yeah. I've been doing it since 2001.

**How did you learn to do that? Orienteering.**

I just tried. Working a compass isn't that difficult, you learn by doing it, just train on the job.

**Just go out with somebody who's done it to give you a few tips and then you figure it out on your own.**

Yeah, pretty much.

**And how is your experience here so far? Is it what you expected it to be?**

Ah, yes. Because of my experience in mountains. I've climbed... many treks in the Alps and Norway, etc. so I knew, and I was here before, so I knew the terrain, but my weak point is the altitude, it doesn't work that well on my stomach.

**So, you have stomach problems.**

Yes, I have stomach problems. So, not that much, it is borderline.

**When did it start?**

I don't know, I think a day after Namche on the ascent. So, pretty much up to EBC, and you lose energy, so you are not as strong as you would like to be.

**Are you typically drawn to these extreme events?**

Ah, yes, I find them very interesting.

**Why?**

I'm a tiny bit adventurous. So take adventure, take running, take mountains, combine them and you have something like this.

**Still, not everybody would do this.**

No, but I like challenges.

**This is really extreme, though.**

Yeah.

**So, do you think your adventurous nature is part of your character or has it developed? Were you always like that?**

Yes. When I was 16, I wanted to join the Marines because of the physical aspect of it, not, of course not, at that age, the political aspect of it, but purely the physical aspect. So I get, um, you have to be vetted...um... vetted, no? um... they check your health, secure your physical.

**Check-up?**

Yeah, a check-up of four days. It's a difficult one. Psychological, etc. And I did it after my school at 20, but I couldn't go there because I have glasses, so and at that time you couldn't have glasses, so I dropped out ...they didn't want to have me.

**They didn't?...but I thought you told me you were in the Marines, then how'd you get there?**

No, I wasn't in the Marines, just in the Army.

**Why would you not want the Army as much? Why are the Marines so much better?**

Yeah, they, they are doing other stuff. They do special stuff.

**More exciting.**

Yes. Yes.

**Okay, so that was a hard time?**

Nah, I just, I had to accept that and choose for an education.

**That wasn't going to be an option before?**

No.

**Really?**

No, not really. I had to switch in a few months.

**You thought, my life is the Marines.**

Yeah, yeah.

**What did you think of the race?**

Good. Very nice.

**Difficult?**

No. The terrain I didn't find that difficult, but the length and the altitude. Altitude is the factor which makes it...sets it apart.

**How did it affect you?**

Ah, weakness. My stomach, for instance.

**Legs, breathing?**

Yeah, breathing. Going up was so difficult.

**Was it the toughest race you've ever done?**

Yes, in that aspect, I'm sure it was. I've done things in the Mountain Marathons which were comparable, but that's of course without the altitude, but in length they were comparable. And some Saturdays, the first days of the Mountain Marathons, with marathons of 12 hours, just walking and at the end of the day it went dark so you have to go down a mountain with your head torch only, so it can be dangerous. It was cold; we did it in winter. Yeah, it is tough.

**But this ranks up there?**

Yeah.

**Okay, what do you think about the organization of the Everest Marathon?**

Pretty good. I think they were excellent.

**Out of 5? 5 is the best.**

Five, yeah, five.

**And the people?**

Yeah, the same. Same, I liked everybody. Yeah, no exceptions.

**Even me?**

Even you, yeah. Ah, you're fishing. (Laughing)

**What's been the best and the worst for you on this trip?**

The worst was my stomach. I just hated it that the altitude had so much effect on my performance. And the best...the best was running. Hiking up is good but I knew that, so it was nothing new. Ah, camping outside with toilets, nothing new, but the running, yeah, that was the best.

**Commentary:** Harry is a software engineer, and his personality can be pretty much summed up by his job description: meticulous, straight-forward, dry. Although he has amazing stories to tell, he does so in a way that leaves all emotion in the gutter and you struggle to keep your eyelids open. If you saw him walking down the street, you'd never peg him for anything outside of mainstream, but the guy has jumped into deep ice crevasses...for fun.

**Conclusion:** Adventurer

*Interview: Recorded post-race in Lukla Coffee House.*

## Mark and Jill Griffin

I'm Jill, I'm 42; I live in Charlotte, NC, and I work for Bank of America. Not a very exciting job but it gets us to places like this. I'm in finance and I used to do management reporting, but now I do stress testing...prove that we have enough capital to survive a stress period. It is exciting.

I'm Mark Griffin, I'm 43; I'm Jill's better half, and I work as a realtor. I sell homes but I focus more on investor purchase, new constructions. We have two children, 8 and 10, Lila and Elijah.

**Sounds like you both have pretty standards jobs...**

Yeah.

**What was your road to the Everest Marathon?**

J: It wasn't until a few years ago that we really got into running, it was up until then more boot camp-style workouts. I ran in high school so I had that history, but nothing like this. When we met 11 or 12 years ago, I didn't even know he ran, and then through a local group we saw other people doing a marathon and you (to Mark) jumped in and did a marathon and then I started thinking to myself, maybe I could do a marathon too, so over the past few years, we've started doing a few a year, the first when I was 37, road races, without knowing how to train. But as we learn how to do it, we start to travel a bit more but still close to home, still US, but somewhere along the way we developed a fascination for Everest. Everyone who came out of that alive (referring to the expeditions in 1996 when 8 people died in one day) wrote a book on it and after reading and seeing the documentaries we began to think how cool it would be to get to Everest.

**M:** Yeah, there was kind of a magical moment, 'cause your question was kind of, why Everest and what drove us here and we share an anniversary date with the first summit and two years ago I was thinking about it to celebrate our 10 year anniversary, but it was too much to do between the point of realization with what's happening on Everest on the 29 of May. Oh shit there is a marathon on Everest on May 29! We need to put this thing together and of course not at 10 years, we'd never been at altitude, then did Pike's Peak to try out altitude closer to home. We had done some other Spartan trail races, but NC trails, not extreme, night and day compared to Everest. We like the physical challenges, the training aspect that leads you to the actual marathon.

**[J best marathon time 3:30; M 2:58]**

**Everest is an extreme event. Do you tend to such extreme events? You (Mark) I can see that you are a bit on the edge, but you (Jill) seem to be more mainstream, is that true?**

**J:** I think we both really like challenges. And believe it or not I'm usually a really competitive person too, but with Everest it was like jumping into the deep end...I don't run trails, I have not only a fear of heights, but a paralyzing fear of heights. So just being here is extreme compared to Boston. So I am mainstream in my day job but I feel like I play along. I feel like this is really more, like we love this, and there may be nothing more like this again but I think that we'll see ourselves to continue to find those races that excite us and plan our next adventure or vacation around that.

**Do you take the kids to some of your races?**

**J:** Sometimes. We've taken them to Colorado. I think it's a great way for them to see the world, too.

**And then you guys become their superheroes?**

**M:** Yeah, I think we're that anyway. But this type of thing, was less about competition, we do well in our AK and compete against ourselves, but stuff like this you have to find a balance: it's our anniversary, do it together, less about competing and just do it together because it's special, but it's hard because we both were sick, so there is no guarantee that you are going to make it, so it was just a 3-week challenge to get through it and we acclimated well, trekked well, but the conditions sucked.

**J:** We really do have fun together.

**M:** Without even recognizing it, in a group of 25 people, we had a 100% success rate, which is crazy, cause you hear about other treks they have like 30% fail rate, and you are surrounded by like-minded individuals that really want to challenge themselves.

**So you were sick at EBC?**

**M:** On the 27th, the night we got to Base Camp.

**(At 11:49. Shaun is sitting with us at the table and he throws that in...)**

**M:** Was it 11:49 that I lost my guts? Throwing up at both ends. The marathon was good. I was thinking between Jill's fear of heights and my poopy diapers, I thought we just needed to move smart, it's a once in a lifetime thing, just take the day, enjoy the day. It was more of a power walk than a run. Once we made cutoff comfortably, we had the conditional elements that would challenge us. Some of the parts that were flat and easy, well, we'd start to run but I got a little light-headed. I felt okay when I woke up, but after 4 or 5 hours I was done with that. In the end we needed 10:25 to reach the finish.

**How do you rate the organization?**

**J:** I thought it was excellent. I don't know what I had in mind but it was great. There were parts a little disgusting, but what do you expect?

**M:** It's whatever.

**J:** They did a great job.

**M:** Overall, very pleased.

**J:** They took care of you when you were sick. The doctors, Ricky Bobby...

**Best and the worst?**

**M:** One and the same: Base Camp. I dreamt of that place, read about it, so getting beaten up there a little bit, well...it's still such a special wonderful place, it's so fitting that all the scenarios that were running through our head, that I got my ass kicked going into BC and then it was getting through that and like okay, one last challenge that I have to overcome going into that race, so

BC was kind of my best and worse cause it's a horrible place but it's just incredibly perfect, just being surrounded by these snow-capped peaks, it just looks painted in, it looks fake. It's just so beautiful and perfect but brutal and ugly at BC.

**J:** It's easy to say the worst when you are sick, but I thought I would have that moment of enlightenment or where I became a better person and that it would happen like a lightning bolt and coming here and I thought it would happen during the race, a moment of feeling really emotional, but I didn't, but that did happen, when I felt really emotional was when I said goodbye to the sherpas and our team and then the tears came and that showed that this is so much bigger than the race. It was the whole trip. But I don't know why I thought a lightning bolt, it is more of a subtle thing and I think when I get home I will realize that, yes, you did change but it wasn't just a moment where you had a big, aha! But just kind of daily like just hoping it will make me more patient and just a better person.

**Commentary:** These two look like pretty rough and rugged outdoorsy North Carolinians, but actually, they are very composed, precise, and sweetly caring of each other. Mark is a little nuts; Jill adores him and, in her own words, plays along. Both have mainstream jobs and a cookie-cutter family life, but they chose to celebrate their wedding anniversary together by running a marathon at the foot of Mount Everest.

**Conclusion:** Adventurers (one by nature, the other by way of love)

*Interview: Recorded post-race in the garden at Hotel Shanker just prior to the post-race party.*

# Raymond (Ray) Lem

I'm 44 years old and I live in New York City. I'm an IT professional for a small real estate lab research company that builds lab research buildings for cancer research.

**IT work, huh? So pretty unadventurous?**

Yeah, you could say that.

**And you are married?**

Yeah, married.

**No children?**

Not that I know of.

**Right. Um, but you did not grow up in NYC, did you?**

Born and raised.

**Tell me about your road to Everest...**

I made a promise to my friend, my good friend in 2014 who wanted to compete in the 7 Continents Marathon in Antarctica in 2014 and he was looking for someone and I was the only crazy one that said yes. So last year we finally got accepted into that cruise, or that class, so that was the first time that I ever ran a marathon.

**You'd never run a marathon before?**

No.

**Half marathon? 10k?**

I ran a 10k in, maybe, 2008.

**So Antarctica, first marathon?**

Yes, first marathon, and I met a lot of really cool people just like this trip and yeah, that's when I found out about this 7 Continents Club so it piqued my interest, so most people choose Antarctica as their last, and it was my first, so I wanted to start my journey on it, hence I ended up on Mount Everest after someone in the Antarctica FB posted a race for Mt. Everest.

**So, your plan is actually to do another five after this.**

Unfortunately, yes.

**But you have no time limit?**

Well, I would like to knock one or two off per year. I'm not getting any younger. So, I did Antarctica and I was fortunate enough to do New York, um, a couple of months after it in November because my company sponsored us for it, so I joined at like the last minute. And so this is my third continent.

**So you've got Europe still to do...South America.**

Yep, South America, Europe, Africa, and Australia.

**And do you know which ones you are going to run?**

Yes, I would like to run Machu Picchu in South America, in Europe I would like to end up at the Greece Marathon, in South Africa the Big 5, and in Australia it should be the Outback.

**And races like this, they are extreme, you know, is this in your character?**

No, not really...No. Like everyone chooses their seven continents a little differently, some choose road races, except for Antarctica because of the nature of the terrain but I like to make mine unique, so I wanted to do Great Wall cause everyone else was doing Great Wall so when I saw the opportunity for Mt. Everest, I thought it was a lot more unique. Same thing with Machu Picchu, there's only about 20 people who do it per year, so I like to make my journey a little more unique.

**But other than that, your character doesn't tend more towards craziness?**

No, I was telling Harry, I'm a Virgo...I'm like anti-chaos. Here, I was constantly cleaning my shoes, I was cleaning my bag.

**So, what drew you to this? Was it the physical challenge? Mental?**

It's just a journey, I think. So next year, pretty much half of my Antarctica group will be doing Everest, but I was just impatient, I don't have time for it next year, I'm doing it this year.

**Well, it worked out well, you met a bunch of cool people...**

(Laughing) Yeah, totally, I wouldn't trade it for anything else.

**Previous race history, you already said New York marathon.
What did you get for a time in NY?**

Um, 4:08...pretty slow.

**No, pretty standard around the 4-hour mark.**

Horrible time, it was so cold.

**Not as cold as this! What do you think about the experience
here so far, the whole trip, has it met your expectations?**

I've learned throughout life not to have any expectations, just
come in with an open mind, so it has totally surpassed whatever
I thought of, but you know, I was telling Harry I learned a lot
about myself, learned to let go a lot of my tendencies of OCD-
ness (obsessive-compulsive disorder). The first two days you
know, my boots were brand new, I didn't want to walk in yak shit,
I didn't want to use my trekking poles because I didn't want them
to go in it. But the second day I was like oh, give that up right
now.

**Weren't you wearing a mask at the beginning?**

Yeah, actually the mask was one of my saving graces, because I
felt it kept the air warm, because I'm asthmatic, so it kept the air
warm and I didn't have to cough as bad as a lot of people because

of that. I was going to leave that at home, the mask, because of the weight restriction. (**I think he was kidding.**)

**How was your health the whole time?**

That was another journey within itself, when we got to Namche I came down with a stomach bug and that knocked me out for about four days. I was on antibiotics, so that drained me a bit. But I'm a mountain man now 'cause I pooped in the woods. That first time when I had to go…it was a learning experience.

**Happy with the organization?**

Yeah, I mean, everyone got up there and everyone came back down. That was good. So, like I said, I try not to have too many expectations because you set yourself up for failure.

**What have been your best and the worst of this trip?**

The best was the views, I mean, that was like mind blowing; this is my first time being introduced to camping and outdoor life, I'm the typical New Yorker, so with Harry's help, I was very fortunate to have roomed with him, 'cause he was like laid back and I was like how the hell do I sleep in a sleeping bag? The worst was getting used to the sanitary conditions and I will not eat potatoes or white toast for a very long time.

**But the food was okay other than that?**

No, I was hoping it would be better.

**Yeah, so did I.**

Like when I saw what the guides and herpas were eating, I was like, that food, I want to have that food.

**Yeah, like the first day in Lukla, the dal bat, I was like this is going to be awesome...that was a tease.**

Yeah, exactly.

Ray then had to rush off to catch his flight home.

**Commentary:** Ray is introverted, organized to the point of being self-proclaimed obsessive-compulsive, structured, sarcastically funny, and from the outside looks like a pretty normal guy. But this average guy just happened to run a marathon in Antarctica on a whim, although he had never run a marathon before, let alone more than 10 kilometers at a stint.

**Conclusion:** Adventurer

*Interview: Recorded post-race at the pool in Kathmandu, Hotel Shanker.*

# APPENDIX III

## Training for the Everest Marathon

Shortly after returning from Nepal, a friend asked me about training for the event. He wanted to run it, but said he worked a lot and didn't have too much time to dedicate to training for it. I told him that if he had time for marathon training, then he has time for *Everest* Marathon training. It's similar, but different. It doesn't need to be heroic. Long runs. Hill work. Strength training. Cross training. Trail technique.

Now let's break that down.

### *Long Runs*

Just as in training for a marathon there should be a long run once a week, built up in time and distance over several months. It is recommended to have 5-7 long runs of 20 miles (30 km), building up to a standard marathon (i.e., run on the road). My recommendation when training for a trail marathon is to concentrate more on a long run based on time rather than distance. If you run a road marathon in about 4 hours, then you can expect the Everest Marathon to take you double that time, at least, so you'll be on your feet for 8 hours or more; thus, endurance training of up to 6 hours should be in your training plan. This doesn't mean that you need to go out and run for 6 hours, since that would be too much for the body to quickly recover from to keep up the rest of the training week. But a 6-hour run–hike combination on trails with some elevation is perfect (e.g., go for a 3-hour trail run then take the family out for a 3-hour hike). If you don't have trails and hills, then a long run can be combined with biking to get the extended endurance without killing your legs.

## Hill Work

Try to incorporate hill sprints at least once every two weeks in the two months leading up to the race. Find a steep incline that is long enough for you to run up at full sprint for 30 seconds and then jog down for 60 seconds. Build up the repetitions starting with 6, then the next time 8, then 10; that's plenty. A 2-km warm-up and cool-down make it a short but effective session.

## Strength Training

This is an important aspect of trail running. You need to have a really strong core to maintain balance on uneven terrain. You are often jumping from side to side, up and down, so adductors, abductors, and quad strength are essential too. Eccentric exercises for the quads (e.g., the downward motion of squatting), and calves are a must, since this is the muscle action required for downhill running.

## Cross Training

Biking, swimming, yoga, tennis, kayaking, climbing. Doesn't matter. Just do what you enjoy. Variety spices things up and keeps different muscle groups in shape, rounding out the package.

## Trail Technique

This has two aspects: hiking up and running down. Of course there are some trails and trail races that are run on very well-groomed trails, but traditional mountain trails are rather tricky and technical. Unlike paved roads, there are stones, roots, loose gravel, grassy fields, and sometimes streams to cross. Plus, there is more often than not uneven ground, this could be side-to-side, whereby one foot may be on a level higher than the other; or up and down in a step-like motion.

1. Hiking up such trails should not be underestimated. You need to know what to expect under each footstep, and balance is critical. This can be learned with practice. Trekking poles can be a huge help in hiking up, though I am not a big fan of them while running (fear of tripping!).

2. Running down is also a technique that can be learned and mastered with practice. There are many good tutorials on downhill trail running on the Internet, so look at a few and then get out there and practice. You need to get a feel for the ground underneath you. Look ahead to scan what is to come then back at your next foot placement. Avoid stepping on wet rocks and roots, steer clear of loose stones and gravel, find a line, make short quick steps, and use

your arms for balance. Laughing and howling sometimes help too—at least, they add to the fun of it.

## Running

On top of the long runs and hill sprints, there should be a day of regenerative easy running of about 75 minutes, a tempo run of about the same length, and a middle distance run between 1.5 and 2 hours in length. Doing too little may well be too little; but doing too much is dangerous, as it can lead to overtraining, illness, or injury. Listen to your body, but know who is boss.

## Medical Check-Ups

A routine blood work-up should be made at least once per year (twice if possible), preferably by a sports medical specialist who knows which blood values are performance indicators and where all your values are optimal. Tell your doctor that you are a long-distance runner and that you want your ferritin levels checked, too, as this is not part of the routine blood test. Many long-distance runners are iron deficient (men as well as women), due in part to a phenomenon called Runner's Macrocytosis, which manifests in increased red blood cell size as a compensatory mechanism for increased red blood cell turnover. The impact forces from running can lead to red blood cell hemolysis and accelerate red blood cell production. This can shift the ratio of red blood cells toward younger, larger cells. This shift may be reflected in higher than normal MCV (mean corpuscular volume) values, an indicator of red blood cell size. This may indicate a propensity toward iron deficiency anemia due to high red blood cell turnover.

Symptoms of iron deficiency may be lethargy, not having the speed nor strength to finish running distances that were previously the norm, or the feeling of overtraining. But this type of iron deficiency is not evident when testing iron serum level, which may appear normal or even high if you are taking small amounts of supplements. That's why serum ferritin should also be tested. Levels below 25 ng/mL are connected with performance drops and injury, while levels above 50 ng/mL are recommended for both male and female athletes. I feel best when my value is over 100 ng/mL. Supplements come in many forms but can easily be taken in a tablet as iron salts: ferrous sulfate, ferrous fumarate, and ferrous gluconate. **Quantity and type should be determined under doctor's supervision.**

# APPENDIX IV

## Trekking and Race Gear for Mount Everest Base Camp Trek and Mount Everest Marathon

### Essentials

- Expedition-grade sleeping bag!!!

- Thermarest (or other good quality) air mattress

- Trekking poles

- Warm down winter jacket

- Mid-season down jacket

- Rain jacket

- Short- and long-sleeved merino wool shirts

- Long-sleeved fleece

- Trekking pants

- Running tights

- Water bottles: at least 2-liter capacity; bottles that can hold boiling water; charcoal water filter bottle

- Running shoes

- Sunglasses

- Headlamp

- Earplugs

- Travel towel (quick drying)

- Snacks: Granola bars, nuts, dried fruit, chocolate

- Hats (for warmth and sun shielding)

- Gloves

- Neck warmer

- Trekking backpack

- Running backpack capable of holding at least 1.5 liters of water

- Water purifying tablets

- Cell phone

- Basic first aid: Band-Aids, pain killers, safety pins, travel antibiotic, antidiarrheal meds, Diamox

- Charging cables

- GPS watch

- Sunscreen

- Kleenex

- *SHITLOADS* of antibacterial hand sanitizer, preferably hospital-grade (e.g., Sterillium)

- Flip-flops for the showers

- Comfortable clothes for chillin' in the lodges

*Tip:* Pack all your clothes in plastic bags. If it rains while on the trek, and all your stuff is on the back of a yak, you will regret it if you don't bag everything.

**Worth a thought or two:**

- Pillowcase (thanks, Shaun)
- Sleeping bag liner

- Toilet paper

- Solar charger

- Trekking boots, if desired...
  (I hiked and ran in the same
  running shoes made for rough
  terrain)

# APPENDIX V

## Notes, Credits, Links...

Our Everest Marathon Trekking company: *www.everestmarathon.com*

Photographer Anuj Adhikary: *www.anujadhikary.com* (Cover photo)

Beatrice Lessi: *www.askthemonsters.com*

Shaun Stafford Fitness: *www.shaunstaffordfitness.com*

Kyaron's family hotel in Nagarkot: Hotel Peaceful Cottage & Café du Mont: *www.peacefulcottage.xyz*

Raemonde's nonprofit Gorilla project: Mountain Gorilla Conservation Society of Canada: *www.mountaingorillaconservation societyofcanada.com*

Sagarmatha Pollution Control Committee (SPCC) and the Mount Everest Biogas Project. Safe disposal of human waste in Gorakshep. Project in design phase. For more info or to donate: *mteverestbiogasproject.org*